D

The Wish To Be Free

THE WISH

UNIVERSITY OF CALIFORNIA PRESS

TO BE FREE

Society, Psyche, and Value Change

FRED WEINSTEIN

GERALD M. PLATT

BERKELEY AND LOS ANGELES · *1969*

University of California Press
Berkeley and Los Angeles, California
University of California Press, Ltd.
London, England

Copyright © 1969 by
The Regents of the University of California

Standard Book Number: 520-01398-0
Library of Congress Catalog Number: 71-83291
Designed by James Mennick
Printed in the United States of America

For Joan and Christina

Preface

T HIS BOOK deals with the problem of social change, link-
ing ideas in sociology, psychoanalysis, and history. The development of our point of view on social change depended
upon classical and modern contributions to theory, and
those who are familiar with sociological and psychoanalytic
thought will recognize our indebtedness to Freud, Weber,
Durkheim, Tönnies, Parsons, Erikson, Hartmann, and others. We are also indebted to a number of teachers, colleagues, and friends, some of whom shaped our thinking
and helped us to develop our general orientation to the
problem of social change; others discussed our most recent
ideas directly with us, contributing to the refinement of the
content and the form of our work by sharing their knowledge and critical insight. Among the many to whom we are
grateful we would like to mention the late Rex D. Hopper,
Talcott Parsons, Ralph H. Turner, Nicholas V. Riasanov-

sky, Thomas J. Cottle, Gerald Feldman, Lawrence Levine, Victor Lidz, Sheldon Rothblatt, Irwin Scheiner, and George Stocking. Special thanks are due Lewis Mangani, Philip Lee Thompson, Stephen Lukashevich, and Lewis W. Sperber, all of whom will recognize many of the ideas expressed in the book. We must also acknowledge the fine editorial assistance of Gene Tanke and Bill Carver, as well as the effort of Robert F. Bales, former Director of the Laboratory of Social Relations, Harvard University, to make funds available for typing, and the work done by Joan Weinstein, who edited and typed several versions of the work, early and late. Gerald Platt would like to thank the Social Science Research Council for a postdoctoral fellowship which provided him with the time and opportunity to develop some of the thoughts in the work, even though that fellowship was awarded for a different intellectual endeavor. Finally, we note the constant encouragement and support of our wives, Joan Weinstein and Christina Platt.

F.W.
G.M.P.

Contents

The Wish To Be Free

Introduction

CLASSICAL WESTERN concepts of freedom characteristically assumed that man has rational control over his faculties, that he can order his actions and effect calculated changes in his environment, and that he does so on the basis of self-interest. In this view, society comprises individuals with diverse interests and goals—goals that are personally chosen and best realized through mutual regard for the principle of competitive autonomy.

This was the ego-oriented view of man advanced by the liberal theorists of the eighteenth and nineteenth centuries, the view invoked to justify their demands for a broader inclusion of individuals in the decision-making processes of society. They insisted, in particular, that power be shared more equably in the political and economic areas of endeavor, for they believed these areas to be crucial to the real exercise of autonomy. And so that this diffusion of power might be effectively implemented, liberal writers insisted also upon an organization of "market" structures in which authority could be established on the basis of free consent, and in which the interests of all legitimate members of the community could be represented.[1]

Neither the sociological nor the psychological basis for the liberal orientation was very substantial. There was no real appreciation of the role of social structure in the formation of these innovative and radical suggestions; and understanding of psychic structure was limited to the notion that autonomous man could act consistently in a self-disciplined and rational way. It was acknowledged that emotional indulgence would affect an individual's capacity to maintain his autonomy and lead to the loss of control. Individuals who could not discipline themselves, therefore, were bound to be dependent upon others, particularly for their economic well-being, and all those who were so dependent were systematically excluded from the social sources of power.

Marx's critique of this classical view represented a significant intellectual advance, for it established in a decisive way the importance of social structure in the formation of ideas and institutions. But in terms of advancing a sophisticated psychology of internal processes Marx had little more to offer than the liberal theorists. Marx believed that man was capable of a high degree of conscious control and that by virtue of this control he could manipulate the external world sufficiently to eliminate anxieties stemming from conflicts at the social level of activity. Marx, however, had no awareness of the unconscious factors that might inhibit the fulfillment of this goal, or distort comprehension of the means by which the goal might be achieved.

None of these views, then, instrumental though they may have been in structuring man's understanding of his environment, included any systematic appreciation of psychic structure. Indeed, until the appearance of Freud's work, no adequate psychological theory was formulated by any of the social theorists. Unfortunately, Freud's biological emphasis, his failure to deal adequately with social structure, and his inability to verify in convincing fashion important aspects of the theory caused his work to be ignored for the most part in the consideration of social questions; psychoanalytic descriptions of personal and familial problems were not seen to be relevant to the crucial areas of political and economic endeavor.

It must be understood, however, that Freud's idea system was as closely related to social developments as the liberal or Marxist systems had been. The theory was itself the result of changes that had taken place in the Western family structure, changes that stemmed from the need for the individual and the family to adjust to the consequences of the earlier economic and political revolutions. Specifically, these changes had permitted sons to become competitive with fathers in personal and familial terms; Freud's awareness of this conflict influenced his thinking to a very great degree.

In effect, demands for autonomy codified earlier in relation to political and economic activity were being extended in the late nineteenth and early twentieth centuries to personal and familial levels of activity. From the vantage point of the present we can see that all these demands are interrelated, that the movement toward autonomy is in fact a comprehensive one encompassing all levels of personal and institutional activity. Our vantage point also allows us to put Freud in proper sociological perspective: faced with the dramatic consequences of the movement toward autonomy in the family, he was led to a radically different kind of theoretical insight; and though his primary concern was the nature of psychic structure his insight was intimately connected to real events in society. His work can be understood as an attempt to relate man's internal wishes to his external existence and to bring both the internal and external worlds under more rational control. From this point of view it becomes evident that at least certain aspects of his work can be used in the analysis of social structures.

When we consider the various movements toward autonomy and inclusion we observe that all of them were generated within traditional social structures—structures, that is, in which the moral and psychological necessity for dependency relations and arbitrary authority was taken for granted both by authority and by its subjects. The question is, What were the social conditions that allowed these innovative demands to be accepted as legitimate and acted upon by masses of people on different institutional levels in different times and places? The question has been posed before, but the responses have been seriously limited on theoretical and empirical grounds. Because the psychological component in particular has not been systematically integrated, and because personal and familial processes have not been understood as comparable aspects of the larger movement toward autonomy and inclusion, the answers that have been offered have left too many problems unresolved.[2]

For this reason we have tried to develop a broad general theory that will explain the modern commitment to the principles of autonomy.[3] In this effort we have drawn heavily upon Talcott Parsons's contributions to sociological theory[4] and upon important aspects of Freudian psychoanalytic theory and post-Freudian ego psychology. There are a number of theoretical contributions in these works that suggest the possibility of a more comprehensive analysis of the questions we have raised.

One theoretical assumption we shall make—an assumption common in certain respects to both psychoanalytic theory and Parsonian sociology—is the existence of a process of internalization. Defined in the simplest terms, internalization means that regulations that have been accepted on the basis of continued interaction with objects in the external world are replaced by inner regulations. This internal acceptance of *patterns* of behavior, as opposed to the content of behavior, forms the basis for consistent orientations to action on all institutional levels. Moreover, the better part of this "common culture" is not available for conscious examination; it exists for individuals on an unconscious level.*

Both Freud and Parsons assume that without this internalization of norms it would be impossible to organize a stable, predictable, and viable social order. Some relationships and some bases of action must remain unconscious in order to prevent the war of all against all that would be engendered either by the expression of unrestrained instinctual behavior or, under conditions of progressive rationalization of psychic structure, by the totally egoistic expres-

---

* In addition to the concept of internalization it will be necessary to refer to the process of identification. Not all psychoanalytic or sociological writers define identification in the same way but, as Heinz Hartmann notes, all seem to agree to this extent at least: ". . . the identifying person behaves in some ways like the person with whom he has identified himself. The likeness may refer to the characteristics, features, attitudes of the object, or to the role the object plays in reality (or to the role it plays in reality according to the fantasy of the person who makes the identification) : it may mean to 'take the place' of the other person. . . . We use the term both for the process and the result." See Heinz Hartmann and Rudolph Loewenstein, "Notes on the Superego," *Psychoanalytic Study of the Child,* XVII (1962), 48-49. This publication will hereafter be referred to as *Ps. St. Chi.* Also see Robert W. White, "Ego and Reality in Psychoanalytic Theory," *Psychological Issues* (New York, 1963), vol. III, no. 3, monograph 11, 95-124.

sion of self-interest. It is not possible for man to accept society's rules on a strictly conscious level, or to become totally rationalized; for were he to do so, he could then abandon the rules the moment it suited his purpose.

As a result of this internalization of general rules of conduct, individuals accept and reproduce the patterns of behavior required by society, and they remain committed to the rules even when the patterns run counter to reason and self-interest. Thus compliance, not force, is the critical determinant of stable behavior; the presence of external authority is not enough to produce "adjusted" behavior through time. And though there has never been any direct empirical verification of this process of internalization, its existence can be inferred from recurrent behavioral manifestations and from the appearance of shame, guilt, and anxiety in situations of transgression.[5]

We shall examine this connection between personal and social levels of action in the terms established by Parsons. Parsons, like Freud, deals with the personality as a system containing internal mechanisms of control, as well as the means for categorizing and evaluating objects and actions and for becoming emotionally attached to them. Personality is integrated with a cultural system of action, comprising symbols and codes that are organized and incorporated in religious doctrines, folklore, art, and accumulated bodies of academic knowledge; and with a social system of action, which consists of patterned norms of behavior leading to the development of roles, groups, institutions, and so on. The cultural system thus establishes for the social system the principles upon which to base its organization, activities, and choice of objects; and the values and norms involved in both systems become a part of the individual personality through the process of internalization.

Another more formally psychoanalytic concept we shall

employ is that of fantasy wish-fulfillment. In relation to the dynamics of social change—the relationship we shall be concerned with—the concept of fantasy wish-fulfillment is a heuristic device by which internal wishes are linked to the social factors that allow them to become conscious and codified. Wishes that have emerged into consciousness can be brought more or less successfully under control, to provide the ground upon which demands for value change can be made. Again by inference, we presume that this movement from fantasy to value change has occurred on various historical occasions, and we may characterize our explanation of the process as an attempt to raise to the level of a systematic socio-psychological framework different manifestations that have been described more exclusively at the personal level by such writers as Erikson, Brown, Feuer, and Marcuse.[6]

The idea that fantasies can become conscious, codified, and directed toward value change in response to social conditions is employed as an analytic proposition. It is presumed that certain social-structural conditions must develop before social action aimed at value change can take place; that these conditions are such as to bring about a violation of the extant morality that binds and relates subjects to authority; and that such a violation constitutes the indispensable social condition for the codification of aggressive wishes, which are then cathected and acted upon in society.

Thus, the values and norms that lead to stable and compliant behavior over time can be attacked, and will be, if the moral code that legitimates and organizes the compliance is violated. If the affectual and status relationships that bind individuals to authority are transgressed by authority, the binding evaluative standards will cease to be effective. Aggressive wishes, ordinarily repressed and unavailable to consciousness, can become conscious and intellectually organized, and it is in this manner that wishes provide the basis for social action.

In classical psychoanalytic theory such repressed materials can become acceptable to consciousness only when they are far removed from the original instinctual impulse; that is, they must appear in some distorted or ambiguous form.* Moreover, the process is dependent wholly upon psychic factors, so that it occurs in individuals in a highly idiosyncratic way. Subsequent psychoanalytic discussions of the process (notably Ernst Kris's "regression in the service of the ego") have not progressed beyond this idiosyncratic level. Thus, so far as psychoanalytic theory is concerned, Freud's original view still holds: "We can lay down no general rule as to what degree of distortion or remoteness [from the original impulse] is necessary before the resistance on the part of the conscious is removed."[7]

It is our contention, however, that a general rule can be

---

* The concept of repression is used here in the psychoanalytic sense to designate unconscious internal processes that withhold psychic materials from consciousness when such materials are the source of conflict intolerable to ego. Strictly speaking, repression is only one of a number of defense mechanisms that serve such a purpose; though the use of the repression concept varies in Freud, he finally proposed that the term be reserved for the mechanism operant in hysteria, and that the concept of "defense" be used as a generic term subsuming all the various techniques employed by individuals in dealing with psychic conflict. Freud would then write of different kinds of defenses rather than of different kinds of repressions. In any case, we have no intention of distinguishing systematically or consistently among mechanisms at the personal level. All we mean to indicate by the use of the more familiar term "repression" is that certain materials are not consciously available. Sigmund Freud, "Inhibitions, Symptoms, and Anxiety," *The Standard Edition of the Complete Psychological Works of S. Freud,* trans. and ed. J. Strachey (London, 1958, 23 vols.) , XX, 163-64 (hereafter cited as Freud, volume, and page). Also see "Notes upon a Case of Obsessional Neurosis," Freud, X, 196.

organized to explain at least one dimension of the problem: wishes that are codified and directed toward value change have become conscious as a result of lapsed repressions; and the repressions lapse, allowing certain materials to become conscious, not in a unique and random way, but as a systematic response to the specific conditions of social-structural violation that we have indicated. It is absolutely vital to distinguish this socially motivated form of expression from idiosyncratic insight. The distinction is not always easy to make, but there are at least two criteria we can use in making it: the extent of conscious control over critical judgments, and the acceptance of these judgments in a general way by society.

The development of psychoanalytic theory itself should be understood in these terms. For example, the special capacity of artists to make available to themselves materials otherwise inaccessible to consciousness is axiomatic in psychoanalytic thought,[8] but the processes and conflicts involved in these internal materials had never been explained prior to Freud; the content had always appeared in symbolic or disguised form and it had had no general effect on society. The same cannot be said of Freud's work. The difference between what artists have been able to achieve and what Freud was able to achieve is the difference between unique, individual perception and perception that is organized and developed in response to external social conditions. Before the sociological conditions were operative —i.e., before the industrial revolution had disrupted the established relationships of the family—it was not possible to codify this kind of knowledge or make it available to society.[9]

In the light of this relationship between structural factors and psychic response, it is possible to say why ideas directed toward social change become common currency at a particular time without reference to personal feelings and predilections. And given the notion that the bases of some relationships must remain unconscious, it is also possible to say why any idea system must be limited in terms of its capacity to analyze the environment.

Freud's theory was itself limited in these terms: there were objects and actions in his environment that were difficult for him to investigate. And in the years preceding Freud the same was true for political theory and political action that sought to achieve autonomy and inclusion— we have noted, for example, that there was a marked absence in modern political and economic theory of any systematic insight into the nature of psychic processes. Thus in both cases there were some authority relations that could be examined critically, and this allowed for a certain level of insight; but there were other relations, perhaps equally oppressive, that remained unavailable for conscious examination. Because all authority relations are internalized and because individuals act in terms of a number of roles and institutional levels, it is possible for one structure to be attacked while others are left inviolate.

This observation leads to the further suggestion that codified demands for independence, and the psychic factors upon which these were based, had to be organized anew in relation to each institution against which such demands were made—including religious, economic, political, and familial spheres of activity. Institutions have tended to democratize largely on the basis of internal structural factors. The degree of autonomy and self-determination achieved within any one institutional area has had only external relevance for subsequent achievements in any other area.

The point of view taken here is opposed to a notion extant in the sociological literature that the personality factors involved in democratic achievements are basically a diffusion of characteristics stemming from the development of ascetic Protestantism.[10] We would argue, on the contrary, that the personality traits in question are a function of withdrawal from traditional authority on all institutional levels, and that for this reason the traits have recurred more than once in the modernization process and have in fact recurred in circumstances where Protestantism could have had at best only a peripheral and external influence—in, for example, the French and Russian revolutions.

These hypotheses have been organized on the basis of observations and suggestions available in the sociological and historical literature. It is impossible, of course, to establish them on firm empirical ground with respect to all institutional levels or all societies. What we can do, however, is to demonstrate, at least tentatively, the usefulness of this sociological frame of reference. Thus, two particular historical periods have been selected for review and analysis, periods that witnessed the codification of theories relating to political, familial, and individual levels of activity: the French Enlightenment, and its extension into the subsequent Revolution and the process of political democratization; and what we call the introspective revolution of the late nineteenth and early twentieth centuries, as evidenced in the changing patterns of authority in the family and the consequent liberalization of controls in domestic life.

These two periods were chosen because they permit us to discuss comparatively the movement toward autonomy and inclusion in two crucial institutional areas, one of which is not ordinarily considered in such terms. At the same time we can make use of the efforts of certain writers and actors (e.g., Rousseau, Robespierre, Freud, Kafka) whose works are rather readily available and who are most likely to be familiar to the greatest number of readers. It should be kept in mind that the two periods are approached from a particular sociological standpoint, one that integrates psychic, social, and cultural levels of activity in a systematic way. These periods are treated as sociological events, and the contents of the events—the political, social, and psychological ideas—are dealt with as sets of proposed normative statements about the universe, and not at all consistently in terms of the accumulation of bodies of rational knowledge or the dissemination of that knowledge. Our interest here is in generalized conditions that account for recurrent forms of behavior. Our explanations, however, will focus on the psychic level of activity. The social level is of course also important, particularly in terms of the tensions that are developed when behaviors are legitimated in cultural but not social terms, or when one social institution is democratized while on other institutional levels resistance to democratization persists. But we have chosen to emphasize the psychic factors because these have been consistently underplayed in considerations of the nature of social movements.

The most important general process we shall consider in this work is the separation of emotional and abstract functions that accompanied the movement away from traditional authority structures toward broader levels of autonomy and inclusion. In the traditional authority structures, the emotional and abstract functions—or what can be called, respectively, maternal and paternal functions— tended not to be separated on personal, social, or cultural levels. In the political sphere this was epitomized in the ongoing symbolic relationship of church and state; in the family it could be identified by the relative lack of distinction between mother and father, in the sense that both parents were internalized as loving and coercive representatives of authority and both were more or less equally referred to in the child-rearing and educative process.

In practice this meant that the moral codes of traditional societies imposed certain nurturant and protective functions on the various authority structures while at the same time expecting subjects to accept a passive and deferential posture. Relationships to the power structure were rigidly, if not ascriptively, defined. Authority was retained exclusively in the hands of king and aristocracy in politics and in the hands of parents in the family. Subjects and children were categorically removed from the sources of power and control.

It follows from this assessment that one of the crucial factors in the development of autonomy and inclusion has been the rationalization of traditional authority, the separation of emotional from abstract factors, and the reorganization of each in more functionally specific roles and institutions. Without this kind of separation and emotional withdrawal it would have been impossible to express the behavioral mandates typically associated with demands for autonomy—rationality, competitiveness, and emotional constraint. The withdrawal of emotional content arising from and directed toward objects permits the abstract manipulation of these objects.[11]

Among the *philosophes,* for example, the capacity for emotional withdrawal was very clearly expressed in a hostility to traditional religion and a demand that religion as such be separated from the political structure. As far as most Enlightenment writers were concerned, politics could not become a sphere of rational activity until this occurred. In the introspective era the capacity for emotional withdrawal was manifested in another way: business generally became the special province of men, while women were confined to the household. Because of this the mother was able to effect a special relationship to the children of both sexes, a relationship which was focused in ego ideal and superego and which remained repressed. The relationship of father to son, on the other hand, became more conscious; centered in the ego, it was therefore capable of a higher degree of control. This control permitted critical examination of the father's position, and on this basis the first steps were taken toward the inclusion of the sons in the family structure.

This process of differentiation of social units occurs along two lines: certain activities of social units relate to internal as opposed to external functions; other activities (referred to as expressive and instrumental) concern the acquisition of resources as means to be employed by a social unit, in contrast to the use of resources for the achievement of functional ends. Both lines of differentiation are linked to the distinctions made above—those between emotional and abstract, maternal and paternal.

Problems arise, of course, in attempting to apply such analytic categories to empirical situations. But taking the modern Western family as an example of this process the following can be said: the father has come to play primarily an external-instrumental role in the family; it is his responsibility to acquire resources for the family from external agencies and he does so ideally in terms of rationality, self-discipline, and emotional constraint. The mother, however, has tasks internal to the family; for example, she must join members of the family to the unit and to each other. Through the manipulation of affect, the mother socializes the children, especially in the early phases of childhood, orienting them emotionally to whatever subsequent obligations society will impose. Thus, external-instrumental-abstract-paternal roles stress active mastery, rationality, conscious control, and, in general, ego-superego functions. Internal-expressive-emotional-maternal roles are related rather to id-ego functions and stress affective ties based on emotional manipulations that are much less amenable to conscious control and much more removed from rational apprehension.

The point is that in pre-modern societies these various functions were relatively undifferentiated. Religion, which provided more or less a set of moral mandates on which behavior was based, was manifestly an internal-expressive function and was not differentiated from the political structure. Nor were "maternal" and "paternal" figures separated within the family in these terms. The successful political revolutions separated the religious function from the political, and the industrial revolution led to similar separations between the economy and the family and then within the family itself. Generally speaking, it is this kind of separation that allows for rational, objective, calculated manipulation of objects in the environment, and allows also for dealing with authority figures on all these institutional levels with some measure of independence.[12]

Of course, the separation of the emotional from the abstract that occurred in the political system could not have occurred to the same degree in the family. The modern political system tends to be instrumental, to be directed toward the achievement of specific goals, and to exercise control on the social rather than the personal level. The family, however, is an "associational" system that tends toward unconscious commitments; activity is directed more to the integration of members than to the achievement of specific goals. Power is more exclusively implemented on the personal level, and the ability to manipulate is based not only on one's legitimate status in the system but on one's special relationships to other members of the system (as among kin, friends, colleagues, and so on). Equivalent abstract mechanisms have not been created for the family, and the process of emotional withdrawal has not been nearly so intensive. These two structures, then, are not perfectly parallel,[13] but they are comparable in that, within the structures, power has become more generally distributed among the members, and relations more generally centered in the ego.

Obviously this process of differentiation has not occurred to the same degree on all institutional levels in all societies. Moreover, when it has occurred, it has been dealt with more successfully in some societies than in others. On the one hand, the separation of the emotional from the abstract has provided the necessary basis for the theory and practice of autonomy, and the assimilation of this separation accounts for the behavioral traits characteristically associated with the modern world. On the other hand, the inability to achieve the separation or to tolerate its psychic and social consequences when it has appeared has led to the most striking forms of personal and social regression.

It has been recognized for some time that this distinction between emotional and abstract relationships represents an important criterion of modernity. In effect this is what Marx was pointing to when he wrote that the egoistically calculating bourgeois society had stripped away the illusions fostered by the patriarchal customs and traditions of feudal society, resolving personal worth into exchange value and leaving money as the only connection between men. Ferdinand Tönnies, following Marx, developed this point, defining the historical process as an irreversible movement from associational to contractual societies, a movement resulting in increasingly mechanistic and instrumental human relationships. In much the same terms as Marx, Tönnies observed that every individual in the modern world must be separated from and opposed to every other individual.

Tönnies also elaborated upon the psychological qualities

that distinguish one social form from the other. The less differentiated associational system produces individuals characterized by spontaneous, impulsive, unreflective behavior; the more complex contractual society produces individuals who act on a rational basis, soberly calculating means/ends relationships before acting. This distinction in psychological types immediately brings to mind Max Weber's efforts to explain the origins and development of rationality in the West and his definition of traditional and modern social forms in these terms.

These different sociological frames of reference have obviously proved fruitful in the analysis of social structure. But none of them has managed to explain adequately why rational processes in contemporary societies are so often disregarded in dealing with the most prosaic, if nonetheless vital, social obligations. It is difficult to say, on the basis of these theories—which indicate a progressive rationalization of psychic and social structures—why certain social obligations continue to be accepted and acted upon without any calculated reflection. The fact is that important aspects of basic social processes are not available for rational examination; and indeed, if they were, if individuals could respond to them in an instrumental fashion, society could not be held together.

Without an appreciation of the complex nature of unconscious commitments, the classical sociologists were unable to locate important sources within the system that provide the basis for stability or change. Moreover, they were unable to explain various ambivalent and regressive manifestations of the social process they were describing, or to isolate the most important element in this process: the separation of the emotional from the abstract, and the insistence on rationality, discipline, and constraint provide the only basis upon which autonomous activity can develop.

There is no way to separate emotional ties from dependence upon nurturant and protective authority figures, and no way to eliminate the unconscious wish to restore such ties. There is no way to acquire or maintain independence except through the rationalized control of affect and the repression of emotional attachments associated with traditional societies—or, in the modern world, with maternally oriented families. The organization of psychic and social-structural conditions within which some degree of autonomy can be expressed, and within which authority can be approached with some measure of parity, is one of the basic factors in the modernization process.

Theories that have been consistently relied upon to explain social change have lacked a systematically integrated psychology of the unconscious—just as Freud and classical psychoanalytic theory lacked a proper appreciation of the importance of social structure. What we have done is to take aspects of both approaches—mediated through Parsonian sociology—in order to arrive at a more comprehensive historical and comparative view of the social process. This interplay between psychological and sociological viewpoints should permit a more balanced view of institutional relationships (exclusive concern with economic and political processes is an eighteenth- and nineteenth-century preoccupation) and should provide new insights into the crucial functions of ambivalent and regressive behavior.

The separation of the emotional from the abstract, then, serves to identify the transition from pre-modern to modern, and thus has particular meaning for us. The development of more highly differentiated societies and more complex psychic structures is a function of the ability to achieve this separation and reflects changes in authority relations and structures on all institutional levels. This is true with regard to increasing levels of personal autonomy based on a private rather than a public morality, and it is true also with regard to the inclusion of ever-widening segments of the population in decision-making processes. The tensions that characterize pluralistic societies and that lead to regressive behavior are related to this changing and increasingly complex morality and to the pressures that stem from the need to tolerate and sustain ever-expanding levels of autonomy in regard to the self and to others.[14]

1

The Sociology of Value Change

As CREATIVE processes, all revolutionary changes share a common basis—they originate in the expression of personal fantasy-wishes. The progression is always the same: wishes formerly repressed become conscious, are systematically codified, and lead to social action aimed at fundamental alterations in the values that had served to organize behavior within a social system.* And in every case the progression is triggered by structural changes in the system.

That change proceeds in this manner does not mean that man's withdrawal from the inherited values of his society must be regarded as in some sense regressive or pathological,

---

* We employ the term "values" in the Durkheimian sense of the moral orders that bulwark a social system, the set of shared rules that guide and orient action, define correct and proper behavior, and in general shape affect and cognition for all the actors in the system. A change in the values that underlie a social system implies a change in the rules governing what members of a society (or some part of the

or that it cannot represent personal and social development.[1] The elevation of a fantasy-wish to consciousness is in fact a normal reaction to certain conditions obtaining even when personality and environment are relatively stable. The codification of a fantasy-wish is also a normal response, given particular kinds of structural change in the external world. It is therefore necessary for individuals to adapt to fantasy-wishes, and the adaptive process manifests in them the same range of response that exists for any tension-producing condition; i.e., they evince attitudes and behavior that will be judged as creative or destructive according to the point of view of the society of the actors, or in this case, the point of view of the historical investigator.

Our focus, then, is on value change that alters the meaning of life for individuals in society, and also the character of society itself. It should be clear, however, that social change as such need not occur at the expense of inherited values. Historically, in fact, social systems have for the most part been interpreted as fundamentally viable, and the

---

society) decide is appropriate behavior, a change in how members perceive and categorize objects, how they feel about objects, and so forth. This formulation is particularly relevant for the argument presented here: value changes in the political and familial spheres we shall be discussing led to the replacement of exclusive, dependent behavior by inclusive, autonomous behavior; the transition was reflected in changes in both social and psychic structure.

Values in these terms are distinguished from "norms." Both values and norms constitute rules or standards, but norms are symbolic codes related to specific roles and are institutionalized with reference to specific components of the "division of labor" within a social system; for example, a work group shares common values that are independent of levels of social differentiation, but each member's role in the group is governed by more specific normative standards; the different work roles are integrated, and on the basis of this integration the group's values are implemented and its goals achieved. Values render norms legitimate, and as standards for conduct are, as noted, more general than norms.

alterations called for by those interested in change have been designed to take place within the extant value system. Social tensions are generally perceived as stemming from the "ineffectiveness" of institutional arrangements; the further evolution of these institutions in the direction of greater functional efficiency[2] is enough to reconcile discontent.

Thus, in the long run, values have enormous staying power and are capable of sustaining a great deal of institutional change. However, given the structural changes that result simply from historical development, and the consequent changes in personality and dispositions among the members of a society, it is reasonable to anticipate that under certain conditions the basis of institutional legitimation will be challenged, i.e., that the values as such will be questioned.

The alternative processes of change, then—one taking place within a given value structure, the other in opposition to the structure—follow similar patterns, the choice between the two being determined by the "actor's definition of the situation." The members of a society may deem it feasible to solve issues through structural rearrangement in the direction of more effective performance within the extant system, or the environment may be felt to be so intolerable that only a basic change in elements of the value structure will suffice.[3] When the latter condition obtains, revolutionary change becomes possible because the values of a society have in some sense failed. At this point fantasy-wishes become consciously available and codified, and are more or less generally accepted in society. Further, it is the internalization of these newly codified wishes that ultimately produces a situation in which no change within the extant system can satisfy the discontented. This condition develops for two reasons: the fantasy is not oriented to contemporary reality (though aspects of the reality may well be called upon, even to a considerable degree, in the formation and codification of the fantasy); and the internalization and expression of the codified fantasy end any *conscious* sense of obligation to the extant moral and social system.[4]

Empirical resolutions of fantasy take many possible forms: a fantasy can remain unconscious or preconscious indefinitely, thus never achieving consciousness; a fantasy can escape personal repression and exist consciously for a great length of time without being codified; a fantasy can become codified and be suppressed by the society to which it is addressed, or it can become codified and be available to society without being accepted as a basis for action by the group that might be, or ought to be, its principal adherents. That is, *the progression from fantasy to social action is not an inevitable evolution.* But once fantasy becomes conscious as a function of social structural factors, the conditions exist for efforts to be made toward its ideological codification, and toward its general acceptance.

On the conscious sociological level, of course, a number of other factors contribute to this process of value change. For example, after those who are seeking such a change define the values that appear to be desirable or that are wished or hoped for, it is then necessary to motivate the important sectors of the population to become committed to the new values. From a structural point of view the movement will have to be independent of the extant social organizations, and, in the end, the movement will have to gain access to or absorb the relevant organizations of society. Moreover, an important factor in the overall process is the emergence of some form of charismatic leadership.

For what follows, it will not be necessary to examine all of these various factors. One, however, will require some elaboration—the function of personality. Personality becomes an especially decisive source for value change because of the emergence of charismatic individuals and because, as we have indicated, certain contributions to change originate in fantasy-wish expression, a non-institutionalized aspect of the social order that becomes structured and made available to the society.

To assert that personality is a critical source for value change and that innovative thought originates in fantasy leads us to a consideration of the internal nature of thought processes. It is not sufficient to accept thought as the result of some given but unknowable process, to be ignored in favor of examining the external circumstances that give thought one particular shape or another. The codified, intellectual form that thought assumes on the conscious level is a result of psychic as well as social causes, and this process must be examined. The basis for a description of the way in which wish-fulfillment is related to codified thought is provided by psychoanalytic theory, including Freud's original contributions and especially his late structural views, and by suggestions from post-Freudian ego psychology. The ideas and the language may be alien to ordinary sociological or historical discourse; nevertheless we must examine these psychoanalytic contributions and indicate their relationship to sociological theory as it is developed here.[5]

Fantasy-thought may be considered to originate as a response to deprivation: in the absence of an object of gratification, a hallucinatory image or idea of that object or of an experience associated with that object arises. It is assumed that the production of these images or ideas depends upon memory traces of earlier gratifying experiences; when a given trace becomes charged with energy it can be cathected and achieve consciousness. The model for the initial phase of the thought process, then, is this: mounting tension in the absence of a need-satisfying object leads to the production of some image or idea of the object, constituting an attempt by the personality to reestablish equilibrium in the face of deprivation. These images can be thought of as safety valves for tension states.[6]

Two critical observations must be made here: first, during this phase of the fantasy-thought process, realization is always attempted in terms of wish-fulfillment, the shortest path to the alleviation of tension; second, the unconscious memory traces in question are to be conceived of as *generalized symbolic categorizations of objects or experiences related to previous modes of adaptation.* This means that the conscious production of images or ideas cannot be infinitely diverse but must be limited to productions linked in some way to important aspects of the past; given the absence of an object, only a finite number or range of symbolic memory traces can possibly be cathected.

Because the image or idea assumes an impulsive, wish-fulfilling form it must be modified at the conscious level before it can be acted upon; the idea must be refined in terms of the laws of logic and causality, and it must be consonant with the demands of internalized morality as well as the demands and pressures of the external world. Since thought can be adaptive only if it is reality-oriented, it is subject at the conscious level to ego and superego processes. In particular, if ego is threatened by anxiety stemming from the impulsive quality of an idea, or by superego punishment because the intended gratification is morally suspect, then the idea will be repressed. The ego, the rationalizing and systematizing function of the mind, strives to exercise control, and it ordinarily does so by mediating between the impulsive claims of the wish and the internal and external prohibitive agencies.[7]

There are some interesting parallels between this psychoanalytic formulation and Parsons's efforts to integrate psychic factors into a systematic sociology. Parsons claims that the internalization process involves the acceptance of several orders of phenomena, each order a part of the inter-action process that takes place between two or more persons: the status of an object, the emotional orientation toward the object, and the evaluative and integrative standards by which status and affect are combined to form a system.[8] The binding qualities of evaluative and integrative elements are referred to (following Durkheim) as moral standards.* These standards work to stabilize interaction, to legitimate and organize relationships between persons and groups, to clarify and structure appropriate feelings, and generally to produce predictable and consistent courses of action through time.

In line with notions that Freud had begun to sketch into his system, Parsons concludes in these terms that not only are moral standards internalized as part of the personality structure, but *all the components of common culture* (affectual, status, integrative, and evaluative standards) are internalized as parts of unconscious personality.[9] Parsons notes further that if his assumptions regarding the internalization of culture are correct, then the following conclusion will relate to Freud's metapsychology: the ego, the organizational aspect of the personality, would "not be derived from the 'reality principle'—that is, from adaptation responses to the external world alone. Instead it would be derived from *two* fundamental sources: the external world as an environment; and the common culture as acquired from [social] objects of identification."

* Evaluative standards legitimate, and within given limits designate, the styles of change in a social structure. Integrative standards determine the organization and allocation of status and affect in a social structure.

From a sociological standpoint this implies an important reorganization of the concepts of id and ego. Parsons states that id-impulses should be considered as an integral part of the ego: "human emotions, or affects on the normal human level, should be regarded as a *symbolically* generalized system, that is, never id-impulses as such. Affect is not a direct expression of drive motivation, but involves it only as it is organized and integrated with both the reality experience of the individual and the cultural patterns which he has learned through the process of identification."

There are, then, two points of convergence between the psychoanalytic and the sociological frames of reference. One point concerns the notion of symbolically generalized expression of id-impulses.[10] The second concerns the mutual emphasis on the internalization of affectual, status, integrative, and evaluative relationships. The integrative and evaluative dimensions of judgment are particularly crucial for both systems because it is on this basis that stability is maintained within a social system; these mechanisms of control narrow the range of acceptable alternative thoughts and actions.[11] Thought and action at the psychic level are inhibited by ego and superego processes: no individual can tolerate unlimited dissonant expression, not even in the context of uncodified fantasy.* It is only in the polar cases of personal or social anomie that behavior can begin to assume unrestricted forms.

In these psychosocial terms the individual perceives, identifies with, and internalizes objects and actions; the process ensues from the very beginning of the development

---

* Restrictions exist at the social level, too, of course; thought and action must be interpreted in the light of commonly accepted definitions of safety and utility. At this point, however, we are referring only to the internalizations that control and inhibit activity at the psychic level.

of the personality and accounts for the formation of ego and superego. In this manner the individual acquires patterns of behavior, and, ultimately, these internalized patterns include not only physical, anatomical factors, or such factors as status and occupation, but all the components of common culture as these are expressed in various forms of social activity. Thus, the objects and actions the individual identifies with and internalizes are not only the familial but also, more generally, the social, and each plays a crucial role in the life of the individual. Religious, political, or economic authorities and relationships, for example, are not to be viewed simply as representations of original family experiences; they develop an existence of their own in the life of the mind, and it is because of the general nature of this internalization process that, historically, attacks could have been directed against religious, political, and economic authorities *without triggering an immediate and equivalent attack against authority in the family.** And although various forms of idiosyncratic behavior may follow from the experience of deprivation, systematic social action becomes possible because of the shared personal and social experiences within the common culture.

* It is axiomatic in psychoanalytic theory that "family relationships become the prototypes of subsequent relationships throughout life." This is not true, at least in the sense that psychoanalysts mean it. Historically there have been relationships to authority on religious, economic, and political levels of activity that were not duplicated or reflected in the family, or were not based on extant relationships in the family. For example, the idea that one could choose, accept, constrain, defy, or repudiate political authority was accepted as appropriate behavior long before a comparable sense of independence was accepted as appropriate behavior in the family. True, the internalizations that support such an attitude to political authority stem initially from life in the family. But that is not the same as saying that relationships to authority in the family are prototypical of relationships to authority on all other institutional levels. The quote is from Gregory Rochlin, *Griefs and Discontents* (Boston, 1965), 8.

In this context, then, if individuals should experience deprivation with regard to *social* objects and actions, hitherto repressed materials will be cathected and made available to consciousness. Codified thought that assumes an ideological form directed at value change originates, therefore, in an unconscious desire for instinctual gratification stimulated by the absence of objects at the *social* level of activity.[12] The cathected ideas will strive for realization in terms of wish-fulfillment, but will be mediated by ego in terms of what the external world and the psychic counterpart (superego) will allow. If the ideas are relatively ego-syntonic, and if the social situation is such that they do not lead to excessive conflict, they will be subject to revision and refinement and will acquire systematic form. In such a form the ideas can be cathected by large numbers of people, who will then act to institutionalize new standards and styles of behavior.

The mediating function of ego must be understood in relation to the symbolic content of the wish and the factor of deprivation. The ego, confronted with the fantasy (wish-fulfillment) response to deprivation, searches out connections with and support from the external world and the common culture in order to exercise control over both the internal and external dimensions of the environment. This is not to say that ego always succeeds. But in general the ego's synthesizing function tries to bring coherence to data: the ego must try to understand deprivation and fantasy in some sensible way. It is the symbolic content of fantasy thought, the normatively defined environmental deprivation, and the need to maintain conscious control over the two that lead to system formation.

For our purpose, then, fantasies related to social structure may be conceived of as relatively nonlegitimate, non-institutionalized ideas codified as ideology and internalized and expressed as solutions to social crisis.[13] However, the alternatives suggested by those offering the ideology and interested in value change will not be the expression of randomly internalized fantasies but will reflect the interaction between personal, historical, and contemporary circumstances, so that in the long run the "answers" will be oriented to the problem raised by the particular agency and level of society provoking the strain.

The internalization and expression of cathected fantasies not oriented to contemporary reality, followed by the acceptance of new status, affective, integrative, and evaluative relationships based on these fantasies, account for the experience of dissatisfaction with a particular social organization. The integrative and evaluative elements are stressed as particularly important factors in social change because demands made in terms of these factors explicitly entail change in the values and norms of a society.

In subsequent chapters we shall be attempting to isolate movements based on fantasy solutions directed toward the changing of values across broad reaches of human endeavor. We have established four empirical criteria for identifying such movements. First, the fantasy solution must be expressed by a single unit. The unit can be a single person or a group acting in a collective manner, i.e., with unity of purpose and commitment, no matter how loosely organized or bound together. A group taking collective action usually responds to a single temporary "spokesman," the member who symbolically expresses the fantasy solution, whereas other members adhere to the group's ideas or activities primarily on the basis of personal and affective, rather than intellectual, commitment. Changes in the choice of spokesman usually occur with the passage of time and with the structural development and organization of the group. In particular, those who are moral innovators are rarely the activists in-

volved in institutionalizing the change. In any case, someone must lead: the group and its ideology must remain
focused and embodied in a single spokesman.*

Second, the content of the fantasy cannot have been
previously accepted in the institutional order to which it
is being directed. Thus, for example, from the standpoint
of the *ancien régime,* human equality was a legitimate
religious doctrine, though an illegitimate political doctrine.
Third, the content of the fantasy used as the basis for
moral evaluation of the relevant institution must cause a
personal and social reaction that can be defined as moral
indignation on the part of self and others.[14] And fourth,
in spite of the indignant reaction, adherence to the codified
fantasy must "desacralize" the extant morality, that is, allow allegiances to be repudiated so that activists can strike
against the morality and against those who represent it.

Given the assumption that fantasies can become conscious and codified, it is still necessary to account for the
relationship between structural violation and the codification of the particular wish for autonomy and inclusion.
The demand for the implementation of these values was,
after all, a significant departure from the mores and practices of the traditional order. This is immediately evident
if we examine the cardinal behavioral mandates involved:
self-discipline, emotional constraint, and rationality. The
individual thus affirms that he is prepared to rely on a
personal capacity to direct his own existence rather than
on an unquestioning response to public morality. It was
the internalization of such content as this, brought on by

---

* When the spokesman is no longer the one who expresses the
values but the one who acts symbolically to implement them, the fate
of the new morality has been given over to the charismatic leader, and
larger factions of the society, those beyond the bounds of the active
collectivity, can be motivated to participate in the movement.

different structural changes, that provided the basis for struggles that led to the transformation of traditional societies—for here was a wish that could not be accommodated to the mandates of the extant moral order.

This is not to say that social conflict directed against traditional authority was unknown in pre-revolutionary societies. But the uprisings that did occur were invariably based on demands for the implementation of traditional values, not on the repudiation of these values. This was true even when the demand was for total equality within the community of Christian believers. This inclusive content, after all, had always existed·at the cultural level in Christian societies and had already been acted upon in significant ways, as, for example, in the monastic orders.[15] However, there was no such equivalent content available to justify demands for political autonomy.

It is difficult to make such fundamental breaks with established order. Values are internalized and they control and legitimate behavior. Moreover, the extent to which they do so varies with the level of institutional differentiation: there exists considerable evidence to indicate that internalization of values occurs most intensively and extensively in relatively undifferentiated groups and communities. The socialization of individuals at such a level implies an unconscious adherence to all the diverse aspects of the common culture. In traditional societies, characterized as they were by sharply defined hierarchical authority structures, this was true particularly of the internalization of the *moral appropriateness of superordinate-subordinate status relationships.*

To the greatest degree, in pre-modern societies, both political and familial authority conformed to this relatively undifferentiated hierarchical pattern. The parents in the traditional household and the leader of the traditional

society had in common a great deal of "political" authority, if this authority and the implied control and decision-
making are understood in a general analytic sense.[16] In
traditionally organized structures not only were the king's
and the parents' status internalized as legitimate, but so too
were the affectual ties and moral (i.e., evaluative and integrative) standards governing the relationships between authority and those subject to its control.

In particular, the traditional forms of authority had
nurturant and protective functions in relation to subjects:
superordinates were obliged to provide systems of control
and also to provide for the general welfare of subordinates
in personal and affectual terms, under the mutually held
principle that the subjects were unable to provide these
for themselves.[17] The subjects had to *appear*, therefore,
to be treated as an end and not as a means. On this basis
it was possible for subordinates to internalize a dependent
posture and act upon it. Traditional societies endured with
tolerable levels of conflict on the basis of compliance.

In these societies relationships to authority figures were,
of course, ambivalent. However, in hierarchically arranged
status systems, the aggressive aspect of the ambivalence
cannot be expressed outside the value structure so long as
authority appears to be fulfilling its nurturant role; except in individual and idiosyncratic instances, aggression
aimed at the moral codes must remain unconscious. As
long as authority can be prevailed upon to act within the
mandates of the system, the internalized affectual ties,
status relationships, and moral standards will permit the
expression of only positive commitments toward what is
held to be sacred in society.

In every society, therefore, the moral mandates are intimately connected with what is considered sacred, just
as the authority legitimated by these mandates is invariably

hierarchically ordered. Those who have the greatest share in and responsibility for the implementation of values also receive the greatest rewards. So long as the representatives of the moral order meet their obligations, neither those at the center nor those removed from it will see the inequities as morally burdensome.[18]

Social stability, then, depends upon maintaining a high degree of integration among institutional systems and within each system. But the unity is never perfect—indeed, if it were perfect it would be impossible to effect change. Social structures are always to´ this degree "unstable"—particularly so when for structural reasons authority may be forced to transgress status and affectual relationships, thereby disrupting evaluative and integrative standards. It is possible, and sometimes unavoidable, for authority to breach the mutually accepted system of psychic and social control, and when this occurs the inequitable shares of power and reward may be viewed as inappropriate and immoral, thus allowing positive affect to be withdrawn. It is at this point that hostile wishes can be cathected and internalized, legitimating aggressive action at the social level.

Freud's classic paper "Two Principles of Mental Functioning" offers an important insight into the workings of this process of structural violation in relation to the wish for autonomy at the personality level. Freud pointed out that unconscious (primary) processes are timeless, a factor expressed in the desire for immediate gratification and in cathectic instability. He observed further that there are no contradictions in the unconscious—thoughts that would be seen as contradictory at the conscious level exist simultaneously without conflict on the primary level.[19] If we add to these conjectures Parsons's emphasis on the moral standards (in brief, *"all components of the common culture* are internalized as parts of the [unconscious] personality"), we have the basis for an analysis of this aspect of change.

What these factors indicate is that not only does the wish for dependence exist at the unconscious level, but so too does the opposite and (from the standpoint of the traditional society) illegitimate wish for independence—in relation to social as well as personal and familial objects. Therefore, when authority is perceived as acting systematically in violation of the moral codes—while at the same time maintaining an insistence on the former status relationships and modes of obedience, loyalty, and submission—the negative wish can be cathected and codified.[20] Aggression will be expressed in ideological terms characterized by a vivid sense of moral indignation.

Where social institutions offer rewards for the control of impulses, the hostile aspect of ambivalence cannot be expressed consciously or lead to action. But when the rewards fail, it becomes possible for repressions to lapse, and aggression can then follow. When this sequence was triggered on the political level in France, the Enlightenment and the Revolution followed; when it took place in the structure of the middle-class family, father/son conflict and the development of psychoanalytic theory followed. Moreover, these withdrawals from authority were carried through even though the failure of authority to fulfill moral obligations resulted from structural changes that no power could have controlled.*

* "Moral obligations" are the appropriate modes of action for the actors in a system, with respect to each other's role expectations. "Authority" represents the legitimate right of command, including the use of power and/or influence to achieve compliance. Further, the legitimate use of authority implies the probability that commands will be obeyed by one or a set of persons. The legitimate scope of authority is at this point not relevant to our discussion. See Max Weber, *The Theory of Social and Economic Organization,* trans. and eds. A. M. Henderson and Talcott Parsons (Glencoe, Ill., 1947).

It was as a result of specific violations of status and affectual relationships that demands for autonomy and inclusion were codified by intellectuals in the Enlightenment era and made available at the cultural level. The public expression and acceptance of these ideas was proof enough that the traditional structure could no longer support certain kinds of practical social activity. Organized as literature, philosophy, social science, or even as journalism, these ideas represented the codification of wished-for innovative patterns of behavior, belief, and thought, the codification of new values for the legitimation and organization of political authority. The content of the ideas was cathected and internalized by masses of people, leading to action at the social level. The ideologies and actions directed toward social change can be understood as wish-fulfillments as we have defined the process, for the wish for autonomy and inclusion became conscious and generalized in society even though the morality necessary to sanction it was not yet available.

The codification of such an alternative value structure led to conflict within the society. Those who had internalized the values of political autonomy took steps directed at the integration of their interests into the power structure. But there were individuals and groups who would not or could not accept the new values, and even disadvantaged elements, who felt themselves more threatened by the attack on traditional morals than by their dependent, subordinate position, could be mobilized to defend the old order. Adherents of the traditional structure denied that change was morally appropriate, and took countermeasures to maintain or restore traditional social practices based on passivity, stratification, and exclusion.

Wherever a society has undergone the organization and

attempted implementation of the values of autonomy, it has occurred in more or less this same way, and on virtually all institutional levels of activity. It is the similarities in the nature of traditional, hierarchical authority, and in the means of withdrawal from this authority, that lead to the general and rather uniform patterns of behavior. Thus we note that those who have internalized the values of autonomy and are in a position to implement the values in practical terms invariably and universally insist upon the expression of such behavioral mandates as self-control, emotional constraint, and rationality. It can also be noted that if the pressures stemming from conflict prove to be too great, then certain other kinds of behavior can be expected to follow, behavior regressive in content and reflecting continued attachments to the mandates of the traditional structure. In order to explain more fully the relationship of these recurrent behaviors to the demand for autonomy it will be necessary to examine them in both their positive and negative forms, and we shall do so in due course. For the present, however, we shall pursue the negative (regressive) alternative in relation to political activity—specifically, the failure of individuals and groups committed to the new values to maintain them when the traditional order has been overcome. This approach permits a continued focus on the function of repression, thus allowing more effective illumination of the vital comparisons that will subsequently be made between the aggressive questioning of political authority in the Enlightenment era and the advent of Freud and the systematic investigation of authority in the family.

The fact that it is authority which initially violates the moral system does not mean that the resulting conflict can proceed without great strain on the psychic level. On the contrary, such strain must follow from the internalization of contradictory evaluative structures. Thus the internalization of traditional affectual and moral ties meant the compliant acceptance of a passive position, whereas the internalization and conscious expression of the wish for autonomy led to opposed moral positions and behavioral mandates—specifically, active mastery and self-control. The innovator, therefore, was forced by his own demands to experience various kinds of personal conflict.

The demand for autonomy and inclusion stands as a public confession of the wish for power, or the wish to share power with formerly inviolable figures. Ego, caught between the claims of the wish and the learned prohibitions, experiences guilt for the violation of the past. Aggression is also manifest—against society to the extent that the wish is pursued to its conclusion but *also against the self,* whether in the attempt to repress the wish or in attempting to fulfill it.*

Ego, striving to impose the values of autonomy, can succeed in its mediating function in spite of such obstacles. The actor(s) can create a tolerant view of the environment if it proves possible to endure the anxiety stemming from the violation of the past. This is accomplished by conceding to unconscious commitments; that is, by insisting at the conscious level on the incorporation of significant elements of the past into the new framework. Indeed, the values of autonomy have been successfully implemented only by moderates whose behavior is characterized by an inability to make unequivocal breaks with important aspects of tradition.

* The revolutionary, in spite of manifest propensities to creation and innovation, must interpret the world to a significant degree in terms of the formally and informally stated modes of interpretation that he has inherited as a member of society and that have been internalized as sanctioned modes of thought and action. Thus aggression against the society must constitute aggression against the self.

In so saying, we imply the possibility that ego will fail in its mediating function; if the guilt and anxiety provoked by the wish become intolerable, the actor is forced to accept regressive solutions. In terms of political organization several such solutions are possible, but two in particular concern us here, both typically associated with the radical-democratic left. These are the creation of a system that expresses the new values in excessive and polarized fashion while according authority a traditional hierarchical form; and the passive, dependent acceptance of this hierarchical and exclusive reorganization of authority on the part of masses of people.

What distinguishes the radical from the moderate is that in defense against unconscious guilt his values become idealized, related to superego rather than to ego. Further, and for the same reason, it becomes necessary for him to deny that any violation of the past has actually occurred. The radical can take action only by repressing his own past, as well as its connection to the cultural past, on virtually all levels. The past is then interpreted in a wholly negative light, and there is a deliberate, conscious attempt to avoid accepting any of it into the new structure; i.e., the past is explicitly abandoned on behalf of an idealized future that, to the radical, is categorically available and even imminent.

The problem for the radical is not yet solved, however. The renunciation of affectual ties and moral commitments to traditional authority, to this degree and with these results, leads to an anticipation of retributory punishment; no forgiveness can be expected from the violated authority and so none is asked for or offered. Any disorder in the external world takes on systematic meaning (the existence of plots and conspiracies), and the method of dealing with the threat takes a form that is quite clearly an expression of unconsciously held commitments to the past: the restoration of the traditional form of authority. It is for this reason that power comes once again to be reserved exclusively for the few and is organized in a rigid and punitive way, employing disciplined violence in order to gain compliance with dictates.

To put it another way, when the external world becomes too problematic, the implementation of the new values of autonomy becomes personally intolerable, and there is a reversion to a less differentiated past. There is, perhaps, an exaggerated and idealized public commitment to the principle of autonomy, but no capacity to invoke it; the leaders respond rather in a traditional way. At the same time, large numbers of people who become involved in the struggle because of the promise of inclusion rather than the promise of autonomy accept once again in a passive, subordinate way this reorganized undifferentiated authority structure. Those who do not are driven from their position by the implementation of terror.

These aspects of control and violence have impinged enormously on the consciousness of the modern world. Violence was certainly not new to anyone, but abstract violence, the sense of disciplined terror organized as a function of conscience, was shocking. What had happened is understandable, however: the behavior patterns associated with autonomy had become internalized, and given the need to express the values in ideal terms, within an authoritarian structure, these rather typical traits—self-control, self-denial, suppression of feeling, mastery, discipline, duty—came to be employed in a rigid and punitive way in the service of terror.[21]

Although we intend to discuss only this radical-democratic alternative at length, we should distinguish at this point another possible solution to the inability to tolerate autonomy—the conscious adherence to traditional values typically associated with the so-called radical right. This reaction is identified by an excessive dependence upon the past, by an attempt to incorporate consciously *all* the features of the past into the present. The attempt must fail in any objective sense because the past as object is gone and cannot be restored. What results, then, are codified fantasies about the past in which an idealized figure of traditional authority is created in order to impose, again in ideal terms, the values and norms of passivity and dependence.

It is for this reason that the emphasis of the radical right is on the customs and mores of the traditional community, on the affectual nature of the simple past that was based on personal rather than abstract and instrumental relationships. This view of the past is opposed to the egoistic complexities of the present—complexities symbolized, for example, by the great cosmopolitan cities that are the sources of diversity and pluralization. The radical right denies the possibility for self-control and demands restoration of the absolute unity that apparently once existed between private and public morality. All wishes directed at the disruption of such traditional relationships are repressed.

Thus there is manifest complete compliance with the traditional values. Violence in this case is mobilized on the basis of identification with the unassailable, punishing, archaic authority, and it is directed toward anyone who might appear to wish or to be the cause of the destruction of these relations. Violence is also important as a means of maintaining some sense of mastery over the environment; this position supports the continued commitment to an essentially masochistic posture.

In objective terms there are many similarities between these two regressive solutions to the demand for autonomy. The similarities have been identified time and again, particularly those respecting the excessive and rigid social control and the use of disciplined violence. But it is clear that the two solutions are based on rather different reactions, and no matter how punitive or coercive the radical-left movements become, the wish for autonomy has become conscious, the values have been internalized, and the identification is always with the historically dispossessed. The continued ideological adherence to the values of inclusion creates a tension between the cultural and social levels of society, and the principles can never be wholly suppressed or denied. The radical right, on the other hand, manifests no such commitment; on the contrary, everything is organized to keep the wish for autonomy repressed.

The failure of certain societies in the modern era to accept movements towards autonomy and inclusion and the failure of certain radical-democratic movements to institutionalize these values when power became available can in part be understood from this point of view.* But,

---

* It is important to consider the institutional, or structural, problem. In two senses, a kind of pluralism was "built into" the traditional societies. First, there were two dominant institutions, church and state, and allegiance to both was encouraged; moreover, in terms of cultural commitments, the two were not reducible to each other. Second, the whole network of concrete, practical, political and social power centers that were built up forced, through time, a distribution of allegiances in traditional societies. The chaotic circumstances of revolutionary upheaval tended to destroy the separate institutions of church and state, focusing affective attachment to the revolution; and of course the turmoil also destroyed the informal power centers so that a total structure could dominate *temporarily*.

The temporary nature of these solutions, especially for left-wing movements, is stressed not only because of the continued ideological

again, these regressive forms are by no means a necessary consequence of the attempt to implement value change. Yet if the demand for differentiation produces intolerable anxiety, the result will be one or another form of a closed world.

We have explained in ideal terms the differences between three types of reaction to value change on the political level. In practice there is considerable overlap in response; and, of course, contradictory commitments and motivations may easily coexist in the same individual or group. In general, however, the distinctions we have made will prove valid, and may be summed up in the following way: if the individual considers the goals of autonomy and inclusion, the means of achieving these goals, and the possible results of his actions in relation to the possibility of compromise, his behavior can be considered ego-oriented; if the individual acts towards the fulfillment of these values in an absolute way, without regard to the means and without entertaining the possibility for compromise, his behavior may be considered superego-oriented; and if the individual denies in an absolute way that it is possible or morally appropriate to realize these values, and insists rath-

---

commitment, at the cultural level, to autonomy and inclusion, but also because these societies are determined to progress in technical-industrial terms; i.e., the process of differentiation continues at least in this area, and the trained, educated personnel required by the process cannot be expected to tolerate passivity indefinitely.

Further, it is necessary to locate in these societies the large groups who have not yet internalized the new morality, or who have accepted it but find the pressure of conflict too great to permit them to act in terms of the morality. This is particularly true for urban working masses who have been deprived of the consolations of the traditional society, and who are, therefore, particularly exposed and amenable to authoritarian solutions. Regimes may rule by terror, but they rule also by virtue of the compliance of such masses.

er on an idealized adherence to passivity, his behavior may be called id-oriented.*

The id-oriented form of the resolution of conflict is interesting for its relevance in another context: it resembles the form adopted in response to the failure to maintain new values in the more affectively based family structure. The inability to tolerate demands for autonomy in the family has again taken the form of the incorporation of the past, though not in terms of rigid control and violence, which have been fairly restricted to the political level of action. This response in the family has brought with it rather an excessive dependence upon a *permissive* past in which the satisfaction of wishes has sufficed to submerge autonomy in both parents and children.[22] This response amounts to a passive acceptance of compliance through regression to another aspect of traditional authority, the idealized loving parent.

We shall not be able to pursue this problem of regression to an idealized past in the family; we will, however, return to other aspects of the familial problem, in relation to the development of psychoanalytic theory.

* The point is that ego faced with the necessity of rejecting received authority is beset by complex pressures—instinctual, superego, and reality pressures. The difficulty is that critical, objective observation is only one aspect of thought; thought can also be used for the gratification of instinctual urges, or to serve purely superego demands. It should also be noted that superego is not necessarily antithetical to ego; rather, superego represents the extant morally sanctioned modes of expression, which may be consistent with ego. However, when ego seeks to codify a formerly repressed wish and to alter the environment on the basis of the wish, ego stands to superego as the representative of nonsanctionable modes of expression and behavior. In part, these distinctions above are equivalent to Weber's distinction between goal-rational and value-rational behavior (Weber, *The Theory of Social and Economic Organization*).

2

The French Enlightenment

*T*HE VALUE structure of pre-Revolutionary France defined a political system in which authority and rewards were
reserved exclusively for a legally defined elite order. At the
center of the structure stood the king, the dominant symbol and the source of power. At this cultural level there
were no political boundaries—the king and his people were
as one, interests and functions were a common concern, and
so long as the king appeared to be fulfilling his protective
role there was no ideological outcry at the periphery for
political and social equality and inclusion.

The French nobles, of course, traditionally close to the
monarch, viewed their relationship to power as morally
appropriate. The nobles, however, never did develop the
kind and degree of *moral* legitimacy commanded by the
king—indeed, from the standpoint of the excluded elements, the power and status enjoyed by the nobles derived

wholly from their relationship to the king. Thus the king's status was sanctified by the moral order but the nobility's was not. The affective and moral commitments that bound the symbolic structure of society concerned only king and subjects; it did not concern the aristocracy.

Society did not necessarily accept the concrete conditions imposed by the prevailing authority relations, but it did accept the patriarchal symbolism, on two levels. The king was accepted as a religiously sanctioned patriarch with absolute authority over his subjects; at the same time, the king was morally obligated to protect his subjects and to see to their welfare. Society also accepted the authority of the aristocracy, but at a conventional level, that is, on the basis of noble connections to the king rather than divine sanction. Thus, as Tocqueville pointed out, the French held it as a maxim "that the king could do no wrong; and if he did do wrong, the blame was imputed to his advisers. This notion made obedience very easy; it enabled the subject to complain of the law, without ceasing to love and honor the lawgiver."[1]

But the eighteenth century witnessed an evident shift in the loyalties and allegiances of Frenchmen. Elements of the population that had hitherto been excluded from the political processes of society began to demand equal participation in the power structure. Their demand evolved because, in the terms we have employed, the monarchy had violated the value structure that legitimated its existence. Specifically, the seventeenth century attempt to organize royal absolutism constituted a violation of the moral commitment that existed between patriarchal authority and society. It is in terms of this aspect of monarchical policy that the events of the Enlightenment century can best be understood.

The situation may be viewed in the following way. The

attempt to establish absolutism was bound to fail; the king could not possibly have succeeded in organizing an undifferentiated political structure. This structure had to evolve to meet concrete economic, technological, demographic, and political pressures. Thus, at the same time that the king was stressing his unqualified power he was forced to share that power—not with the aristocracy as such, against whom the absolutism was at least in part directed, but with a bureaucratic machinery that had neither sacred nor conventional justification for being included in the authority structure. This need to create an abstract administrative structure and to share authority with it was the initial, critical step in the failure of royal authority to carry out the moral imperatives that justified its right to rule.

The process had unfortunate consequences for traditional authority, for nurturant, affective ties were broken as a result of the bureaucratization of politics. In addition, status relationships were also affected: people who could never "belong" to the traditional society were asked or required to participate in and contribute to it in important ways. Equal contribution in the absence of traditional emotional bonds should have led to the granting of equal prestige at the social level, thereby enhancing individual self-esteem. But this prestige was not forthcoming, and though the situation remained more or less stable so long as a degree of mobility was afforded by the system, it would inevitably deteriorate to the extent that this mobility was threatened.

At the same time, the monarchical policy forced an identity crisis on the aristocracy: the nobles were threatened by the loss of function in a differentiating society that was in a position to link positions of power to competence rather than to birth. Aristocratic hostility was directed against the symbol that appeared to be responsible for the threat; it was the aristocracy that initially justified the violation of received authority. Rather than face oblivion in terms of social change over which they had no control, the nobles proceeded to redefine an identity on the basis of race and blood. They insisted that as a class they were peculiarly suited to rule, and they took positive steps to institute that rule.

The nobles wanted a sphere of independent authority, *but they wanted it within the extant moral order.* They understood that they had no right to rule unless they remained bound to what was sacred in society. It was for this reason that they sought to buttress their position by invoking ancient rights, privileges, and charters, even going so far as to invent mythical ones. The nobles wanted concrete, practical political power, but they did not want to change the value system. However, their desire to establish an independent sphere of power, in the light of the king's reliance on a bureaucratic machinery, produced an unexpected reaction. The aggressive demands of one segment of society, and the inclusion of a second one, indicated to other equally non-sacred elements that the rights of participation in the political structure could be extended even further. The way was opened for a demand that everyone be included.

There was, of course, a host of concrete events that contributed to and sharpened the growing hostility to authority. To begin with, royal policy had simply failed. Economic hardship, which peripheral elements could not justify to themselves, and defeat in war, which always reflects against authority's ability to protect, led to the withdrawal of positive affect and the disruption of moral and psychological commitments to the monarchy. The initial (aristocratic) withdrawal was precipitated by the policies of Louis XIV, and the situation was evidently critical by the late 1750's, judging from the government's continued inability to dominate military and economic events, the efforts of the Parlement to control the government, the encyclopedic enterprise, and, symbolically, Damiens's unsuccessful attempt to assassinate the king, in 1757.[2]

Monarchical policy and concrete events had created an insoluble dilemma: to resolve the discontent in any final way it would have been necessary either to return the authority structure to its earlier form, which was impossible, given the economic, demographic, and political complexities, or to include the common man in the political structure, which the extant value system simply could not legitimate. In this situation of conflict both the king and the nobility were able to find support in eighteenth-century French society, but a newly organized ideological demand to extend the rights of participation to the common man found support, too.[3]

It was, of course, the writers of the French Enlightenment who were responsible for the codification of this demand. One part of a social process, initiated at a personal level by publicists and intellectuals, the Enlightenment expressed a desire to end the commitments to passivity and dependence in the area of politics. This desire to reorganize the traditional affectual, status, and moral relationships was nothing less than revolutionary.

One should not, however, infer the necessity for any direct connection on the level of ideas between the Enlightenment and the Revolution that followed. In fact, there could have been but few specific congruences between Enlightenment speculation on the nature of autonomy and the form this actually took with the advent of the Revolution. Several reasons can be given in support of this statement. When the authority structure is perceived as failing or having failed, each individual perceiving the failure experiences a heightening of anxiety in his own unique way, so that, for example, a writer seeking to solve social problems on a speculative level is forced to articulate in terms of his own anxieties. The writer speaks for a developing ideology, but he cannot formulate his solutions so that they cover the totality of people involved or the possible range of alternatives they will be faced with. Then, too, psychological alternatives change in relation to changed circumstances, so that the affectual disturbances provoked by an actual revolutionary situation can never be adequately predicted. And, finally, sociologically feasible organizations depend upon compromises between aspiration and circumstances, and in these matters the writer is bound by the objective world far less than the activist.*

In general, however, the *philosophes* did make the values of *political* autonomy and inclusion conscious and available. Though they did not originate the hostile sentiment against authority, they did crystallize it and give it a direction and a language; and by elaborating unrelentingly on the inequities of the existing system and on the possibility of man's capacity to reorganize the system, they helped to justify a new basis for legitimating and distributing power in society.[4]

It must be pointed out, however, that the Enlightenment writers were not comfortable with this radical role. They were manifestly ambivalent with regard to the struggle against traditional authority, and it is this fact that is central to an analysis of the period and the Revolution that followed it. The *philosophes* indeed sought autonomy for themselves and for other men. But in order to discover the bases upon which autonomy ought rightly to be organized it was necessary to contemplate the violation of all the preroga-

---

* In terms of what follows, these factors will account for the relationship of Rousseau to Robespierre.

tives of traditional authority, an authority that considered itself divinely instituted and absolute. It was the necessarily unconscious adherence to this value system, along with the desire for inclusion, that provoked anxiety and ambivalence among those who were determined to effect change.

If one can imagine an ideal rational individual, a prudent calculating person who chooses in each situation the means most appropriate to a desired end, one would have to imagine a man with complete control over ego and superego. Of course, such control is not possible. Ego may promote objective knowledge, but because of the requirements of identification, dependency, and social adjustment it also takes on the conventional prejudices of the culture. Ego pursues independent goals, but it also pursues goals centered around other persons and things which may be internalized and unconscious.

Moreover, values (superego, ego ideals, identity) as directives to action remain unconscious even though ego comes under progressively more rational control. While means move into consciousness the social directives as ends remain internalized and unconscious. The Enlightenment writers declared the sufficiency of ego, but they could not truly appreciate the limits of the rational capacity to deal with the environment. In particular, the values of the old order remained a part of the Enlightenment even as the bases for new values were being expressed. Thus there could be no autonomy without aggression, and the *philosophes* could not demand it for themselves or others without experiencing ambivalence and guilt.

Values are objectified in society as symbols. For the *philosophes* to offer new values meant to violate symbols of a very powerful, obviously "paternal" content. Not even the most minimal demands—the right to speak and write freely, to make ideas available to the public—could be made without transgressing against traditional authority. But what they wished was far more than this: they wished to put an end to the bases for that authority. Each *philosophe* had therefore to struggle with himself as well as with the environment, and although some succeeded better than others in maintaining balance, none wholly escaped the consequences of the struggle. The group did claim for men the right to participate in society if they had the ability, regardless of origin, and they did aim to obliterate the secular and religious bases of traditional authority. But the content of the ideological statements that served as explanation and justification for their demands was indicative of a great deal of anxiety and ambivalence, manifest particularly in the inability to manage any ultimate, unequivocal public break.

This difficulty can be appreciated more readily in its more social aspect, in terms of identity. The Enlightenment generation was in a situation in which previous modes of adjustment were inadequate, while new ones had not yet been legitimated—in which old rewards had no relevance or merit, and no new ones had yet been created. Moreover, there was no on-going movement external to these writers for which they could speak and whose numbers could justify their behavior. A value crisis on this order creates internal conflicts that can be controlled or exploited only if society offers the opportunity for a reconciliation between self-conception and culture. In the France of the Enlightenment no such reconciliations were possible, and in the absence of such a possibility the radical critics were compelled to rationalize a position in which they could not be defined as destructive.

In other words, an individual must be in a position to identify with himself and with his own behavior. Any threat to identity resurrects old conflicts (often with tragic consequences, as in the case of Rousseau), and it becomes difficult to see or to maintain a continuity of character. Diderot, for example, was quite able to articulate the wished-for values, and in the *Encyclopedia* he wrote that "no man has received from nature the right of commanding others. Liberty is a present from Heaven, and every individual of the same species has the right to enjoy it as soon as he enjoys reason." Further, Diderot observed that "true and legitimate power necessarily has limits. . . . The Prince holds from his subjects themselves the authority that he has over them. . . . Besides, the government, although hereditary in a family and placed in the hands of a single individual, is not a piece of private property, but is public property, which in consequence can never be wrested from the people, to whom alone it belongs essentially and in full ownership. . . . It is not the state which belongs to the Prince, but rather the Prince who belongs to the state."[5]

Still, it was difficult for a man like Diderot to venture as far as he did; he felt compelled to cover his position by making repeated references to his virtue, by denying any revolutionary purpose, and by putting aside his most threatening manuscripts. Diderot could make radical statements on the problem of authority but he could never allow them to become manifest at the level of action. Rather, he tended to defend himself and his good nature with moderate behavior. Hence, the advice he offered in his conclusion to the "Supplement to Bougainville's 'Voyage' " was, for him, entirely consistent: "We should speak out against foolish laws until they get reformed, and meanwhile we should obey them as they are. Anyone who takes it upon himself, on his private authority, to break a bad law, thereby authorizes everyone else to break the good ones. There is less harm to be suffered in being mad among madmen than in being sane all by oneself."[6]

Few of the Enlightenment writers would or could say what they really meant; they preferred to find means to protect themselves from the consciousness of what they were doing—even if this amounted to protestations of loyalty to the culture. The most deceptive of these means was the drafting of a beneficent paternal authority into the Enlightenment camp. The more moderate the demands against the *ancien régime,* the more logical the notion that the autocrat himself could expeditiously introduce change—although France had to experience a revolution before even Voltaire's relatively moderate demands could be realized.[7] By contrast, the more radical and more universal the demands, the more obvious the basic reluctance to take responsibility for the violation of traditional values. The conflict was then resolved by expressing the wish that the king himself become the chief radical and preside over the termination of the old order and the social structure that supported it, in concert with the *philosophes,* who would instruct him as regards appropriate means and goals.

The Baron d'Holbach, for example, wrote that government owed its legitimacy neither to possession nor to divine approval, but to the consent of the governed. Government simply borrowed its powers, and society could revoke, limit, or extend them according to its needs and interests. Government existed solely for the benefit of the governed, to secure the advantages of "liberty, property, and security."

Holbach, to be sure, refused to consider the possibility of revolutionary upheaval as the means for realizing such radical change. But though it is possible to appreciate Holbach's unwillingness to involve the masses in bringing on the desired social change, it is impossible to understand how this concept of government could have been imposed without this involvement. Holbach thought that "by rectifying opinion, by combatting prejudice, and by showing the ruler and the people the rewards of equity," reason itself could cure "the evils of the world and firmly establish the reign of liberty."[8] In other words, Holbach wanted to arrange the elimination of a hereditary aristocracy, the extirpation of religion, the installment of a public functionary to take the place of the traditional monarch, and the organization of a social democracy—and all these changes were to be supervised peacefully by the monarch himself.

Helvétius, for another, plainly wrote that men hate dependency, that it is in man's interest to be independent, and that the best form of government within which to express this independence is the government of all. Government by a single man or by a group of men is intolerable because it cannot work in the public interest. Furthermore, Helvétius indicated the most radical connection between the external environment—politics, law, education—and virtuous, responsible behavior. The art of creating good citizens is everywhere so intimately connected with the form of the government that it is impossible to imagine any substantial change in man's actions without some considerable alteration in the constitution of the state. But having admitted the principle, Helvétius refused to draw the corollary. Again the wish was that the "legislator" could be approached, that he could be persuaded to adopt the principles of a moral and legal science that would achieve human harmony.[9]

The wish was that society could achieve equality in a peaceful way without violating the central symbol of the structure, the monarch.[10] This wish was stated in its most perfect form not in any treatise on political theory but in a utopian fantasy, Sebastian Mercier's *L'an deux mille quatre cent quarante*. In Mercier's "dream" of the future, the whole of society had been reformed in the direction of

equality, autonomy, and inclusion by a revolution peacefully effected through the heroism of one man, a philosophic
prince. "Absolute sovereignty is now abolished; the chief
magistrate preserves the name of king, but he does not
foolishly attempt to bear all that burden which oppressed
his ancestors."

The simple and effective laws by which man ought to
be governed had long since been discovered, so that although Mercier's visionary society was not yet perfect, none
of the familiar abuses existed. All the citizens were equal,
distinctions having arisen naturally among men from the
diversity of talent, virtue, and capacity for work. Moreover, the king invited to his court those men from whom
he could receive instruction, and these philosophers were
rewarded by being invested with a special dignifying symbol. It was a fundamental law of the country that these
intellectuals could approach the throne at any time, and
though others might have accrued more wealth, the philosophers commanded the greatest respect.

Mercier promised in his book that the vile herd of kings
that then sat upon the thrones of Europe would one day
be no more, and his model king illuminates the essence
of the enlightened wish—the king walked about the streets
in plain dress, mingled with the people, rested in their
shops, and visited in their homes. Above all, the king met
with his people once a week for several hours, and any
man could speak to him, making complaints or suggestions
without fear of reprisal, unless what he said was unjust or
self-interested.[11]

The inability to achieve change without aggression provoked the ambivalence manifested in the wish that the
king make himself responsible for the change. What the
Enlightenment generation wanted, in short, was basic value
change, not merely institutional readjustment. These writers sought to create a secular morality and, by separating

authority from its religious base, to organize abstract criteria by which authority and subjects could be guided in their judgments. What the *philosophes* wanted, therefore, could not be realized within the institutional framework of the old order, but they could not say so directly. In fact, the revolutionary desire was expressed to the limit only on a metaphoric level, as literature or in a life of sexual transgression. The implications were not clear to the contemporary actors—but when traditional authority has lost the power to persuade, there is no better way for its subjects to declare their freedom than through violations of the sexual codes of the society.

Every form of sexual practice, everything the culture was maximally organized to prevent, made its way through the contemporary literature, the incest theme being dominant.[12] The use of sexual themes to express aggression was manifest in two particular styles. One, usually related to the fear and anger of the contemporary aristocracy, was deadly, antagonistic, concerned with the sadistic expression of power—Laclos's *Les liaisons dangereuses* is precisely this kind of work.[13] The other was a taunting defiance of traditional values, emphasizing freedom from authority and a declaration of autonomy—Diderot's "Supplement to Bougainville's 'Voyage' " is an excellent example of this style, expressing as it does transgression through sexual violation within the context of autonomy. When Diderot described the aberrations that derived from unnatural demands made by the institutions of the old order—as for example in *La Religieuse*—he evoked the same oppressive and despairing sense that is found in Laclos. But when Diderot wrote in terms of new values, feeling his way through to answers outside the traditions and mores of the *ancien régime,* the aggression, though still present, took another, more tolerant form.

The "Supplement" is an exercise "on the undesirability

of attaching moral values to certain physical acts which carry no such implication," and it is full of the eighteenth-century preoccupations with the relativity of cultural values, the sufficiency of other than Western modes, and the insufficient and even corrosive nature of rather typical Western, Christian attitudes. Part of the dialogue is devoted to a confrontation between the ship's chaplain and a native of the island of Tahiti, where the ship has visited. In the midst of the discussion the chaplain, already taken aback by the relaxed sexual mores of the island, discovers that what was forbidden in the West as incest was an accepted practice here; in fact the native could not understand why anyone would object.

The chaplain asks the native, Orou, "May a father sleep with his daughter, a mother with her son, a brother with his sister . . . ?" And Orou replies with the innocent query "Why not?" When the chaplain asks if it is very common for a man to sleep with his mother the native replies "No, not unless he has a great deal of respect for her, or a degree of tenderness that makes him forget the disparity in their ages and prefer a woman of forty to a girl of eighteen." Actually, intercourse between father and daughter was not likely either, "unless the girl is ugly and little sought after. If her father has a great deal of affection for her, he helps her in getting ready her dowry of children."[14]

The sexual play in the "Supplement" has been described as "pleasurable yet innocent, not debauched, without deleterious consequences for moral character or order."[15] But it is impossible to imagine incestuous relations having all this charm for Western societies, or to imagine incest as one aspect of genital maturity. Diderot's purpose in the "Supplement" was aggression against the dominant values of his society, and the form of aggression is indicative of the inability of authority to command on the psychic level.

This kind of literary expression—a private vice striving to become a public virtue—had its reflection in the contemporary political theory. Helvétius argued that restriction imposed on sexual freedom was an error because it limited human pleasure, that women ought to be available to the state (to serve as rewards for virtuous conduct). Helvétius also argued that since man experienced a conflict of loyalty between the family and the state, the family ought to be abandoned and all kinship bonds terminated. Further, he indicated that marriage as an institution should be abandoned as well.[16]

No argument could possibly demonstrate more clearly or more dramatically that the enlightened generation was after the destruction of patriarchal values. However, this assertion must be viewed in the proper perspective; that is, though there were attacks on the family in the Enlightenment, and though there were many more critiques of sexual mores that ultimately involved the family, the wish for independence was codified and accepted and led to action only in the area affected by structural change—political institutions. Such Enlightenment ideas on marriage and the family as those of Helvétius should be viewed as idiosyncratic expressions, reflecting the escape of a repressed wish on the personal level. Moreover, these ideas were unmediated by ego—they represented a barely disguised demand for an unrealizable gratification and were therefore unacceptable to the culture; the oedipal content was too startlingly direct. From the standpoint of society, such ideas appeared, then, as nonlegitimate ideological statements and were not seriously considered. More specifically, no attempt was made to realize these ideas in any institutional form.

A brief examination of Sade's opinions on the subject will illustrate the reason for the rejection of these ideas. Sade also wanted to abandon the conventional ties of marriage and the family, to allow every man and woman to be available to each other whenever desire was stimulated. Sade knew that the logical conclusion to this line of reasoning was that any mother would then become accessible to her son. However, unlike Helvétius, who would have choked at the thought, Sade simply went on to make a positive virtue of the possibility; incest was no barrier to him. Reflecting Helvétius's concern over division of loyalties between family and state, Sade demonstrated how incest would indeed help to solve the problem. Incest "loosens family ties and the citizen has that much more love to lavish on his country. . . . I would venture . . . that incest ought to be every government's law—every government whose basis is fraternity."[17] Sade drew an Enlightenment idea, one that could never be realized, to its psychological conclusion, thereby pointing up a facet of the problem: rebellion leads to the elaboration of the incest theme, a theme reflecting the general hostility toward, and withdrawal from, patriarchal values.

Because the wish could have no legitimate expression on this level, the attack on the family was abandoned, while the attack on political authority was carried through. Logically, the demand for inclusion in the political processes should have been accompanied or followed by a demand for equal status in the family. This did not occur because, sociologically, structural changes in the family similar to those that had occurred on the political level had not taken place; the individual's commitments to the family had to continue. Nevertheless, these ideas on the family reflect accurately the content of the political rebellion, the extent of that rebellion, and the kind of anxiety that was precipitated by action and thought directed against the traditional values of the society.[18]

If the ideas made available in the eighteenth century are

viewed from the standpoint of literary excellence or profundity of content, then it is possible to select a handful of men—Voltaire, Diderot, Rousseau—and relegate everyone else to a secondary status. If, however, Enlightenment ideas are viewed as responses to a social crisis that had exacerbated individual anxiety, and if it is understood that the anxiety directed the organization of the ideological statements as a mode of defense, then all eighteenth-century ideas have an equivalence because they all represent contingent possibilities to the solution of crisis.

There were writers in the Enlightenment era who were not overly threatened by the implications of the struggle, who organized and maintained a liberal, tolerant point of view. However, a good deal of the writing, and especially the work concerned with the restructuring of moral and political authority, was directed at the creation of closed systems. The writers who devised these systems justified their work on the basis of deductions from a priori psychological assumptions that indicated the perfect or near-perfect possibility of manipulating the external environment. The fact is, though, that the problems raised by the Enlightenment assault on authority so impinged on these men that ambiguous situations became intolerable, and they therefore directed their theoretical constructions to the permanent resolution of conflict and anxiety.

Such writers as Helvétius, Holbach, and Morelly tended to maintain a defensive control over the threatening environment through their ideas and symbols. They attempted to put boundaries on an infinitely dangerous world, overcoming guilt on the conscious level through the manipulation of concepts that appeared to them to be empirically based and wholly right. The fact that these systems were closed is indicative of the need to maintain ego control through a precise structuring of the external world, and the aspects of control and authority so prominent in their constructions are indicative of their lack of success in resolving attachments to the values of the old order.

The logic in Helvétius, for example, goes as follows: the moral universe responds to laws of self-interest in the same way that the physical world is subject to the laws of motion. Since self-interest motivates all of man's decisions, and since man strives for all things productive of pleasure and eschews all things that cause pain, the wise legislator should organize society so that self-interest and pleasure become consistent with social and public ends.

Helvétius pointed out that if morality was more backward than other sciences it was because men had been forced to form a social system before they could learn correct moral principles; and now it was simply in the interest of certain powerful persons to keep these principles suppressed. The moral science was in its infancy, according to Helvétius, but it could be brought to perfection. The first step was to recognize that the conduct of men would always be the same—that is, always based on self-interest—and the virtuous man is not the one who sacrifices personal pleasure but the one whose pleasure is consistent with public welfare. Therefore, "the legislator may assign so many punishments to vice and so many rewards to virtue that every individual will find it in his interest to be virtuous."

Further, because all men were deemed to be equal in their physical organization with regard to pleasure-pain sensibility, all men were educable to the same degree. Observable differences in education were not due to natural endowment, but to chance and circumstance. There is no truth in Locke or Newton that could not be understood by every man, and every truth, no matter how apparently difficult, is essentially comprehensible to every mind.

All false judgments were thought to be the result either of the sway of unruly passion or of ignorance. The first weakness could be overcome by adjusting private interest to public good, and the second weakness was remediable because all men were educable to the same degree. Happiness therefore depended upon law and education; virtue and genius were both products of instruction. The moral education of mankind had hitherto been abandoned to chance; now it could be founded on these simple, invariable laws. Legislation could be a science, and perfect legislation was only a matter of time and experience.

Helvétius wrote that men are what they are designed to be: they are under the necessity of pursuing their own happiness. He noted that "Men are wicked, full of contempt, and consequently unjust whenever they can be so with impunity." That, however, is a result of the unfortunate organization of society. Men are wicked because it is in their interest to be wicked; but interest can also tie them to virtue. "If pleasure is the only object of man's pursuit, we need only imitate nature in order to inspire a love of virtue. Pleasure informs us of what it would like and pain what it forbids. Man will readily obey these mandates. Why cannot the legislator, armed with the same power, produce the same effect?" If the legislator, tutored by the moralist, would substitute the soft voice of interest for noisy invective he could establish a nation based on virtue.[19]

Holbach's psychological assumptions were different from Helvétius's, but his assumptions too, led straight to the power of an external agency to mold man's behavior. Holbach posited a diversity of organic structure in man that accounted for differences in aptitude and desire; so long as these aptitudes and desires were directed to the common good they should be rewarded. This inequality, which stems from unequal organic natures, is useful to society; if men were all the same they would have no need of each other and would live in isolation. "The diversity and inequality of our faculties, both bodily and mental, therefore makes man necessary to man, makes him sociable, and makes clear to him the necessity for morality." Holbach thus offered a theory of social organization based on diversity of function and differentiation, contrary to the Helvétian equality.

Nevertheless, man was seen as motivated by passions of self-interest, by pain and pleasure, so that politics properly understood was still the art of regulating passions and channeling them toward the welfare of society. The legislator could shape sound, understanding people, and morals could be organized on a scientific basis. Moreover, it could be demonstrated incontestably to man that his interest consisted in being virtuous; obligations, no matter what their nature, could be founded on the certainty of obtaining reward for good and punishment for evil. "Morals would be a chimera and would have no certain principles if they were not founded on the knowledge of the motives that must necessarily determine the actions of human beings." The key factor was necessity: men do only what they must do—and it was this necessity that established, for Holbach, a firm basis for morality, so that, man's nature being known, government could be organized for his welfare.

Pleasure and pain, the hope for happiness, and the fear of being held in contempt are the motives sufficient to compel man to virtuous behavior. Furthermore, "It is evident that nature has made man susceptible to experience and consequently more perfectible"—i.e., there is also posited an eternal law that pushes man forward and accounts for progress. Though there is not in Holbach the extreme optimism of Helvétius, there is certainly the sense that man is manipulable to a great degree, and that the legislator can go a long way toward the creation of a harmonious order.[20]

This kind of theorizing was based on a few psychological notions that may be summarized as follows. One, concerned with the rational analysis of ideas in terms of the sensory perceptions from which they arise, derives from Condillac, who assigned no differential role to the physical apparatus of sensation or to the organic in general, the influence of the organism being constant in all normal people. Further, he did not admit any innate psychological factors. Condillac regarded the experiencing mind as an abstract receptacle, explaining individual differences solely with reference to sense impressions in a given social and physical environment. We can observe the extreme use of this hypothesis in the analysis of morals and politics offered by Helvétius.

Writers like Diderot and Holbach did not accept this psychological structure; rather, they insisted upon differences among men in organic composition and therefore in perception and ideation. They rooted their psychology in physiology rather than in sensory experience, thus allowing for all kinds of differences in temperament, aptitude, and capacity. This second basic psychology was a physical one, however, so that Holbach could conclude, for example, that there was no doubt that a man's temperament could be changed by causes as physical as the matter of which he was constituted.

Man was therefore seen as a mechanical entity in which psychic events were regularly caused by organic factors; moral man is a purely physical being whose actions can be explained by organic structure and environment. Life was considered a long succession of necessary and associated movements, the essential principles of which were physical, contained in blood, nerves, tissue, and so on. The physical qualities of sympathy, antipathy, attraction, and repulsion had direct counterparts in the moral qualities of love, hate, friendship, and aversion.

There are several factors deriving from this kind of theoretical speculation that should be made explicit. The models for individual control suggested by Helvétius and Holbach were regressive to the extent that self-esteem was regulated from outside the individual, in the form of approval or rejection issuing from external agencies. The notion of an independent internal regulating mechanism was not entertained: man was absolutely controlled by the principle of self-interest and therefore could have no sense of justice. And because the feeling of having done right or of not having done right depended solely on objective sources in the environment, remorse could not be conceived of as a genuine internal repentance.

Since by these constructs the fear of external punishment is the only fear engendered by wrong-doing, there is no true conscience.[21] With conscience the fear is internalized, and danger threatens from within, in the form of a fear of the loss of well-being or of the loss of pleasurable feelings that derive from self-control, characterized in general as a feared loss of self-esteem. Since neither Helvétius nor Holbach conceived of a conscience, the mode of control over human activity had to take the form of psychic manipulation; in the absence of conscience the development of abstract and rationalized social relationships is impossible. Virtue, therefore, became the concern of the state, not of the individual, and society was regulated by the manipulation of emotions stemming from the desire for esteem and the fear of disgrace.

These psychological notions, combined with the wish that the "legislator" make himself responsible for change, represent, in turn, an archaic view of authority relationships. These writers conceived of political authority in a traditional, almost familial sense, that is, the leader's power is undifferentiated in executive and legislative terms, and in economic, political, and social terms. Authority in this form is the patriarchal ideal. It is the patriarch who treats all subjects with equal kindness and firmness, who is, in effect, both maternal and paternal in strictness and goodness. The implications in this for external authoritarian control have been overshadowed and softened by the egalitarian and universal content of the social theories.

Morelly's work represents another excellent example of this tendency, although his criticism was offered more at the social level than the psychological level. His *Code de la Nature* is a most direct statement of the wish for equality of condition, for harmony and oneness, and for inclusion in the decision-making processes, in terms that were simultaneously democratic and authoritarian. Morelly had a rather extravagant notion of the possibility of organizing society in a way that would end social disharmony. Predicating the existence of all vice (vanity, pride, ambition, duplicity, hypocrisy, dishonesty) on the passion of self-interested avarice, which takes its dominant form in private property and is sustained and nourished by that social institution, Morelly concluded that "where no property exists, none of its pernicious consequences could exist." This proposition was so evident to Morelly that he could "almost mathematically" demonstrate that the division of goods in the form of private property, whether in equal or unequal portions, was the substantial source of all evil.

Once the "legislator" revoked private property, the evils arising from its existence would also be eliminated, and "all the prejudices and errors" that attended the possession of property would disappear. There would be an end to unrestrained passion and vicious behavior, and neither evil nor the idea of moral evil would remain. If evil should happen to reappear, it would be only as a result of accident, and society would quickly contain it.

The properly organized society would put an end to anxiety. For this purpose Morelly outlined a rigid, painfully thorough, mathematically precise organization of the social structure based on the absence of private property (with the exception of those effects the individual would find immediate need for, effects necessary for pleasure or for work). Every citizen would contribute to the extent of his talent and would live within Morelly's rather rigid distributive laws.

Everything in Morelly's society was specified, including habits of dress and nourishment. All children would leave the paternal home at the age of ten and enter workshops, where they would be clothed and fed. Young people between the ages of twenty and thirty would dress uniformly in terms of occupation (after age thirty, one could dress as he pleased, "but not in any excessively fancy way"). No one would be exempt from marriage, and every head of a family would become a senator at age fifty and have a deliberative voice in the working of every regulation the senate was organized to preserve. This was explicitly a simultaneous demand for inclusion and for an authoritarian structure.

No moral philosophy would be countenanced other than that worked out within the system of laws. There would also be a public code concerning all the sciences "in which nothing beyond the limits prescribed by the laws will ever be added to metaphysics or to morals." Regulations related to study would, in general, prevent all aberrations of the human mind, all unworldly reveries.[22]

The rigid organization of thought that served to abate the writers' anxiety[23] raises some important questions with regard to the level of conscious control over intellectual materials. The attempt to deal with the environment, to search for means of bringing the environment under greater control, can be motivated by rational or irrational factors. The quest for mastery can be the expression of autonomous capacities but it can also be a symptom or a defense against pressing anxiety. Indeed it is impossible to assume that such a recognition of external reality as we have described constitutes an effective adaptation to reality. Rather, because the anxiety that stemmed from the demand for differentiation was intolerable, it led to the tendency to structure a closed world.

It was under these conditions that Helvétius, Holbach, Morelly, and others considered the external world, a world that provided them with a particular conceptual language and a choice of rationalizations. It was these conditions that enabled them to speak of democracy while organizing repressive authority, to demand autonomy and yet fear the human ability to tolerate it. At the same time that they were demanding an end to the sacrifice of self and accepting the individual and his passions, they were threatened by those passions and sought to control them through repressive means.

The most consistent characteristic of Enlightenment thought was the preoccupation with the projected external environment and the physical world as these are evident to the senses. The rational, empirical ideal for these writers was to consider only those things that were susceptible of demonstration; they would not, if they could in any way avoid it, fill in gaps in knowledge with metaphysical speculations. In keeping with this ideal, the Enlightenment psychology assumed that man could think and act only in terms of those things impinging upon him from the external world.[24]

All this was predicated on a psychology of consciousness —there was no behavior that was not immediately available for examination if man had only the courage to face up to the principles of his own true moral nature. Thus Helvétius could write that "To understand oneself, one must make a long study of oneself; moralists are practically alone in taking an interest in this examination, and the majority of people are ignorant of themselves."[25] However, by this he meant not what classical introspective thinkers have always meant—the confrontation with unconscious human nature—but simply the examination of materials which he thought were capable of being quickly understood by any individual so inclined.

The psychic structure was thus understood as perfectly manipulable, so that appropriate behavior could be arranged "automatically." In the absence of appropriate laws man acted for himself without regard to the public welfare. But given the organization of the external world in terms of man's nature, it would be possible to manipulate reality so that pleasure sufficient to sustain any normal man through his life could accrue from an adherence to the moral codes of his society.[26]

What is offered in Helvétius and Morelly, and to a lesser but still determining extent in Holbach, is a caricature of reality, a highly limited, defensive view reflecting the inability of ego to meet the increasing demands and the consequent necessity for greater reliance upon repression. The content and the structure of the ideological statements protected the writer from the fear of his own impulses, and the irony of the situation was that authoritarian democracy became possible at the same time as liberal democracy; both points of view could have been expressed by the same man at the same time.

The Enlightenment had demanded the implementation of values of autonomy based on a perception of ego strength. This was not altogether a vain ambition; the ego qualities can be identified. There was in fact an ever-increasing ability to distinguish objective relationships and to distinguish rationality from irrationality. But the excessive "idealness" evident in the works of many of the writers was clearly a function of the inability of ego to tolerate its own demands. The Enlightenment prided itself on the abandonment of illusions, but too often its goals were unreasonable and its appraisals of the possible were immoderate. The Enlightenment writers had to compromise between internal claims and the claims of the external world from which came real threats of injury, punishment, loss of status, and so on. For those who could not tolerate the pressure, the evaluation of the world became a superego rather than an ego function, a factor identified in the promise of a virtuous, harmonious society. This promise was founded on the denial of subjective, internal experience and consequently on distorted perception. There should have been an enhanced ability to test and evaluate both external and internal reality, reasonably and with some tolerance. This was not possible, owing to the need to maintain the repressions; reactively, the greater the demands the greater the repression.[27]

In addition to this denial of internal reality, a second, related factor became operative during the Enlightenment —the distortion of the past in terms of some preconceived future. This problem of the past is epitomized in an interesting way in Mercier's utopia. In this new society, history, the "disgrace of humanity," was all but obliterated —very little history was taught because every page was "crowded with crimes and follies." In addition, Mercier pointed out that since the mind is embarrassed by a thousand external circumstances, and a great library would have to include all manner of idle fancy and malicious notion, it would be necessary for society to burn all books that might threaten good order. "By unanimous consent we gathered on a vast field all those books that we judged either frivolous, useless, or dangerous." The citizens formed a huge pyramid and "this tremendous mass was set on fire and offered . . . as an expiatory sacrifice to veracity, to good sense and true taste."[28]

Mercier's citizens, acting with "enlightened zeal" as the barbarians had once acted from ignorance,[29] removed the possibility of finding in the past any indication that society had furnished the people with any positive sources of support or that men had derived benefit from such institutions as monarchy and the Church. The need for violence in order to impose new values leads to the repression of the past at the same time that the future is perceived to be the repository of all good.

The idea of progress as explained by Condorcet must be understood in this way. The idea of progress was the one product of the tensions we have been describing that still maintained a clearly liberal orientation. But in Condorcet there is again the tendency to distort the past in terms of a predictable future. With all due respect to intellectual antecedents, this kind of thought, in Condorcet and in the others we have been considering, was a result of the conflict generated by the need to be violent in order to be free. Past and future were distorted—more accurately, the idea of progress represented a flight from the past into an unreal future. The present was used only as the means to organize an escape.

Condorcet's capacity to ignore the evidence offered by the Revolution when it opposed his notion of perfectibility was quite remarkable. In spite of the fact that he had seen Robespierre in operation, and that Robespierre and the

Terror controlled France at the time he wrote his sketch for a history of progress, in spite of all the vagaries, equivocations, and brutalities of the Revolution, he clung to his notion of the perfectibility of man and even to his belief in the great good that would eventuate from this cataclysmic interference with history. The Revolution was but another demonstration of man's progress, "a happy event suddenly gave impulse to human hopes; a single instance put a century of distance between the man of today and the man of tomorrow."

Condorcet justified his prediction of the future on the basis of the fact that physical phenomena could be predicted if the laws were known, that the general laws directing the motion of the universe were regular and constant, and that this principle must also hold for the development of the intellectual and moral faculties of man. But Condorcet's hopes for the future represent a mixture of realism and fantasy, unaffected by objective evidence—realism in the form of pragmatic guesses relating to such physical goals as equality between sexes, an end to poverty, improved medicines leading to increased life span, and so forth, and fantasy in the form of deducing from changes in the external world a radical change in the subjective life of man, i.e., objective change terminating subjective anxiety. Thus Condorcet was able to foresee the abolition of inequality among nations and within nations and the "true perfection of mankind"; the world, which had hitherto been "the prey of imbecile scoundrels believing nothing," could look forward positively to liberty, equality, sanctity of property, and national and international harmony. Progress was conceived to be unlimited.

Fantasy is always rooted in the past, but if past and future are linked to possibilities offered by the environment, fantasy can become the basis for realistic goals, and there are realistic goals in Condorcet's notion of the future. But there is also the overriding wish for an end to conflict, a wish untempered by reality. Many writers have in fact wondered how Condorcet was able to manifest such optimism in the face of personal and cultural tragedy. Condorcet succeeded in this by repressing the past, both personal and cultural, and by using the present—hardly less frightening—as a means for organizing the future, where he was safe.

"How consoling for the philosopher who laments the errors, the crimes, the injustices which still pollute the earth and of which he is often the victim, is this view of the human race, emancipated from its shackles, released from the empire of fate and from that of the enemies of its progress, advancing with a firm and sure step along the path of truth, virtue, and happiness! It is the contemplation of this prospect that rewards him for all his efforts to assist the progress of reason and the defense of liberty." The past, personal and cultural, is nothing but the source of terror, and the present is hardly better: there is only the future. The future is an "asylum" in which the memory of his persecutors has been left behind: "there he [the philosopher, Condorcet] *lives in thought* with man restored to his natural rights and dignity, forgets man tormented and corrupted by greed, fear, or envy; there he lives with his peers in an Elysium created by reason and graced by the purest pleasure known to the love of mankind."[30]

Though the future does not exist as object, it is a criterion of reality-thinking to anticipate it, to plan for it, and to forgo immediate gratifications in deference to it. However, in the sense that Condorcet was able to predict perfectibility and harmony, his view of the future was unrealistic. His prediction must be understood as a wish resolving all the conflicts and anxieties of the past. Neither does the past exist as object, but the emotions that derive from it are very much alive; memories long inaccessible to reality-thinking are extant in the mind and even preferred by it.

The perfect harmony of the future, therefore, must be seen as an intellectualized resolution of a past wish, a resolution untroubled by the evidence afforded by external and internal conditions. In many cases, then and later, the wish was clearly aimed at an end to separation, at returning to some infantile unity with the past environment, and therefore was aimed at an end to the very autonomy originally sought. On the one hand the ideologist may derive from his anxieties some basis for insight into immediate problems; on the other hand he will often be forced by his anxieties to pose perfect solutions to those problems.

The kind of thought we have examined so far is, to a degree worth considering, dereistic thought—thought that disregards reality and operates in terms of subjective wishes, the essential ideas corresponding to affective needs. These Enlightenment theories presented man as virtually omnicompetent to deal with the environment. Contemporary intellectual achievements indicated the possibility of a science of man, and on this was predicated ideas that we can now observe to have been unreal, that were in fact used to mask reality. Though none of these men considered their systems immediately applicable in terms of the contemporary society, they did consider that they had described reality on the level of theory; their ideas thus represent wish fulfillments relatively unrestrained by reality.

These several instances of the reaction to demands for value change reflected an inability to tolerate the consequences of struggle against internalized authority. Helvétius, Holbach, Morelly, and others were committed to the Enlightenment quest for a secular morality organized on the basis of a rational capacity to deal with the environment.

But these men were too ambivalent, and the psychological "laws" of behavior that they discovered and that they hoped would be used to arrange stable social process turned out to be a means for controlling behavior in a rather rigid way. There was no tolerance for the ambiguities of political and social existence.

The self-interest theories are particularly interesting for the reason that, generally speaking, they reflect the principle that buttresses moral commitments in highly pluralized societies. In these societies man tends to act on his own behalf in terms of different means/ends relationships which he selects and over which he has some control. However, in these societies man also acts in terms of a part of this morality that prevents the total rationalization of the process—the ego-centeredness never reaches ultimate aggressive conclusions. It was this aspect of the question of moral commitment that Enlightenment self-interest theorists could not comprehend. Their frames of reference indicated rather automatic responses to stimuli on the basis of pleasure-pain, and it seemed to them that only through the guidance of external agents could man ever be persuaded to act on behalf of society. They could not see that man can be emotionally committed to the social structure at the same time that different relationships are being dealt with on an abstract level. There is no insight into this process at all, and, caught in their own projections (the fear of loss of control), the self-interest theorists were able to argue for total inclusion but not for individual autonomy.

This inability to achieve any significant degree of introspective awareness, or any knowledge of unconscious processes—or, as we have noted, any insight into the way that personal emotions and anxieties are related to familial (and religious) processes—was a generalized factor in the Enlightenment era. This was not the "failure" of individual writers; rather, the whole problem was related to structural conditions beyond the control of any individual. We have emphasized the radical responses of particular writers because this sociopsychological factor of repression is more clearly evident among radicals; the extent of their demands and the manner of phrasing their demands are directly related to the need to repress insight as well as to the failure to maintain the commitment to the values of autonomy under pressure. Thus, by examining radical rather than moderate reactions to demands for change—moderates are typically more tolerant of impulses and of the cultural and personal past—we can distinguish with greater clarity the structural factors that separated the Enlightenment from the introspective era in terms of the kind of information that became available and the institutional levels against which demands were made.

The emphasis on radical alternatives should not obscure the important instances of ego control that were also manifested in this period—instances, however, that were not nearly so brave as the grand systematic statements on the ultimate organization of politics. We refer here to something rather less pretentious—primarily a tolerance of ambiguity, a flexibility of judgment, a desire to arrange feasible reforms in terms of a believable future, a desire, at any rate, to open society to personal and civil liberties guaranteed by abstract laws applicable to all. The moderates realized that man in society is an uncertain factor, but they were more, rather than less, willing to accept the uncertainty. Voltaire and Diderot were two such men.

Diderot is especially interesting because of a highly visible interplay between his ideas and his emotional responses to them. Diderot pursued the problem of man's moral relationships in society more faithfully and more capably than any of his contemporaries except Rousseau, and in various of his dialogues one can find Diderot debating with himself over the logic that led to the denial of the possibility of a true morality. Up to the 1770's at least, Diderot's essential point of view was deterministic and materialistic (though even then he was reluctant to hold to all the inevitable conclusions), and based on the physical and the organic. From his premises it had to follow that man is the only thing he can be and does the only thing he can do. There can be no question of moral responsibility for an act or moral justification for restraint. There can be only relative, conventional, and social ends served by a system of rewards and punishments, the good being encouraged and the wicked chastised.[31]

Diderot pushed this logic to its limits and discovered in the process that "this world is only a mass of molecules, loaded like dice in an infinity of different ways. There is a law of necessity that works without effort, without intelligence, without purpose." If Dr. Bordeu ("D'Alembert's Dream") could say that nothing that is can be against or outside nature, and Diderot's neurotic conversational friend ("Rameau's Nephew") could say that "I have become completely convinced that uprightness and humanity are everywhere only conventional expressions which at bottom contain nothing real or true," then force was the only basis on which to organize society.[32]

Once the assumptions are granted, everything quickly follows: there is only one cause, which is physical, and only one necessity, which is the same for all people. Further, nature knows only survival: "In nature all species devour each other; in society all classes devour each other": a weak man is a strong man's dog. All these conclusions Diderot put into the mind of the dreaming d'Alembert, and all were confirmed by the attending and very conscious Dr. Bordeu. There could be no difference between what a sleeping philosopher might concoct and what a wide-awake scientist would have to admit.[33] Diderot assumed that all things were determined, regular, and constant, and therefore capable of being analyzed. But he analyzed behavior in terms of physiological factors, and these had few implications for a moral nature. In the absence of an introspective psychology, moral nature was equated with inherited nature, and therefore had to be denied. [34]

In the end, however, Diderot refused to abide these conclusions, and here his ambivalence was revealed.[35] He was finally constrained to endow man with a moral nature: he conceded that man had causes peculiar to himself and that man was removed from any purely determined physical origin. Diderot concluded with a moral sense that made conscience effective, that indicated to man his responsibilities, and from which man could derive an internal sense of well-being. Virtuous behavior gave man a pleasurable feeling; it enhanced his self-esteem. It should be noted that Diderot wanted to understand this without reintroducing a metaphysical assumption—hence, he indicated a physiological location of the moral sense. But for all the empirical evidence he had, this notion is hardly more than a metaphysical one, a notion he found necessary because he wanted to believe that possibilities existed for man in society.[36]

Diderot, then, was as ambivalent about man and society as any of his contemporaries—but he did not allow himself to be pushed to extreme conclusions. On the psychic level the difference lies in the fact that Diderot did not deny his past; rather, he was tempered and constrained by the past, by his attachment to his family and even, in a highly emotional way, to the religion he had abandoned. Thus, Diderot resolved his ambivalences differently from some of the other writers we have considered. He felt that his arguments made him an "apologist of wickedness"; if he had been right about the necessary impossibility of morality he would have betrayed the cause of virtue, he would have encouraged men "in the ways of vice." Rather than face this prospect, and in order to explain motivation, Diderot fell back on an essentially metaphysical conclusion, which he supported with eighteenth-century conventions of bad education and bad legislation. "If that is an error, at least I am glad to find it at the bottom of my heart and I should be very sorry if experience or reflection ever disillusioned me. What would I become? Either I should have to live alone or believe myself constantly surrounded by wicked men; neither prospect suits me."

This internal dialogue reflects Diderot's dilemma: he could view his logic only as an attack on society, and he could not separate the attack from his feelings about the past. Thus, Diderot moved from position to position, leaning first one way and then another. He felt the struggle very keenly, but unlike the others we have referred to he refused to solve the problem through ideology and would not surrender to the past. Diderot managed to work out a position that was radical in terms of the *ancien régime,* but which was politically moderate, and which allowed for the freedom of the individual. He managed to live with his anxiety.

As far as this generation of writers was concerned, the ego ideals, the cultural authorities, were no longer viable. In coming to grips with the problem of organizing a new authority structure based on broader autonomy and inclusion, some of these writers were able to maintain realistic control, others were not. Their capacity to accept the struggle varied widely, and the Enlightenment era manifests a range of response that spanned moderate liberalism, utopian liberalism, and egalitarian authoritarianism. And though the Enlightenment writers never achieved autonomy and never participated in the established political processes of society, their failure was personal and extended only through their own generation; the democratization of French society moved ahead, if ambivalently, with the Revolution and after. The Enlightenment struggle for autonomy was one episode in a social process leading to independence at large; but it was in any case one of the sources for democratization and pluralization in the West.

3

Rousseau: The Ambivalent Democrat

THE WORK of Jean-Jacques Rousseau stands as the most elaborate eighteenth-century attempt to legitimate a new source of moral authority and to establish the social basis for individual autonomy. Rousseau set out to organize a social structure in which men could avoid dependent relationships, one in which questions crucial to the community would be decided on the basis of parity, and in which all men would be equally obligated to and protected by the law. To put it simply, Rousseau's political theory represents the outstanding Enlightenment statement on the desired reorganization of society.[1]

Rousseau's work is therefore important as an index of the break with the values of the *ancien régime,* and as the maximal codification of the decisive aspects of Enlightenment aspiration. But the theory is also important because of its very evident ambivalence. There is a patent tension in Rousseau between freedom and control, between autonomy and authority, that is manifest in *The Social Contract* and other of his works.

This conflict in Rousseau's work reflects another, more basic conflict between his rigorously moral, austere, and critical self-image and his need to be passive, self-indulgent, and dependent. It was this unresolved crisis of identity that prevented Rousseau from making a consistent commitment to theoretical work and to the community for which this work was intended.[2] Only for a short period during his middle years did he manage to sustain a certain degree of freedom from this conflict; he wrote as critic and theorist essentially between 1749 and 1762 (or perhaps 1764), but even in that span the content was not free of equivocation. It can certainly be said that by the time Rousseau wrote *The Social Contract* the inclination to dependency had assumed renewed prominence, and even as he advocated the new values of autonomy he was forced to insist upon repressive means for their institution and maintenance.

The fact that Rousseau could weave such apparently antithetic attitudes into his work is indicative of the crisis in Enlightenment society, a society that furnished values in support of either pole of the ambivalence. Rousseau, in effect, was caught in this value conflict, and although he wanted freedom for himself and other men, he simultaneously sought security in a society in which choice was limited and controlled.

Rousseau himself was never wholly persuaded of his own autonomous capacities; he was uncertain of his maturity, his self-control, even his talent. Before he could specify the paths to autonomy for society he had to discover them for himself; he had to mold his own identity as an independent person. This was the most difficult thing Rousseau ever undertook. He had to experience enormous anxiety before he could see himself as a separate, valid person who could determine the solution to his own problems or those of his society.

The quality and depth of what Rousseau accomplished during these dozen years of working as political theorist and social critic sheds considerable light on the earlier and later periods of his life. Until 1750 he had done relatively little, nothing that satisfied him and nothing that was indicative of his true genius. In the next dozen years, under difficult physical and psychological circumstances, he wrote the best part of what he is recognized and remembered for. The difference between the early period and these years of great theoretical contribution was Rousseau's determination to become autonomous. The difference between this theoretically productive middle period and the one that followed, one in which he ultimately all but lost control over his intellectual processes, was his inability to maintain ego control, to sustain the struggle that autonomy implied.

It was in spite of a desire to remain dependent that Rousseau was finally able to work. The severity of the internal combat is illustrated by the unique experience that precipitated the writing of the first *Discourse,* an experience that Rousseau described later in a letter to Malesherbes (1762). Rousseau wrote that he had chanced upon the prize question put forward by the Academy of Dijon as he was walking to Vincennes from Paris to visit Diderot, who was imprisoned there. "If anything ever resembled a sudden inspiration, it was the emotion aroused in me by that reading; suddenly I felt my mind dazzled by a thousand flashes of enlightenment; swarms of vivid ideas presented themselves to me with a force and confusion that threw me into a state of indescribable turmoil. I felt overcome by a giddiness resembling intoxication. A violent palpitation oppressed me. . . . Unable to breathe as I walked, I sank down under a tree in the avenue and there spent half an hour in such a state of agitation that on getting up I saw the whole front of my jacket wet with my tears although I was unconscious of having wept." And, Rousseau continued, "had I been able to write down a quarter of what I saw and felt under that tree, how clearly I would have shown up all the contradictions of the social system; how forcibly I would have exposed all the abuses of our institutions; how simply I would have demonstrated that man is good naturally and that it is by their institutions alone that men have become wicked."[3]

The work that followed this experience, the *Discourse on the Arts and Sciences,* is not nearly so important for its ideas as for the feelings and attitudes that surrounded the completion of the work: Jean-Jacques came to feel that he could compete, that he could be an important individual, a man people would heed. It is characteristic of the man, however, that his great intellectual career was initiated by an event in which he had apparently lost control. It is significant also that Rousseau's first work should have been a profound attack on cultural and social institutions.[4] The *Discourse* was an act of aggression, and while it was a display of anger at the moral decay man suffers in society, it was also, and more importantly, Rousseau's declaration of independence against the society, the definition of himself as an independent individual opposed to the dominant values of the culture. This is what Rousseau meant when he later recalled that the instant he read the prize question he saw "another world and became another man."[5] He became an autonomous person: "I have taken my stand," he wrote in the preface to his first *Discourse,* "and I shall be at no pains to please either intellectuals or men of the world."[6]

The remarkable incident that Rousseau described in his letter to Malesherbes served to crystallize his identity. Previously he had not been able to marshal the energy for this kind of intellectual work, nor had he been able to commit himself to the society for whose sake his work was done. Rousseau reported in his *Confessions* that there was one time before 1749 when he might have been able to manage a commitment—a time when he had served as secretary to the French ambassador at Venice. The language he used in the *Confessions* to describe this earlier failure epitomizes the identity problem he faced up to the time of writing the first *Discourse*: "I drifted for some time from one idea to another, from one plan to another. . . . I am easily discouraged, especially in difficult and long-term undertakings. My failure in this [his work as secretary to the ambassador] disgusted me with everything else; and since . . . I looked upon distant goals as fool's bait, I determined henceforth to live without any fixed plan, as I no longer saw anything in life that might have tempted me to exert myself."[7]

With the triumph of the first essay, however, Rousseau began to emerge as the man he wanted to be, filtering out from a bewildering assortment of identity fragments and failed roles a self-image of an honest man with a disinterested heart working for the public welfare in a vocation that called on him "to tell the public hard truths, hard but useful."[8]

Rousseau was, after all, a man who did not discover "the charm of study" until he was in his twenties, and who, after almost forty years, could boast of nothing but a few unimpressive attempts at artistic creation. From a past as abandoned child and dependent adult, runaway and wanderer, Protestant citizen of Geneva and Catholic adherent of France, from positions as secretary, tutor, and musician, Rousseau organized an identity: moral, Protestant, Genevan, independent. The circumstances surrounding the acceptance of his first work brought to the surface, he wrote, the "heroism and virtue" that had been dormant in him. "Nothing appeared great in my eyes but to be free and virtuous, superior to fortune and opinion, and *wholly sufficient to oneself.*"[9]

The public acclaim that Rousseau received encouraged him to greater confidence in his talent and in his independent position, enough so that he began to adopt a style and attitudes consistent with his role and identity. He was determined to avoid situations that could compromise his principles: he took on work as a musical copyist, spurning the more lucrative possibilities that were offered him.[10] He also divested himself of the accoutrements of polite social life, visibly and forcefully breaking connections with the society around him.

Rousseau reports that he was transformed: his friends scarcely knew him. He was no longer timid and bashful, but bold, intrepid, and confident. The results of his meditations inspired him with contempt for the manners and morals of society, and he was strong enough now, he thought, to rebuff easily society's attacks against him.

But Rousseau was never altogether comfortable with his hard-won independence. Autonomy meant transgression and it meant the kind of isolation that autonomous people must experience, consequences he could not completely tolerate.[11] He had never been able to demonstrate his effectiveness before because he had accepted the need to be deferential and dependent in order to avoid being separated from people and to avoid their hostility. But to have continued to experience such relationships would have threatened his identity. This accounts for his exaggerated rejection of society; his break was a means of avoiding the conflict that was bound to result from personal relationships and a measure of his fear of being forced back into a passive position.

In other words, once Rousseau took the initiative and made himself competitive, his former modes of control had to be abandoned. Thus he could live as an autonomous man, but only by accepting severe internal pressure. He could not help feeling that self-assertion was bound to lead to punishment, or that the only way to secure affection was by docile behavior. Such feelings led him to fear personal relationships, and certain consistent kinds of behavior followed. For example, gratitude was linked to submission and dependence, so that Rousseau could hardly accept anything from anyone without great apprehension. All too often he found cause to regret someone's generosity, and the kindness was inevitably interpreted as an attempt to rob him of his independence.

Later this apprehension took on an added dimension; by the time Rousseau wrote his *Confessions,* he was convinced of the existence of a universal plot organized for the purpose of destroying him. He attributed the plot to the greatness of his work: his success had led to the anticipated retributory aggression. Thus, in order to abate the attacks he felt were being directed against him, he tried never to appear as a man to be envied; he declared openly and often that no one had ever suffered as much as he, and in particular he insisted that he had become famous against his will—he had never intended to be great.

It was this insoluble conflict between the desire to exercise competitive mastery and the need to remain dependent that forced Rousseau to abandon his autonomous position.[12] His great gesture of defiance had made him fearful and suspicious of the environment, and because he had failed to control the situation satisfactorily he was forced to withdraw from it. The situation was progressive, of course, and it grew worse with time, but as early as 1756 Rousseau felt the need to leave Paris to avoid the conflict he feared was inherent in his life there. He moved to the countryside in April of that year, hoping never to live in cities again.

Rousseau later wrote to Malesherbes that only at this point had he begun to live. The move was supposed to be the final step toward the independence he had sought since public acceptance of the first *Discourse*,[13] but he could not abide the loneliness and isolation. He complained bitterly that he could find no friends, and he complained just as bitterly about those who might have been his friends. Rousseau had moved away from Paris in order to control his external world, to maintain quiet surroundings, and to allow into his life only those he pleased rather than a whole importuning crowd. He hoped that by living virtually alone he could create a condition of calm and order and escape the anxiety that threatened him when others were close.[14]

But the plan did not succeed. Though Rousseau had come to fear the company of men, he found also that he could not tolerate being isolated from them. He therefore found it impossible to work as consistently as he would have liked, for these conflicts drained much of the energy and enthusiasm he might have applied to his critical and theoretical investigations. The ambivalence began to overtake him, and he became "fearful, complaisant, and timid —in a word, the same Jean-Jacques I had been before."

Rousseau was thus trapped, and the anxiety stemming from these circumstances tended to force him out of his world of critical investigation into a subjective world where he could exercise a wishful control over aggression: *La Nouvelle Héloïse* was an expression of this posture. "The impossibility of grasping realities threw me into the land of chimeras, and seeing nothing in existence that was worthy of my enthusiasm I sought nourishment for it in an ideal world, which my fertile imagination soon peopled with beings after my own heart."[15] Thus, Rousseau would find it increasingly more difficult, as time went on, to keep his anxieties under control. He was forced too soon to give in and lead the kind of life he had sought to avoid and had admonished others against. "Everything combined to plunge me again into that too seductive indolence, to which I was naturally inclined, but from which the hard and austere frame of mind [which he hoped to have developed in the years 1752-56] . . . should have delivered me once and for all."[16]

Rousseau always felt himself to be essentially ineffective. He lived with two feelings in conflict: the desire to enjoy innocent pleasures in a world free from aggression and the desire to behave like an adult and be effective. In the latter mood the contemplative life appeared to him to be a retreat he would rather have avoided. Man was made for action, Rousseau said, not meditation, and action meant to him the clash of ideas, the discipline of self-control, and a "hard and austere regime" that allowed life to match principle. Anything else was a withdrawal from the identity he had struggled so hard to achieve.

Rousseau's reversal in style turned dependence into revolt but it extended only to the conscious level of activity; actually, Rousseau was as securely tied to the past as he had been before. Independence, put forth as the goal, could not be maintained. Though the new path looked right, it was taken much too abruptly; the contrast was too sudden and too complete, and far too scrupulously observed, to be seen as anything but defensive. Therefore, the pleasure that accrued from the work, and from the commitment to new allegiances, could not last, and did not for any great length of time. Compulsive opposition had become more threatening than the former submission had ever been, and as Rousseau's critical opposition increased, so did the anxiety and guilt, and the psychological conflict became intolerable.

After Rousseau left Paris in 1756 he wavered for the next six years between independent activity as a rigorous, selfless moral critic and his need to be passive and retiring; after 1762 the fight was all but over, and Rousseau for the most part withdrew. When the environment was more or less under control he could manage critical thought—even quite late, as with his *Considerations on the Government of Poland.* But when the external world was too threatening, the dominant condition thereafter, he could work only in his private world, writing highly subjective pieces in defense of his good nature—toward the end, almost wholly in the service of his delusions. Rousseau lost the capacity to invest himself in society, to think in positive theoretical contexts or in terms of the future. He was unable to venture beyond the present, which he clung to with all his energy.

Our concern here is with the autonomous Rousseau, for it was as social critic, moral philosopher, and political theorist that Rousseau epitomized and codified so much of the aspiration of his generation. But before we go on to examine Rousseau's social theory in this context, we must make three points relative to the connection between Rousseau's ambivalences and his social criticism.

When Rousseau lost control over the environment he tended to remain fixed in the present and past, narcissistically cultivating his feelings, wholly concerned with himself. Unlike classical introspective thinkers—Nietzsche, Dostoevsky, Kafka—Rousseau never saw that man is faced with radical internal problems that may have a determining relationship to the environment. That is, what may pass for Rousseau's introspective examination afforded him no insights that contradicted his original assumption on human nature—man is good and institutions corrupt him. Whatever occurred to him that might constitute evidence to the contrary was excused by his concept of morality, which insisted that morality is a function of intention and not action. Thus Rousseau could conclude that no matter how wicked an act might appear, man was, in his heart, just and good: he had no need to pursue the problem of motivation beyond that.

In political thought, therefore, Rousseau operated on the premise that all problems were external to man—i.e., external to man's innate composition and personal character and intrinsic to the social and cultural levels of society. "I had perceived everything to be radically connected with politics and that, no matter on what principle these were founded, a people would never be other than what the nature of their government made them."[17] Thus, when Rousseau asked rhetorically why, in three-fourths of the world, ignorance and vice prevailed, and "if the latter are not in man's nature, what gave birth to them," he had the fixed, invariable answer—external conditions that could be altered and improved.

Second, the more Rousseau withdrew into himself the more he tended to inflate his own value and the importance of his work; he began to have ideas of grandeur, fantasies of unlimited accomplishment. These notions he coupled with his identifications with the dispossessed, so that it became his responsibility as social critic and moral philosopher to terminate, insofar as it was possible, human anxiety caused by the destructive pretensions fostered by society. That is, Rousseau saw what was and understood what ought to have been, and on the basis of omnipotence[18] convinced himself not only that the gap could be closed but that, at least on the theoretical level, he had closed it. For example: "even if I am again to be regarded as wicked for daring to assert that man is born good, I think it and I believe that I have proved it."[19]

The third and most important point concerning the content of Rousseau's political theory is his inability to tolerate an ambiguous situation. It was specifically this inability that prompted him to include rigid authority structures in his work even while he explained the nature of autonomy. His own ambivalence forced him to suspect the human capacity for self-regulation and self-control. Indeed it was his dominant apprehension that man did not possess the moral courage to be free. Man was motivated by passions, which in their destructive form threatened at every instant to overwhelm him. Quite simply, Rousseau had projected the inability to control his own inclinations, his fear of weakness, onto society at large, believing that the impulses pressing within him must be equally crucial for society and crucial in the same way.[20]

Rousseau's anxieties tended generally to be manifest as important considerations in his work—for example, his hatred of cities, which he identified with his feared breakdown, his fear of intimate relationships, and his fear of social differentiation. Thus, if human nature was equivocal, if the ambiguity was too problematic for him, the solution was to insist on absolute moral boundaries, and, fearing the insufficiency of this, to exert control from the outside. Rousseau's fear of the failure of conscience led him finally to the traditional, internalized values, values historically available in the culture—authority and external control.

External circumstances, of course, reinforced Rousseau's fears. His unique path of criticism—indeed, his unique manner of living—was opposed not only to the values of the old regime but also to the point of view of all the other Enlightenment writers. His ideas were attacked, and his sensibilities were mocked, by those who might have given him support. Society at large declared his works subversive (even his beloved Geneva defined his *Emile* and *The Social Contract* as "rash and scandalous and tending to the subversion of government") and threatened him with punishment. The net effect was that Rousseau now stood alone, unable to identify with his own behavior, the victim of hostile criticism from within and without.

On this basis it becomes possible to understand the task that Rousseau had set himself: to identify the characteristics in man upon which his judgment of man's good nature was based, to show how these became distorted as society evolved (indeed, to show how they would inevitably be threatened with submersion and distortion, no matter in what society), and to show what measures would have to be adopted in order for man to achieve the moral excellence of which he was capable and which freedom required of him.

In his essay on the origins of inequality, Rousseau wrote that "contemplating the first and most simple operations of the human soul, I think I can perceive in it two principles prior to reason, one of them interesting us deeply in our own welfare and preservation and the other exciting a natural repugnance at seeing any other sensible being, and particularly any one of our own species, suffer pain or death. It is from the agreement and combination which the understanding is in a position to establish between these two principles, without its being necessary to introduce that of sociability, that all the rules of natural right appear to me to be derived."

Rousseau deliberately excluded "sociability" as a natural factor: life in society is not natural to man. For some reason, probably natural disaster or the real threat of it, the organization of societies was imposed on man. In the natural state man had been simply a peaceful brute, living for himself alone. In this condition man was an isolated wanderer in the forest, without industry, home, or speech. He could take care of himself and he could feel for others if they were hurt, but he could develop no further affective or intellectual capacities. Natural man was not even in possession of curiosity and foresight; there was neither the need nor the opportunity for natural man to develop any of the conscious capacities by which he is identified in the social state.

Once man began living in societies, however, the psychological functions that were active in the state of nature—self-interest (self-love) and compassion—became corrupted, while hitherto dormant functions—reason and conscience—began to develop. In society, the quality of compassion (which in the state of nature moderated self-love and contributed to the preservation of the species) tended to disappear, and self-love (which in the state of nature implied only the desire for self-preservation, without reference to others and thus without the possibility for aggression against others) turned into selfishness and vanity. This process led to continual dissatisfaction with one's own condition, to an incessant desire to improve one's condition relative to others, and, consequently, to aggression against others. In society, man's needs grew, they became more difficult to satisfy as man became more dependent upon others for their satisfaction, and the basic sentiment of self-interest (self-love) became distorted.

Vanity, self-esteem, and love led to competition, rivalry, and contempt for others; distinctions began to be made, and inequality became a fact. As society differentiated it began to seem advantageous to have enough goods for two men, and the idea of property was introduced; those with less became the satellites of those with more, and work became indispensable. Out of this network of related circumstances the familiar social tyrannies developed—chief among which was the tyranny of dependence. Human understanding improved as man became depraved—man became sociable even as he became wicked.[21]

In society, man became the victim of a multitude of destructive passions that did not exist in nature but appeared only with the emergence of communal life. Because the evolution of society is irreversible, these destructive passions remained by definition a permanent threat. A society could be organized to defend against them but no society could be organized to exclude them, and that is the crux of the political problem for Rousseau.

Rousseau's notion that the thinking man is a depraved animal becomes clear in this light. Complex reasoning reflects a complex culture, which in turn means that man has assuredly become a victim of his passions. The culture that lauds the arts and sciences is misguided; such pursuits are indicative of man's decline and nothing more. Though Rousseau was ambivalent about the argument he had developed in the first *Discourse,* he could nevertheless write to Voltaire that "the love of letters and the arts arises in a people from an internal weakness which it only augments; and if it is true that all human advance is pernicious to the species, that of the mind and intelligence, which increases our pride and multiplies our errors, soon speeds the coming of our misfortunes."[22]

With the development of society, man became heir to the malicious passions; in society men hate each other in proportion as their interests conflict. To organize a society equipped to combat man's nature as it must become in society it is necessary to take these weaknesses into consideration. "Fanciful notions are all very good in books," Rousseau wrote, "but when it is a question of forming a body politic one must begin with knowing men well and taking them as they are."

In simplest terms, "taking men as they are" meant to Rousseau that the functions of reason and conscience were not a sufficient basis upon which to predicate a human capacity for self-regulation.[23] When Rousseau considered man in the political state he did not concede to him the potential for self-control implied particularly in the notion of conscience. Rousseau's fear of the power of the passions never ceased to dominate his appreciation of man's positive moral capacities. That is, although reason allows men to know the good, and conscience to love it, there is no guarantee that men will act in terms of it. Rousseau ascribed to man free will (a wholly metaphysical notion), which gives him a choice between good and evil, and the organization of society is such that to choose the good is the most burdensome task of all. Neither conscience nor self-interest *automatically* regulates behavior, but society imposes such forbidding psychological and social obstacles that virtue must suffer. To choose the good, to prevail against self-interested passion, putting duty before everything—that is virtue. To say the least, Rousseau conceived this to be extraordinarily difficult to accomplish.

It was at this point, in fact, that Rousseau gave up theorizing in a positive context. He was not able to look beyond his fear of human weakness, not even in his most optimistic moments.[24] Rousseau, therefore, presents a clear example of a problem that has recurred in radical democratic theory no matter where it has appeared, a problem we have already alluded to. The demand for autonomy and independence, necessarily predicated on aggression against traditional (internalized) authority, has provoked such anxiety that the fear of the failure of or separation from conscience has stimulated serious doubts about man's capacity to tolerate freedom.

In Helvétius and Holbach the issue was conceived of in terms of the absence of conscience; conscience simply did not exist. Social control had no internal dimension; it had to be external to man and it had to be rigid. Rousseau, however, did pose an innate psychic structure; he did endow man with conscience, the first necessary step to the creation of abstract social mechanisms of control. But by projecting his own fears onto society he was led to doubt the ability of conscience to contain passion or to be sufficient for self-control.

Two points must be made clear in this connection: wherever Rousseau indicated that man was capable of self-government it was only on condition that conscience dominate all aspects of existence; man was asked to live in terms of absolute moral ends and means with no relief or alternatives. However, Rousseau felt at the same time that human conscience was not strong enough to rule over the passions—and he therefore added to the extreme superego demands the authoritarian repressive mechanisms external to man.

Reason and conscience are demonstrable, perhaps even measurable, qualities; will is not. Reason and conscience expand in society; will does not. Will allows man the freedom to be moral,[25] but because of social demands it is more likely that he will prove immoral. The empirical, socially developed faculties of reason and conscience help, but they are not nearly decisive; there is no way to guarantee virtue so long as men are free to choose, and because the passions engendered in society have such endless power, the issue must remain in doubt.[26]

Man is a double—allowed free will, he can choose virtue or vice. One principle raises man to the love of justice and the moral good, the other lowers him, makes him a slave

to the senses and passions. "No, man is not one; I will and
I do not will, I feel myself at the same time slave and free;
I see the good, I love it, and yet I do evil." Man is complex,
he is ambivalent, and "if to place oneself above everything
is a natural inclination in man, and if, nonetheless, the
first sentiment of justice is inborn in the human heart, then
let him who considers man a simple being explain away
these contradictions."[27]

In order to achieve the moral excellence necessary to be
autonomous in the social state, man must recognize the
limits imposed by nature and by society (as objectified in
law) and freely accede to them as a function of will. However, in all cases and under all conditions, even the most
perfect, the human grip on virtue is uncertain. This is why
Rousseau wrote that the greatest lesson he ever learned was
to avoid situations in which duty conflicted with interest;
at any time, with the best of intentions, interest may prevail.
"It is certain that in such situations, no matter how sincere
our love of virtue, we must, sooner or later, inevitably
grow weak without perceiving it and become unjust and
wicked in act, without having stopped being just and good
in our hearts."[28]

In any case, it is not enough to be good; man must be
virtuous, and that is another problem. In *The Social Contract*, in the *Discourse on Inequality*, and in his projects
for Corsica and Poland, Rousseau made use of two techniques calculated to deal with the problem of virtue, thus
demonstrating his anxiety over man's ability to remain free.
In the *Contract* it is particularly the social repressive mechanisms that are evident; elsewhere it is the manipulation
of the passions, sentiments that Rousseau otherwise abhorred (pride, love, vanity), that is pre-eminent. The use
of these techniques represents the defensive, dependent side
of him.

It is difficult to appreciate Rousseau's political and social speculations unless the democratic intent of his work is conceded.[29] In particular, Rousseau considered it to be absolutely essential in a democratic community to defend and protect "with the whole common force the person and goods of each associate [in such manner that] each, while uniting himself with all, may still obey only himself alone and remain as free as before." This statement of Rousseau's is the epitome of eighteenth-century aspiration. It is the demand for inclusion in the political processes on equal terms, wholly free of social or political subordination. It is the demand for the creation of a political "marketplace" where the individual, freely exercising his political rights, can himself mediate between desire and circumstances, for the good of the community. The democratic essence of the theory was the establishment of equality among citizens so that all those who pledged to observe the same conditions could, therefore, "all enjoy the same rights."

Consistent with this democratic basis, Rousseau also suggested the organization of a body of abstract law, applicable to all citizens, as the means for guaranteeing the maintenance of such a structure. All the members of the community would have to adhere *freely* to this law; whoever refused to accept the conditions was free to leave. Rousseau required, in addition, the total alienation of the rights of each man to the community; for if any man retained any particular right there would be no common superior to judge between him and the community. Each man's being his own judge on some one point would soon require this to be so on all points, and men would be thrown back on the passions.[30]

The law would objectify social and physical necessity: it would make explicit the moral purposes of the community and what each man would have to do in order to attain virtue. This law would be severe in its moral requirements;

for society by definition makes unnatural demands, demands difficult for men to manage.[31] In any case, it is only through the free, mutual acceptance of the law that man can achieve freedom. Then, though the demands of society may be great, the people have acceded to them willingly; and though the community may have maximum power (since by agreement no one individual has power over any other, and since private interest is most likely to be bound to the public good), man can be autonomous.[32]

The public that is so organized is sovereign; its sovereignty is indivisible, it cannot be delegated or represented.[33] The people are responsible for making decisions that pertain to the community, each man deliberating for himself. Rousseau advised the prohibition of all interest groups, all bodies intermediate between the public and the government, so that no persuasive partial will could command the public interest. To the same end, Rousseau advised economic adjustments between the extremes of wealth and poverty so that no man would have to be dependent on any other in this obvious way.

Given the modification of self-love by the accepted law, the presence of conscience and reason, the easy dissemination of education and information, it is possible for the deliberating community to find the one right thing for it to do in each case that it decides to act upon. That objective right thing to do, the moral choice most conforming to the public welfare, is the general will. The general will is not the majority of votes, nor is it necessarily expressed by a unanimous vote—it is the right (moral) alternative that exists for every situation, an alternative that can be found if desire is subordinated to justice. The physical and psychological preconditions predispose men to find the common good at the expense of private interest.

Given all this attention to universal inclusion, it is difficult to deny Rousseau's democratic intentions. But because his demands were ideal there could be no compromise with principle, and there was always the fear of impulse. The problem was to induce man to live with laws of great severity, laws that would prevent him from giving in to selfish desire. No one in Rousseau's time could find such a government, and, so far as he was concerned, if none existed or could exist, then there might as well be a despot—in fact, the perfect despot, God if possible. In no case could Rousseau see any "tolerable mean between the most austere democracy and the most complete Hobbesism, for the conflict between men and laws which throws the state into continual civil wars is the worst of all political conditions."[34] It was necessary, therefore, to find the means to maintain virtue in the face of human weakness, and Rousseau's proposed manipulation of the passions becomes relevant in this connection.

The most violent of these was love, "a terrible passion that braves dangers, surmounts all obstacles, and in its transport seems calculated to bring destruction on the human race which it is really destined to preserve." Love did not exist in the state of nature; it is a social phenomenon, dependent upon man's ability to reason, to compare, and to have preferences, and although it is a tender feeling the least obstacle turns it into an impetuous fury. "With love arose jealousy; discord triumphed, and human blood was sacrificed to the gentlest of all passions."[35]

Love represents a threat to stability and order among individuals. If, however, sound relationships could be organized on some other basis, this energy could be directed instead to the community. Julie told St. Preux *(La Nouvelle Héloïse)* that it was wrong to imagine love's being necessary for marriage: "this is a gross mistake; honor, virtue, a certain conformity, not so much of age and condition as of temper and inclination, are the requisites for marriage; nevertheless it must not be inferred from this that such a union does not produce an affectionate attachment, which, though it is less than love is no less agreeable." Julie pointed out that the intent of marriage is not that man and wife should always be taken up with each other, but that they should jointly discharge the duties imposed by civil authority.[36]

The energy devoted to love—those who are involved are necessarily withdrawn and exclusive—is better spent on what is socially necessary. Rousseau therefore consistently desexualized people as he made them better citizens. Moreover, he was wary of every kind of relationship that required energy to be spent independently of the political community. His experience with the anxieties of friendship, for example, led him to be hypercritical of this kind of expression.

Rousseau was equally anxious to break the hold of institutions that required affect on the social level. The Christian ethic might be favorable to humankind at large, inasmuch as it was founded on benevolence and humanity, but one could not be interested in humankind as such, since the world is not organized in that way. Men live in civil, political societies, and these are based on different principles: "They are purely human institutions from which Christianity consequently detaches us as it does from all that is merely of this earth."[37]

Christianity requires that all men be regarded alike, and charity does not allow men to make invidious but necessary distinctions between compatriot and stranger; it does not make for either good republicans or good fighters. Christianity by its nature is opposed to the social spirit, and if the religion is successful in its competition with the human attachment to society, then the latter must be the loser, and "in default of a suitable support, the political state falls into decay."[38]

Emotion attached to the state is attenuated in proportion to its attachment elsewhere. Love and friendship are restrictive; the number of people these can be extended to is limited. Religion, with its panoply of competing symbols, is also restrictive; religion demands the kind of devotion that must be offered only to the community. Rousseau even protested, on this score, d'Alembert's suggestion that the theater be promoted in Geneva because he believed that the depiction of sexual love would compromise Genevan virtue. "The continual emotion which is felt in the theater excites us, enervates us, enfeebles us, and makes us less able to resist our passions."[39]

Since love ought rather to be directed to the community, Rousseau's society became an institutional structure designed to maximize affective attachment to the political unit. Rousseau had shrewdly suggested the withdrawal, the serious curtailment, of libidinal energies from individuals and the redirection of these energies toward the community, the fatherland. This redirected love would have all the passionate intensity that characterizes love among individuals—it would be as exclusive, as hostile to external influences, as suspicious of the intrusion of outsiders. "The patriotic spirit is a jealous spirit which makes us regard everyone other than our fellow citizens as a stranger and almost as an enemy. . . ."[40]

It was because Rousseau could not ultimately trust in man's ability to manage the necessary sacrifices that he employed this kind of manipulation.[41] Thus, his statement that "it is to the laws alone that men owe justice and liberty" cannot be taken literally. It is rather that men would owe their liberty at least in part to the manipulation of the passions: the noble ones that inspire goodness, but also the baser ones that can be used to attach people to the law.

In part also, men would be constrained to live rightly in the community by the implementation of external repressive mechanisms *(The Social Contract)*. Thus Rousseau could write, for example, that the people must be made to see things as they are "and sometimes as they ought to be," and he could support this notion with a censorship that would sustain morality "by preventing opinion from growing corrupt, by preserving its rectitude by means of wise applications, and sometimes even fixing it when it is still uncertain."[42]

The Social Contract includes that "which alone can give force to the rest; that whoever refuses to obey the general will shall be compelled to do so by the whole body—this means nothing less than that he will be forced to be free, for this condition . . . secures him against all personal dependence."[43] This injunction means that those who have entered into the communal agreement have thereby expressed readiness to accept in advance decisions which are not unanimous and which run counter to individual interest. But all states are organized to prevent certain defections from the law—the point is that no state wishing to call itself free and its citizens autonomous can invoke a censorship that is used to fix opinion.

Rousseau finally allowed the state to impose itself even in the matter of a civic religion: the state would have to fix the articles of a purely civic profession of faith, one that could, through rigidity and intolerance, be designed to reinforce the affective attachments without which a man could not be a good citizen. The state could not compel a man to invest his faith in this construct but it could banish him for not doing so (on grounds not of impiety but of his being antisocial, incapable of loving the law). Any man, morever, who had publicly recognized the civic faith and then behaved as if he did not believe what he professed would be executed for lying before the law, the worst conceivable crime. The principles of the civic religion would encourage the citizen to continue to conform even in the face of a difficult objective situation.

This matter of a civic religion is a critical aspect of the regressive features in Rousseau's work. As we have noted, the Enlightenment aspired not only to open the society to "new" people but also to separate and exclude the religious function from the political. To the *philosophes,* separation was an important step toward the creation of "rational" politics, and in practice it did eventually permit both diversity and stability. But Rousseau, his attacks upon Christianity notwithstanding, disapproved of the kind of pluralism implied in the separation of religion and politics, and for him the civic faith became one more mode of control.

What this means is that Rousseau could not imagine a viable community comprising networks of private interests within some kind of general consensus. The objective world, therefore, was organized to prevent breakdown to subjective desire. There was an implied perception that a lapse in virtue was not perhaps dangerous in itself, but represented rather a temptation to others: if one or several should fall, the rest would be compelled to follow.[44]

Rousseau was afraid there would be no way to organize substantial harmony on the basis of man's internal strength. It was not enough to understand that judgment is fallible and institutions flawed; against this Rousseau did not believe that freedom could prevail. As a result, he could not envision a pluralistic society held together by mechanisms at the social and cultural levels and not profoundly dependent on the binding character of affect. If one axiomatically distrusts the human capacity for self-regulation and infers from this the automatic failure of social mechanisms, then one cannot theorize in a positive way. Rousseau's model of society shows the effects of this predicament: it is a rigid society, because it became necessary for Rousseau to control the social and cultural levels of action.

Rousseau's political structure was organized to guarantee the unity of political aim—the end of dependence and the reliance on individual autonomy. But it was also organized to eliminate the uncertainties that arise the moment man becomes free. The critical concept of the general will should be seen from this point of view. The general will was Rousseau's myth or, at best, his wished-for morality. But the general will has no counterpart in reality; social process is too ambiguous and too complex for that. The general will was the means by which Rousseau could manipulate the hostile environment through ideas: it was for him the resolution of doubt in politics, a device created to deal with that aspect of reality most problematic to him.

It is tempting to consider Rousseau on the level of logic— in terms of contradictions rather than of ambivalence—for then one can resolve the contradictions in Rousseau by claiming that he really meant freedom, or that he really meant control, adding and subtracting according to one's preferences. *But Rousseau is crucial precisely because he did mean both: he was strongly committed on an emotional level to both alternatives.* Rousseau, therefore, is a critical figure in the Western tradition of posting abstract, impersonal, representative institutions, the maximal form for the expression of pluralistic interests. But he is also an early and certainly very dramatic instance of the failure of ego to live with the wish for independence.

4

Robespierre: The Retreat to Authority

THE FRENCH Revolution and the Enlightenment were both characterized by the same wish for autonomy and by a similar range of ambivalence. The Revolution, the necessary violation of legitimate authority and traditional custom, provoked, therefore, a value crisis in French society, and what might have concluded with a reasonable termination of violence developed into a bewildering complexity of motive, anxiety, and interest that protracted the revolutionary unrest.

The Revolution destroyed all political manifestation of hereditary privilege, and the representative government that was organized should have been able to integrate the expression of pluralistic interests. However, the Revolution failed to achieve a consensus, in part because the aristocracy would not abide the consequences, but more significantly, because those who agreed on the Revolution in principle could not agree on the extent to which the new values were to be implemented. There was no action taken after July 1789 that did not exacerbate the fears of some bloc, which then proceeded to conspire against, threaten, and violate constituted authority. Because of the unending succession of issues and crises, substantial elements of the right and the left were unable to invest allegiance in common authority.

The revolutionaries were ambivalent. In all classes, at all levels of society, men were drawn between the internal attachment to the old values and the desire to implement the new. The future of the monarchy was particularly affecting; the revolutionaries were unable to decide on the extent to which the king's authority still obtained, if indeed it obtained at all.

The value conflict brought on by the Revolution is apparent also in the relationship between economic crisis and mass action, particularly in Paris. On the one hand, the various assemblies, anxious to institute the new values of autonomy and inclusion, had no ultimate intention of imposing economic restrictions on society.* On the other hand, insofar as the *sans-culottes*[1] declaimed against profits and

---

* The preamble to the Constitution of 1791: "Neither nobility, nor peerage, nor hereditary distinctions, nor distinctions of orders, nor feudal regime, nor patrimonial courts, nor any titles, denominations, or prerogatives derived therefrom, nor any order of knighthood, nor any corporations or decorations requiring proofs of nobility or implying distinctions of birth, nor any superiority other than that of public functionaries in the performance of their duties any longer exists."
The Chapelier Law, June 14, 1791, articles 4 and 8: "If, contrary to the principles of liberty and the Constitution, some citizens associated in the same professions, arts, and crafts hold deliberations or make agreements among themselves tending to refuse by mutual consent or to grant only at a determined price the assistance of their industry or 'their labor, such deliberations and agreements, whether accompanied by oath or not, are declared unconstitutional, in contempt of liberty and the Declaration of the Rights of Man, and non-effective. . . ." "All assemblies composed of [continued on page 110]

big business, or thought in terms of a just price rather than the price the market could bear, they referred to and acted upon the values of the *ancien régime*.

The king's attempted escape, the flight to Varennes (June 21, 1791), was decisive for the continuing political role of the *sans-culottes*. The king's defection gave objective content to their persistent fears of betrayal and justified their withdrawal from authority and their aggression against the symbol. The masses practiced a rough democracy, but the defensive qualities were evident. The *sans-culottes*, especially, reacted with a rigidity of perception to economic and political crises—which accounts for the exclusive and authoritarian overtones evident in their behavior.

Rigidity under these conditions was not necessarily an ineffective process, for rigidity helps to mediate tension and leads to ego control. But in this situation it led also to premature judgments against the environment at the expense of reality—the September massacres being a case in point. The behavior of the masses may therefore be described as "paranoid" (stemming from the projection of aggression), though our caveat on rigidity is worth repeating: we do not mean to suggest that "paranoia" cannot have positive functions or that there were not good and substantial reasons for fear.[2] We use the term here chiefly to indicate the mood —the feelings that existed toward authority—a mood that prevented the development of affective commitment to any

---

artisans, workers, journeymen, day workers, or those incited by them against the free exercise of industry and labor appertaining to every kind of person and under all circumstances arranged by private contract, or against the action of police and the execution of judgments rendered in such connection, as well as against public bids and auctions of diverse enterprises, shall be dispersed by the depositaries of the public force. . . ."

government. So long as the motives of government were suspected there could be no stability.

The Revolution made great strides, in objective terms, in instituting the new values. But obviously whatever was done was not sufficient to settle the revolutionary turmoil. There remained areas of change that the Revolution found more difficult to deal with—in particular, the necessity of creating an interim authority structure that could command allegiance and pacify factional interests until final aims were agreed upon.

The problem the Revolution ultimately could not solve, then, was the organization of a civil authority that could command obedience from the various groups in French society. The *sans-culottes,* for example, had already violated church and king; there was no reason why they should accept the new politics if it too promised to threaten their security. The Revolution had violated constituted authority in order to effect change; it thereby sanctioned the continued violation of authority by any group that felt itself excluded from the consideration of those in authority.

The most important element in the formation of such a civil authority—a long-term, consistent, charismatic leader—was not to be found. None of the revolutionary leaders, for personal reasons, could play an unequivocally charismatic role; none could act as spokesman for the new values until the upheavals in society were calmed.[3]

Robespierre's attempts in this direction, however, are worth examining. Robespierre had come to conceive of himself as peculiarly suited for this charismatic role, to see himself as singularly equipped to become the conscience of the society, the man who could inculcate in the people the standards of democratic behavior invoked by the principles of the Revolution. He believed he had the moral power to settle the social unrest and institute the new values; he expected to be able to withdraw when the people were in a position to accept a permanent, legally constituted body and no longer needed to resort to violence.

For a time, Robespierre did play a charismatic role, but in the end he was unable to implement the values for which he stood—there emerged no symbol of the Revolution and its values which could reconcile the diverse interests of society and be responsible for the creation of a permanent representative form of government. We cannot, of course, deal here at length with the failure of the Revolution to solve the problem of authority; but we can examine the fate of the wish for autonomy *in the light of repression and personal fears,* and for this purpose Robespierre presents us with an excellent focus. It was because of his own ambivalence that he failed in the charismatic role, and it is the nature of this ambivalence that we must explore. Robespierre was, after all, a dominant spokesman for the new values, anxious to make autonomy succeed, but he was also intensely authoritarian.

Robespierre took the popular position on virtually every issue that arose after 1789. In August of that year he stated that freedom of the press was the necessary corollary of freedom of speech; in September and October he opposed the royal veto and any property qualifications for voting rights; and in December he insisted that it would be better for a hundred guilty men to go free than for one innocent man to be punished. He also attacked the proposal that theatrical performances be censored by municipal authorities ("Public opinion is the sole judge of good taste"); he defended privacy of the mails; he inveighed against capital punishment; he demanded a more equitable jury system; and he insisted that political clubs be left inviolate as the most responsible source for political criticism of the power structure. He consistently identified the Revolution with the people, and in so doing identified himself with the people, stating simply, "I have always held that equality of rights belongs to all the members of the state."[4] He was indeed so consistent in his points of view that he seriously jeopardized his own political chances by decrying the advent of the war, very astutely identifying the counterrevolutionary dangers inherent in such an involvement.[5]

Robespierre, then, plainly identified himself with the democratic cause, and he was courageously outspoken against anyone who seemed to threaten the Revolution or who appeared unwilling to fulfill what he considered to be the purpose of the Revolution, the inclusion in the decision-making processes of the greatest number of people.[6] However, the charismatic influence he enjoyed stemmed not so much from his demands as from the way in which he made them—from his ability to manipulate popular anxiety, an ability which drew upon a violent, punishing moral tone, a manifest moral superiority marked by uncompromising rigidity, and a capacity for structuring the world in absolute terms.[7] Not the least productive of Robespierre's talents was his ability to "identify" plots and conspiracies, the first of which he denounced in a speech before the Constituent Assembly on October 20, 1789. His immensely fertile imagination kept the public supplied with objects upon which to fasten its fears.

These qualities are recognizable aspects of an authoritarian personality—and Robespierre was indeed a sectarian, given to dogmatic certainty of ideas, intolerance of opposing views, an all-or-nothing perception of the world, and a profound conviction that some absolute good would come from revolutionary interference with history. There was nothing moderate about his demands; in spite of the democratic idiom, his evaluation of the world stemmed from a punishing superego—Robespierre was rigid, punitive, and absolute. These traits were a part of his equipment, and they help to explain the great measure of popularity and support he managed to achieve.[8] In his capacity as the tireless critic of a wavering, ambivalent regime, he made good use of these qualities; they allowed him to keep democratic ideals squarely before the public eye and to remain patently undeviating. Once he assumed power, however, these traits became destructive, and it is in terms of them that we can understand his downfall.

Robespierre's most significant exercise of influence before assuming power was in the debate over the future of the king: the formation of the Republic required a definitive solution to this question. So long as the king was available as a potential source of authority, the goals of the Revolution would be approached with indecision and hesitancy. If the country was to be organized, the king had to be accorded some specific role (which meant incorporating significant aspects of the past), or be eliminated.

Robespierre had been projected into political prominence in the winter of 1792, chiefly by reverses in the war and the general radicalization of politics. Under the dual pressures of at least some responsibility for political action and the continued failures of the government, he came to show less and less tolerance for instability: the more the Revolution appeared to be floundering, the more unsettled the people became, the more the suspected counterrevolutionary activity threatened the gains achieved and those to come, the more Robespierre conceived of himself and the Montagnards as the ultimate alternative. But he could take a leading role only if the king were eliminated; given his personal qualities and the mood of the people this was psychically and socially consistent.[9]

When the question of the fate of the monarchy came to a head in the Convention, Robespierre and his colleague Saint-Just were able to take the most radical position. They were absolutely lucid on this issue; the death of the king (and kingship) would confirm the Revolution—most particularly in terms of the advent of the Republic—and permit the final reorganization of the state. While the king lived, men would refer to him and by doing so would refer to the past, to an order and morality that were dead.*

There was trepidation in the Convention; it was not easy to imagine that the king must die. And it was not so much a political question as a psychological one. The king had already demonstrated that he and the people around him would destroy the Revolution if they could. Nonetheless the attachment to the symbol prevented decisive

* Robespierre's continual either/or ultimatum on the issue of the king is quite complicated, but essential elements can be profitably abstracted and explained. The ultimatum constituted first an attempt to coerce all possible authority types to a confirmation of his point of view, a move that was necessary to him for two related reasons: approval justified his actions and acquitted him of guilt. Anyone who failed to comply with commitments heightened the anxiety and became an aggressor, one who had to be destroyed (note also the remarkable encounter between Robespierre and Desmoulins). Second, independent power centers always represented a threat, the loci of the anticipated retributory punishment. After all, as noted earlier, the assumption of political power implies a public confession of the wish to dominate, to achieve equality with those who traditionally hold the power. Therefore, one so bold cannot expect mercy from the violated parties, nor does he offer any (they may return to harm him); further, power cannot be shared with or accepted from anyone, since that implies gratitude, and gratitude again is linked to submission, dependence, and passivity and must be denied. Hence the necessity, in Robespierre's mind, for the execution of the king. See Jules Nydes, "The Paranoid-Masochistic Character," *The Psychoanalytic Review*, L (1963), *passim*.

unified action, a factor evident in at least one of the questions the Convention was supposed to resolve: Was Louis guilty?

Robespierre had already settled this to his own satisfaction. He reminded the delegates that Louis was not on trial, that the insurrection of August 1792 had already decided his fate. Louis was not the accused and the delegates were not judges. Louis was king, but now there was a Republic, and the existence of the Republic was categorical condemnation of the king. Louis had simply' to be eliminated. Saint-Just added, for his part, that the king was not a mere citizen, but an enemy, less to judge than to combat. The right to dethrone was the right to punish: one was impossible without the other.[10]

The final, unequivocal withdrawal from monarchy constituted a necessary and extreme change. The change could be implemented by the radical leaders, but only at the characteristic cost of losing control over certain aspects of reality, especially the past. The ideological attack was therefore broadened from kings to kingship, past and present. Kingship had not become criminal since the Revolution; it had always been criminal, and all kings were rebels and usurpers. Saint-Just pointed out that Louis had not been condemned for the crimes of his administration, but simply because he was a king. Louis was a stranger among the French: he had never really been a citizen, and he was even less a citizen in 1793. Monarchy had become an eternal crime which nothing could excuse.[11]

The past was denied; the king, it was claimed, had never meant anything to the people. The argument ran that there never had been and never could have been an alliance between king and people. The king had done nothing but enslave, and if France had a history it was one of denigration. To remember the past was to have feelings about it, and if one judged it fairly, then there was the good as well as the bad. But if one could remember the good, it became difficult to act, and both past and feelings were therefore denied, at least in their positive aspects; because the past was not available to him, Robespierre could act.

The same obliteration of the past (and the same conception of a perfect future) which occurred in the Enlightenment recurred in the Revolution, and for the same reason: it was necessary to repress affective attachments in order to act, and the greater the demands the more perfect the repression. The attempt to blot out the past was felt eventually in every area of culture connected to the old order. It was a generalized phenomenon, and its expression this time was not limited to the verbal level. In October 1792, for example, the Convention decreed that all references to pre-Revolutionary times were to be removed from place names, the statues of kings and ministers were pulled down, and Barrère went so far as to declare, "We will burn all the libraries; we need only the history of the Revolution and the laws."[12] This aspect of the Revolution reached its peak toward the end of 1793, in the so-called de-Christianization movement, which aimed specifically at uprooting every form of religious worship that had been a part of the old France.[13] The most indicative event in this assault was the promulgation of the Revolutionary calendar: the Convention voted to substitute a Republican calendar for the Gregorian calendar.[14] The new calendar, as it was finally adopted, declared September 22, 1792 (the date of the proclamation of the Republic) to be the beginning of the new era. The basic intention was obvious—to escape the past, to deny that anything of significance had occurred before the year I of the Revolution, and through Republican fetes and holidays, to fix the public in the struggles of the present and point them toward the future.

But the violation of the past went much further: in the provinces and in Paris the de-Christianizers aimed at the deracination of every vestige of Christian worship, maximally intending either to close the churches or to use them as temples devoted to the worship of the Revolution and its principles. It is not necessary to review the record of all these activities, but one incident is worth noting for its particularly patent distortion of history: the representative on mission at Reims, a man named Rühl, destroyed the consecrated oil that had been used to anoint the kings of France. "I have broken, in the presence of constituted authorities and a numerous throng . . . the shameful monument created by the perfidious trickery of the priesthood in order better to serve the ambitious designs of the throne; in a word, I have broken the sacred phial on the pedestal of Louis the do-nothing, fifteenth of that name."

Robespierre was opposed to the de-Christianizing movement; he had no sympathy for the clergy or the church,[15] but he thought it better to brake the momentum of the movement lest it provoke the people by depriving them too soon of a form of worship they still required. Furthermore, Robespierre had no patience with atheism. Nevertheless, in his way, he too felt compelled to withdraw from the past, as we have indicated, and to invest himself in the future.

Saint-Just, who was close to Robespierre in all this, gave icy, laconic expression to the need to identify only the negative aspects of the past, to abandon the past and use the intolerable present only as the means for organizing the harmonious future. "Believe me, everything that exists around us must change and come to an end, because everything around us is unjust." In language reminiscent of Condorcet's on the same theme, Saint-Just wrote that "obliged to isolate himself from the world and from himself, man drops his anchor in the future and presses to his heart the posterity which bears no blame for the evils of the present. . . . I have left all weakness behind me; I have seen only the truth in the universe and I have expressed it."[16]

Robespierre and Saint-Just, finding both past and present unbearable, denied that the pressures which led them to such a judgment had any internal dimension at all; everything they felt and perceived resulted from events and factors external to them. It was of course necessary to remain tied to the environment (to avoid withdrawal), but only a negative identification with the environment was possible. They could realize neither pleasure nor sense of achievement from the present; nor could they narcissistically indulge the past, whether the cultural past or their own. Since the perceived injustice had no internal causes it had to be a function of events in the external world; given the appropriate principles then, they could, by suitably manipulating the external world, bring about an end to anxiety. Thus, all the while that they were exaggerating what could be done to and with the environment (which guaranteed the future) they were denying that there was any internal reality.

This inability to perceive internal life was expressed in a characteristic way, in terms of political speculations based on a priori psychological assumptions concerning human nature. The style resembled that of the Enlightenment, and Robespierre and Saint-Just were no doubt familiar with that literature. But the resemblance had less to do with the merit of the ideas than with the similarity of the anxieties.

Such a relationship between the Enlightenment and revolutionary eras should not obscure the most crucial differences. The Enlightenment writers could never have conceived of the problems the activists would be faced with. Besides, there are significant personality differences between those who articulate values and those who seek to implement them. Robespierre, for example, had certain charismatic qualities, which immediately distinguish him from his intellectual predecessors. He also had to motivate ever larger segments of society to committed ideological action, and to provide the legitimation for their action. Robespierre was capable of the kind of aggressive behavior the *philosophes* encountered only in dreams.

Still, it was stated again, as it had been by Enlightenment writers, that the creation of appropriate laws and institutions would terminate anxiety, end injustice, and create human harmony. Just what, in this sense, the laws and institutions were supposed to do is again more quickly understood in the writings of Saint-Just, where the ideas are more formally stated. Saint-Just had made it clear quite early in his career that he had no tolerance for a world in which the strong exploited the weak, in which innocence was violated, in which rewards had no relationship to virtue.[17] In order to reestablish the congruencies upset by the old order and the Revolution, he undertook to specify the correct objective organization of society in his *Institutions.*

Here again Saint-Just employed the notion that control over the external world would lead to control over human motivation. He was able, therefore, to envision an ultimate solution to the political question: "The legislator commands the future, to be feeble will avail him nothing; it is for him to will what is good and to perpetuate it, *to make man what he wishes him to be:* for the laws, working on the social body, which is inert in itself, can produce either virtue or crime. . . ."[18]

Saint-Just's stated goal was the release of men from dependence on other men. On the conscious, verbal level he was wary of power and he feared the ease with which individuals can abuse power; he therefore sought to organize controls, in the familiar Western tradition, through the creation of abstract social mechanisms.[19] This was the purpose of the Republic and of the laws and institutions he would have liked to organize for it. "Institutions have as their object the practical establishment of social and individual guarantees for the avoidance of dissension and violence; they are to substitute the power of morals for the power of men."[20] Saint-Just pointed out that though the Terror might settle the question of the monarchy and the aristocracy, the real concern was for the future, which could be systematically structured. The institutions, the alternative to the despotic will of men, would unquestionably deal with passion and self-interest. Without the institutions, society would be in a precarious pósition, i.e., in the hands of fallible men.[21] To Saint-Just the institutions were an abstract and impersonal means of creating and preserving the harmonious society.

It is noteworthy that the primary means of guaranteeing an external world capable of influencing men to the maximum degree was again the redirecting of affective energies toward the state. The proposed civic religion, for example, would direct people to love of the community (the religion would be subordinate to the community), and the educational ideas of both Saint-Just and Robespierre were calculated to encourage this response. Education was theoretically aimed at attenuating the cultivation of the self through the imposition of ascetic rigor, and also at mitigating jealousy in the group by applying the same harsh standards to everyone.[22]

According to Saint-Just, men love either glory or fortune: if glory, the state is fortunate and strong; if fortune, the state is ruined. The state must impose the appropriate attitudes—modesty rather than pride, virtue rather than shrewdness. Since the people had been adversely affected by the old order, it became necessary, in Robespierre's words, "to effect an entire regeneration and . . . create a new people."

The new people, as one might imagine, would sacrifice self-interest for the public good, while the community that protected their freedom and justified their sacrifices would become the object of veneration. The binding tie was love of the nation; the competing symbols, monarchy and church, were, or soon would be, gone. Moreover, the vision of the utopian community was never one of opulence and luxury, but rather of spartan, ascetic self-control. Self-indulgence, by withdrawing energy from the community, would lead to the expression of self-interest.[23] Thus Saint-Just wrote that indifference toward the community and love of oneself is the source of all evil, whereas indifference toward oneself and love of the nation is the source of all good. For this reason he urged that the Revolution punish not only the guilty but the passive as well.

It was from such assumptions that Robespierre and Saint-Just derived their politics. Liberty was impossible without virtue. This meant that there must be an end to the arrogant passions of pride, ambition, and cupidity, an end to indifference, factionalism, and self-interest when not consistent with the needs of the community. Virtue sprang from the organization of law and institutions, and thus could be realized if the external world was appropriately structured.

Since he thought it was the responsibility of society to create citizens, and necessary for it to impose the steps leading to virtue, one can appreciate Robespierre's eagerness to assume power and his anxiety in the face of continuing popular disturbance. The first rule of political conduct was to direct all operations of government toward the maintenance of equality and the development of virtue.[24] It was necessary to stabilize the laws and institutions of the state, creating thereby an objective environment in which virtue could be expressed. And the goal would be met regardless of cost, since anything less, by definition, meant dependence and depravity.

The related distortions and denials (of the past and of internal reality) were brought up originally in connection with Robespierre's demand that the king be executed. In affirming the existence of these distortions we have used materials that properly belong to the period after Robespierre, Saint-Just, and the Montagnards came to power. The more inflexible, more omnipotent tone that emerged at that point must be understood in terms of a political technique that developed with their accession to power— the Reign of Terror. All these qualities became more obvious in the light of the coercive and violent means employed during the Terror to gain social compliance and cohesion.

The creation of the Republic (the elimination of the competing political symbol) was an important step in the attempt to organize postrevolutionary stability. But with the war and internal rebellion there could be no stability— the Republic was not coping with the problem it had been instituted to solve. The Republicans, or Jacobins, clearly controlled French politics. But the Jacobins themselves were divided on the critical issue of responsibility for policy and the implementation of policy. Two distinct groups had formed: one, the "right," generally referred to as the Girondists, was identified with Brissot; the other, the "left," referred to as the Montagnards, was popularly identified with Robespierre. Though Brissot's group controlled the Convention until June of 1793, it never commanded the trust of the Montagnards or the Parisian *sans-culottes*.

The *sans-culottes* distrusted the Brissot faction because it had come to be identified with failure in the war, with refusal to deal with the economic anxieties of the masses, with reluctance to terminate the monarchy, and with the idea of ending the political power of the *sans-culottes*. All this was interpreted by the *sans-culottes* as treason, and by putting the word to it Robespierre reinforced their interpretation.

The Girondists were distrusted by the Montagnards not because the basic social aspirations of the two groups were so different (the better part of both factions agreed on such questions as universal suffrage and they shared similar views on what postrevolutionary society should look like), but because the Montagnards felt that those around Brissot were indecisive, not fit to lead. The *sans-culottes*, on the other hand, could tolerate the Montagnards, who in their view had not become identified with failure (treason) and who were willing to be decisive in speech and action. From the point of view of the masses, the Montagnards' extremism consisted, in effect, in their apparent lack of ambivalence with regard to the implementation of policy.[25]

When Paris rebelled for the third time, from May 31 to June 2, 1793, the Montagnards took power as well as responsibility for the vigorous moves that the situation required. Because of Robespierre's charismatic power, the Jacobins now appeared to have a chance to stabilize the country. But Robespierre failed to sustain his charismatic control, and he failed because of the complex of attitudes described above, attitudes exacerbated by the continued unrest in society—a situation that can be understood only in terms of the Reign of Terror.

Given the reputation the Terror has acquired, it would be a mistake to underestimate the importance of the objective conditions that existed when Robespierre and the Montagnards came to power. France was involved in a losing war, and the country suffered from the disunity provoked both by the war and by the Revolution. The revolt in the Vendée was alarmingly successful, Dumouriez had defected in March 1793, and the Convention seemed incapable of dealing with the situation. It was actually under these political conditions, and the omnipresent condition of economic hardship, that Paris rebelled in May and June of 1793.

The Girondists, who had insisted upon pursuing the war and then had failed to prosecute it adequately, were driven from office. And the Montagnards, who had felt all along that they alone possessed the strength to settle the war and the Revolution, found themselves with the opportunity to prove it. Danton and others deemed too moderate for the enormous struggle ahead were replaced on the Committee of Public Safety by more radical Montagnard deputies, including Robespierre.

The Committee had to deal immediately with the invasion of France and the Vendée revolt. In July and August, Mainz fell, along with Condé and Valenciennes. Not only was northern France invaded, but the Spaniards and Piedmontese were also moving against the Republic. The British put Dunkirk under siege, and in October Alsace was invaded. Worse, Lyons and Marseilles were in the hands of the Revolution's internal enemies, and on August 27, Toulon had surrendered the fleet and the arsenal to the British and declared Louis XVII king.

The Committee had to deal with defeat, treason, and espionage, with too-radical demands from the *enragés* and too-moderate demands from the indulgents, with English agents and refugee Bourbons, with speculators and fraudulent war contractors. When in September it proved impossible to placate the Girondists, and the masses threatened the Convention from the streets, the Montagnards undertook to satisfy *sans-culotte* economic demands provisionally—and they also instituted the Terror. The Law of Suspects, September 17, 1793, gave them the legal basis, and Saint-Just, in a speech on October 10, justified its purpose: "Liberty must prevail at any price. . . . You must not merely punish traitors but the indifferent as well; you must punish whoever is passive in the Republic. . . . We must rule by iron those who cannot be ruled by justice."

The Committee of Public Safety conducted a successful war against Europe, settled armed rebellion at home, introduced France's first democratic constitution (though it was never put into effect), and at the same time conducted the Terror. The Committee and its agents undertook this remarkable task in order to rescue the Revolution and the country, but each of these men was in the struggle for his own reasons. The objective crisis can explain the Terror, but it cannot explain the sadistic excesses of men like Carrier and Fouché. Nor does the objective crisis as such explain the basis of the commitment of men like Robespierre and Saint-Just to means that seemed to violate the principles for which they stood.

Robespierre justified the Terror and the revolutionary government that sponsored it, to the public and to himself, in the following way: constituted government is concerned with civil liberty, revolutionary government with public liberty. The former has only to protect the people from the public power; the latter must defend itself against enemies who are determined to destroy it. The public power must be preserved, to survive the Revolution and the war, or there will be no constitutional government worthy of the cost of the struggle.[26]

The revolutionary government had been organized, in a period of maximum crisis, to defend the Revolution. Any man who invoked the constitution or who charged the government with being arbitrary or tyrannical served only to confuse the issue. If popular government is based on virtue during peacetime, it must be based on virtue and terror during crisis, for virtue is powerless without terror. Since the enemies of the Republic did not hesitate to murder liberty in order to rule, innocence had to protect itself through maximum control and disciplined violence.[27]

Clearly, Robespierre acted with the principles of the Revolution in mind—but his absolute psychology converted relative and contingent principles into absolute truth.[28] The French Revolution to him was unique—if all that could be attained was what England and America had achieved with their revolutions, then there was no point.[29] The other revolutions had ended with the triumph of a faction; the French Revolution would end with the triumph of justice over all factions. For Robespierre the Terror was not simply a revolutionary tactic, aimed at stabilizing a chaotic internal situation; it was part of a political ambition to terminate human anxiety.

Robespierre did not conceive of the Terror as a means of preserving the Revolution in a relative sense. If the principles of the Revolution were merely contingent, then he could be wrong, and the Terror would be criminal; Robespierre was altogether too moral to tolerate that. He undertook these tactics because his principles were (or had become) absolute; the Terror was therefore innocent. Robespierre dignified the argument with language that has since become familiar: the Terror was the despotism of liberty against tyranny.[30]

The absolute moral sense, the need to maintain total control, and the determination to eliminate dissonant elements were exaggerated reflections of qualities that had existed in Robespierre before his advent to power. These qualities stemmed from anxieties that grew worse as the situation grew worse. Robespierre had always been excessively distrustful of those around him, a trait which predisposed him to exercise total control, and which was quite evident to his contemporaries. Pétion said of Robespierre that he saw everywhere "conspiracies, treason, and plots; he never forgave an insult to his self-esteem . . . and always believed that he was being watched and persecuted."

Moreover, in defense against his impulses ascetic tendencies were invoked. At the height of the pressure Robespierre could still distinguish what was vitally necessary in terms of what he would allow himself; but even the morally permitted pleasures were eliminated, and total war was waged against any deviation from the most ascetic standards of moral purity (for example, Robespierre's hostility to Danton).[31] At the same time, he withdrew all libidinal energies into himself, which inflated his self-image and led to the expression of notions of grandeur, to omnipotent, world-saving fantasies. Robespierre could be confident of the prospects for the future because there could be no difference between what he thought and what could happen.

His affectual commitment was thus withdrawn from people and attached to ideas against which people were judged. Since there was no emotional connection to any individual there could be no possibility of appeal except to the moral standard; anyone who failed to meet Robespierre's moral criteria was expendable. It was no coincidence that the Terror came to operate with only two possible sentences: acquittal or death.[32]

Because Robespierre's fears and anxieties were internal, nothing that happened in the external world could satisfy him. The situation was so structured, through his enormous demands, that there would always exist something or someone to justify his punitive rigor and his need to maintain maximum control over the hostile environment (the permanent emergency of the totalitarian).[33] This in turn led to a need to withdraw the sense of achievement or gain from a particular aim the moment the aim had been reached. Robespierre shifted the goal of action to the most remote ends; he continually postponed for the future the gratification normally experienced with the achievement of something good or significant. Each step in the unending process was reported to be incomplete or provisional until the ability to distinguish the possible was lost, and those around him could no longer believe in reasonable attainment—or, rather, they could not believe that Robespierre would settle for reasonable attainment. The language he used underscored this feeling: "The Revolution will come to an end in a very simple way, and without being harrassed by factions, when all the people have become equally devoted to their country and its laws." The Revolution would come to an end, he said, when it had perfected public happiness.

On October 10, 1793, the Convention had declared that "the government of France was revolutionary until the peace." This government included primarily the Convention and two agencies, the Committee of Public Safety and the Committee of General Security. It was well understood that this was a provisional, emergency organization of authority that was allowed to function outside constitutional limits until the crisis had passed. The Committee of Public Safety, for example, had been created in April 1793, as an interim executive body (originally composed of nine men, later expanded to twelve). It could hardly have existed as a permanent executive, and it was justified as a body only so long as the country was grievously threatened.

When the victory at Fleurus relieved France of the threat of invasion, the moderate members of the Convention were convinced that the apparatus of the Terror could be abandoned. But even after Fleurus, even after the Hébertists and the Dantonists had been eliminated, it was necessary for Robespierre to continue the Terror. His last remarks on the organization of the country, his final statement before political defeat in the Convention, said nothing about restoring constitutional procedures or regularizing the government. His program aimed instead at continuing the provisional government, at maintaining the machinery of the Terror under the law of 22 Prairial, and at eliminating the competing power center (The Committee of General Security), leaving the Convention and the Committee of Public Safety under his own domination; finally, the program aimed at eliminating still other groups judged to be enemies of the Republic.

It was these commitments that brought about Robespierre's downfall and marked his failure to maintain charismatic leadership. In the end he could not obtain popular compliance with his dictates through commitment to himself as symbol because his ambivalence regarding the goals and means of the Revolution threatened the masses at the periphery and his colleagues at the center.[34] The authoritarian content had overtaken the democratic, especially insofar as the Convention was concerned. Robespierre's refusal to return politics to legitimate channels, so that the values of the Revolution might be implemented, finished him as a political leader; the masses on one side and the Convention on the other combined to end the dictatorship of virtue. The psychological qualities that characterized Robespierre won him popularity and support while he was the critic of authority; these same qualities, compounded by the enormous pressure, made him intolerable as leader.[35]

Robespierre's politics have been called totalitarian,[36] and it is in terms of the combination of internal and external circumstances that the structure can be so understood. When Robespierre assumed power he had some idea of being able to render democratic values effective. However, though he appeared to have been given a substantial mandate to supervise the necessary change, social unrest and even rebellion continued: important segments of the population remained disaffected either because they refused to accept the implications of autonomy, or because they wanted a wider interpretation of autonomy. The Revolution was therefore faced with possible defeat, and for Robespierre this fear intensified a fundamental conflict on several levels. He wanted to effect the democratic values but he had no confidence they would work. Given the extent of the unrest, it could be doubted that the democratic values were functional. Robespierre's sociological solution to the crisis was the institution of an authoritarian structure and an almost exclusive reliance on violence to achieve social control.

Robespierre's attitude toward economic activity is interesting in this connection. He claimed that he had no intention of depriving anyone of honest profit or legitimate property. He declared that it would be impossible to equalize the distribution of wealth, and that such equality was not necessary for either public or private virtue. It was his view that property could be accumulated and used in any way that did not prejudice the life or liberty of other men. Property rights were limited only to the extent that all other rights were limited; there was, for example, no question of attempting equality in productive or distributive terms.[37] But these principles could not be realized because demands for economic controls from the street had threatened the government. At the same time that the Terror was initiated, economic controls were imposed on the society, for tactical reasons.

However, to Robespierre personally, the coercive means played an additional role: by sustaining the Terror he sought to attenuate a personal anxiety generated from two different but related sources. Robespierre experienced the wish to institute the values of autonomy as a transgression against the old authority; he also viewed the manifest unrest, the conspiracies and defections, as punishment, as retribution for his desire to implement the wish. The repressive structure he helped organize was therefore meant to repress both the mass unrest *and his own anxiety.* At the same time, of course, it served to suppress the wish for inclusion and independence. Through authoritarian control, Robespierre sought to eliminate both political opposition and the sources of anxiety. In the face of mass disaffection and possible defeat, he resorted to a solution that was all too readily available to him—a society organized in terms of the old (internalized) values along lines of authority and hierarchy.

We must bear in mind the connection between the chaotic conditions in the external world and Robespierre's fear that the chaos had resulted from his desire to implement the wish. He had created—or, at least taken advantage of—a structural situation in which the demands of his personality and the demands of the social crisis could be resolved at the same time. He legitimated his behavior in terms of the revolutionary ideology (freedom, autonomy, independence), and he justified the authoritarian structure, to himself and to the people, as a necessary but temporary stage. But as we have seen, it became impossible to estimate the limits of the "temporary," especially as the ideal goals that were posed were unmediated by any sense of compromise. In fact, because it not only suppressed dissidents but also served to abate his own anxieties, the authoritarian structure became indispensable to Robespierre. He could not afford to abandon it.

We have defined Robespierre's authoritarian social structure as totalitarian because it was characterized by several features indicative of this kind of organization. First, Robespierre completely denied the internal nature of the conflict and even the possibility of internal conflict; certainly the possibility never figured in any of the solutions he offered (therefore the external world could justifiably be manipulated to an unlimited degree, and whoever failed to meet the moral standards could be defined as wicked and self-interested). Second, Robespierre's commitments were entirely devoid of the possibility of compromise; he was rigid and punitive, and he could tolerate neither dissent nor deviation, conditions nor qualifications. Note, for example, his speech of 8 Thermidor, so characteristically unyielding, narcissistic, and omnipotent: "I would abandon life with no regrets. I have experience of the past and I see the future. . . . Why live in an order of things where intrigue eternally triumphs over truth, where justice is a lie?" Finally, Robespierre incorporated, as a crucial feature of his solution to the problems raised by the Revolution, a critical aspect of the past he was otherwise determined to destroy— an authoritarian, hierarchical political structure. Repression had obscured the inconsistency between the democratic wish he intended to implement and the repressive solution he organized in order to realize it.

More than a century ago, Tocqueville posed a sociological generalization to account for the "foolish hope that a sudden, radical transformation of a very ancient, highly intricate social system could be effected almost painlessly, under the auspices of reason and by its efficacy alone."[38] His generalization is based on two propositions: social isolation of the radical prevents him from participating in the power structure and therefore from understanding the complexities and the potentials of power; and social repression prevents the formation of any clear perception of the way in which society is evolving (with the corollary that the greater the repression the more radical the demands). The kind of dogmatism evident in Robespierre's politics has invariably been ascribed to these two causes.[39]

It can be argued, however, that Robespierre had not been all that isolated from the machinery of government, nor had the *ancien régime* been so closed that its repressiveness could account for the development of Robespierre's rigid attitudes and radical solutions. Robespierre's political style is better explained in the terms elaborated here: the authoritarian impulse stemmed from the failure of ego to deal with its own demands, to deal with anxiety aggravated by chaotic external circumstances; when the anxiety became intolerable, the reorganization of a closed world became necessary.[40]

The ability to employ at the same time the rhetoric of freedom and the machinery of authoritarian control accounts for Robespierre's actions while he enjoyed power. There was for him no inconsistency between his opposition to the death penalty in 1791 and the Terror he implemented in 1793-94, just as there was no inconsistency between his earlier demand for freedom of the press and his later demand for its suppression, or between his earlier insistence on a more equitable jury system and the subsequent legal practices of the Terror, particularly those involved in the law of 22 Prairial.[41]

Robespierre never abandoned the democratic idiom. But what he might have aspired to do before he took power became impossible to do when he held it. The language did not change; the goals and means did. Therefore, in the midst of the Terror, when Robespierre spoke in his customary way of "la genie du peuple Français, sa passion inaltérable pour la liberté," there can be no question that he was referring to people as they could become if the appropriate conditions were organized. The people were "good"; presumably they had qualities that would enable them to tolerate freedom. For the moment, though, they were easily led astray and needed to be protected—even from themselves. The people were predisposed to virtue, but under the circumstances virtue could not yet be anticipated. The objective situation had yet to be created— and as we have seen, it was to all intents and purposes unrealizable.[42]

Robespierre held firm to the related ideas that the environment could be manipulated and that the people embodied qualities which would allow them to become and remain sovereign. Though as a member of the Committee of Public Safety he received many reports describing the resistance of the people to the government, he saw nothing intrinsic to the people that could account for the unrest. He consistently ascribed this resistance to forces external to the people. In general he had one answer to such reports: "The people are everywhere good; hence at Bordeaux, at Lyons, at Marseilles we must blame only the constituted authorities for the misfortunes which have arisen."[43]

In order to maintain control it was necessary to suppress the forces that were spurring on the defections of the people. In his speech to the Constituent Assembly on April 29, 1791, Robespierre had argued that in a revolution it was necessary to tolerate all political parties. In the midst of the Terror, however, he defined opposition as the expression of private interest opposed to the public good; thus factions were by their nature intolerable and had to be eliminated.[44] It should be understood, however, that he intended not only to end factions but to terminate politics as such, restoring thereby that undifferentiated unity between authority and people that characterized the ideal of patriarchal society. But perception of this was blocked by repression (of the past and of inevitable, internal, affectual commitments to the past), and Robespierre never came to perceive the analogy he had created between kingship and his dictatorship of virtue.

5

The Introspective Revolution

THE INTROSPECTIVE writers of the first decades of this century consistently invested themselves in precisely that mode of thought which the French Enlightenment and Revolution had repressed. These writers turned the social and psychological focus from external to internal reality, creating a language to express the content of nonconscious thought; dwelling on the "terrible recreative power of memory" they showed that the past in its unconscious form exists as much for man as the external world does, and sometimes more so.* Proust concluded, in contradiction to generations of utopian aspiration, that the only paradise is a paradise lost.

Virtually every generation has produced some example of the awareness of nonrational, nonconscious processes and of the extent of the influence of these factors on moti-

* These include Marcel Proust, Henri Bergson, James Joyce, D. H. Lawrence, Dorothy Richardson, Virginia Woolf, Arthur Schnitzler, and Franz Kafka.

vation and action. This generation, however, must be particularly distinguished from the rest, not only because of the depth and prevalence of awareness among the artists, but because for the first time psychologists supported artistic insight and developed a systematic and rationalized statement on unconscious processes, making the information finally available as a critical tool.[1]

One dimension of recurrent perception among the contemporary writers was the feeling that ego is not strong enough to withstand the pressures brought against it by the environment. "Things fall apart, the center cannot hold," Yeats wrote, epitomizing the central experience of a generation. Earlier it was T. E. Lawrence who found himself dissolving into parts, a feeling echoed by Hofmannsthal, who complained that everything fell into parts, the parts into more parts, and by Rilke, who saw that "the things we live with are falling away." Kafka, whose vision tended to be more demonic than the rest, also commented: "I see the small horned devils leaping out of all the gates of the land . . . everything gives way in the center under their feet . . . the ground begins to yield. . . ."

This perception in particular has provided the basis for an explanation of the work of the introspective generation at large. That is, the artist's fear was a response to peculiarly oppressive cultural conditions—breakdown in the external world impinged on individual consciousness, forcing men to critical self-examination. Heinz Hartmann, for example, has suggested that under such cultural conditions as then prevailed, ego will attempt to fulfill its organizing functions by increased insight into internal processes.[2]

Such a proposition is by no means self-evident; it can be argued. But granting its accuracy, one still cannot infer from it the consistency in thematic concern manifested by this group of writers—the concern with time, the past, the unconscious, and oedipal conflict. There is one factor in particular that interferes with analysis and interpretation in these terms. Psychoanalytically, introspective insight depends upon that idiosyncratic quality that Freud called "flexibility of repression"—the greater or lesser availability of material ordinarily subject to repression, the difference varying with individuals.[3] It is hard to conceive, therefore, an interpretation of the work of this generation from a psychoanalytic standpoint as such; the interpretation must rather be in sociological terms.

The organization of psychoanalytic theory itself provides the most important clue to an understanding of the work done in this period. Freud's interests were related to social processes that provided a structural impetus for this kind of introspective investigation, and the contemporary literature can be understood from the same point of view. Before the structural conditions are specified, however, it is necessary that we understand the nature of introspective insight as psychoanalytic thinkers have explained it, in order to determine the kind of information that may be derived from it and to identify its peculiar characteristics.

To begin with, there can be no direct knowledge of unconscious processes; it is only possible to infer these, or, as Proust put it: "we feel in one world, we think and name in another. Between the two we can set up a system of references, but not fill the gap."[4] That is, defenses keep thoughts, images, and instinctual drives from entering consciousness when they are threatening to ego. When defensive processes lapse, or fail, the mental elements and certain connections of these elements become amenable to recollection and reconstruction.[5] However, the material never appears in direct form; if such a thing should occur, one could anticipate at the same time a serious breakdown. A direct, spontaneous lowering of resistances to such an extent that unconscious materials become preconscious* and then conscious leads to psychotic states of mind. Freud insisted, therefore, that the maintenance of certain internal resistances is absolutely indispensable for "normality."[6] The resistances cause such materials as do become available to be expressed symbolically rather than directly, and this accounts—in art, for example—for particular levels of ambiguity.[7]

Repressed materials cannot enter into communication with other intellectual processes; they are inaccessible to consciousness. Still, the repressed retains an upward urge; it tries to force its way to consciousness, and it can do so, but only under the following conditions: "(1) If the strength of the repressing force is diminished by pathological processes which overtake the ego, or by a different distribution of repressing energies in the ego, as occurs in sleep; (2) if the instinctual elements attaching to the repressed receive a special reinforcement; (3) if at any time in recent experience impressions or experiences occur which

* Although descriptively there is only one unconscious, dynamically Freud distinguished two: the unconscious proper and the preconscious. Presumably, unconscious materials are turned back on the frontier of preconsciousness by a first censorship. However, derivatives of the unconscious can be permitted into preconsciousness. A great part of the preconscious therefore originates in the unconscious and has the character of its derivatives. Such materials can achieve a high degree of organization and can be cathected and emerge into consciousness, though if they are recognized as derivatives of the unconscious they will be repressed again by a second censorship that operates between preconscious and conscious. When such materials are allowed into consciousness, it is because they do not violate ego; when they are not ego-syntonic, they can still emerge, but perhaps at a high cost in symptoms; and when they simply erupt, psychotic breakdown becomes possible. There is other material in the preconscious that can become conscious with no difficulty at all, e.g., a host of facts or memories to which no conflict is attached. Ernst Kris, *Psychoanalytic Explorations in Art* (New York, 1964), 24-25, 60, 304-6.

resemble the repressed so closely that they are able to awaken it. *In none of these alternatives does what has hitherto been repressed enter consciousness smoothly and unaltered;* it must always put up with distortions which testify to the influence of the resistance (not entirely overcome) arising from the repressing force, or to the modifying influence of the recent experience, or both."[8]

In psychoanalytic theory the artist has always been acknowledged as possessing a special capacity for uncovering and refining the kind of material that ordinarily remains repressed—the artist is indeed characterized by this "flexibility of repression." What the specific path to consciousness is, what it is that occurs in artistic work, has puzzled psychoanalytic thinkers from the beginning. After devoting considerable energy to the problem Freud could, in the end, only express his admiration and grant the artist priority in the domain of nonconscious processes.[9] Freud wrote to Schnitzler wondering how the latter could have "come by this or that piece of secret knowledge which I had acquired by painstaking investigation."[10]

What the artist can accomplish, however, is qualified by the conditions cited above. Materials originating in the unconscious become available only when they are at a considerable distance from the original impulse—the derivatives of the original impulse must be acceptable to ego before they can become conscious, and they therefore appear in altered (ambiguous, symbolic) form.[11] The primary processes, the unconscious content itself, remain unknown to preconscious and conscious thinking.

What introspective insight implies then, from a psychoanalytic point of view, is the suspension or perhaps even the failure of ordinary repressions.[12] It is clear that the great introspective artists—Baudelaire, Kafka, Strindberg, Nietzsche, Dostoevsky—all suffered from the failure of repression, the lack of control, the "too easy" communication with unconscious materials. Dostoevsky said that it was to his horror that he understood these things; Kafka's work can sometimes be so obscure, so virtually autistic, that one can infer a dangerous proximity to the loss of control; and Nietzsche too paid a high price for his insights.[13]

These men were driven to introspective examination; they gained the knowledge (Freud claimed Nietzsche had more self-knowledge than any other man who ever lived or who was likely to live), and they paid the price. Their impulses were not acceptable, conflict was not mitigated, and there is manifest, among the many invariable results, a good deal of self-hatred. Kafka wrote, for example, that "at a certain point in self-knowledge, when other circumstances favoring self-scrutiny are present, it will invariably follow that you find yourself execrable. Every moral standard . . . will seem too high. You will see that you are a rat's nest of miserable dissimulation. . . . These dissimulated intentions are so squalid that in the course of your self-scrutiny you will not want to ponder them closely. . . . The filth you will find exists for its own sake; you will recognize that you came dripping into the world with this burden and will depart again unrecognizable—or only too recognizable because of it. This filth is the nethermost depth you will find; at the bottom will not be lava, there will be filth."[14]

In these writers there are other familiar signs of profound introspective combat: the shock of discovery, especially upon perceiving the extent to which life depends on repression and sublimation, and awe and fear in the face of a process that is all but intolerable. Nietzsche said that man could not know himself because nature had thrown away the key —and that, speaking for ordinary men who need the illusions, it was just as well. "Woe to the calamitous curiosity which might peer just once through a crack in the chamber of consciousness and look down and sense that man rests upon the merciless, the greedy, the insatiable, the murderous."

Examine, for example, these statements by Strindberg, Dostoevsky, and Kafka. Strindberg: "Self-deception seems a necessary evil in order to exist; for when one's eyes occasionally are opened and one sees humanity in all its horrible nakedness, one shudders and wants to get away from it all."[15] Dostoevsky: "If it were possible for every one of us to describe all his secret thoughts, without hesitating to disclose what he is afraid to tell . . . the world would be filled with such a stink that we would all be suffocated."[16] Kafka: "If ever the deception is annihilated you must not look back in that direction or you will turn into a pillar of salt."[17]

It is clear that the closer the artist gets to what we might call "analytic" knowledge, the more he is marked by intense personal dislocation—and still the material is presented in an "altered" form. The question is, then, how did Freud manage the knowledge that, as far as it went, was direct? At the same time, how did he manage his stability and longevity? His critical discovery was also a result of introspective examination,[18] the progress of which, in relation to the oedipal complex, can be followed in his letters to Fliess, May through October 1897. Freud's hunch that he was about to locate the "source of morality" as a result of his self-analysis culminated in the clear perception of "love of the mother and jealousy of the father in my own case too, and now [I] believe it to be a general phenomenon of early childhood." From this point Freud went on to explain the "gripping power of Oedipus Rex."[19]

Presumably what Freud found out, no one was supposed to know. Just how he did it no one is sure—Kurt Eissler, for one, has insisted that the solution to the Freud riddle will not be found, by this generation at least.[20] However, an answer can be attempted, on the basis of the paradigm of superordinate-subordinate relations explained earlier. The answer will have to proceed on two levels, in relation to both internal and external reality, because two different aspects must be explained. The first level questions why Freud emphasized the conflicts of fathers and sons to the exclusion of other possibilities; the second, how Freud could have discovered and described unconscious processes in the light of repression.

To begin with, we must consider that contents originating in the unconscious and still threatening to the ego will be turned back by the censorship, or will appear in some distorted form. Therefore, Freud's discovery of the oedipal complex, a result of his own self-analysis, must have been acceptable to ego. Why this should have been so is related to how much Freud actually knew, to what in fact he was able to learn.* The point is that Freud's knowledge was, relatively speaking, restricted to the male, to father and son—female psychology, and especially the relation of mother to infant, was still as subject to repression for Freud as the father had been earlier. It is interesting that the father became as accessible to critical examination in the first decades of the twentieth century as political authority had become in the eighteenth—but only the father. Repression

---

* The maximum conditions for availability of internal knowledge are: ego-syntonicity, i.e., freedom from id-superego conflict and from conflict among various ego functions; and full cathexis with neutral energy as the prerequisite and consequence of integration. Ernst Kris, "On Preconscious Mental Processes," *The Yearbook of Psychoanalysis,* VII (1951), 113. This is not to say that Freud did not experience difficulties. But his troubles were slight in proportion to what he discovered; he went much further than others who paid a great deal more for the insight.

continued to operate in Freud in other areas, just as it had continued to operate, for example, in terms of the family in the revolutionary era. Certain information was still not available for conscious consideration.

The reason the father became exposed to critical insight at this point has already been hinted at: this was made possible by changes in the family structure precipitated by the economic and political revolutions of the eighteenth and nineteenth centuries. Just as structural change triggered and legitimated the Enlightenment assault on traditional political authority, so the father's changed role in the family allowed for the demand of the sons to be included in the family processes and made possible Freud's description of the relationship that existed between father and son.

Prior to the economic and political changes of the eighteenth and nineteenth centuries, the family in Western culture was patriarchally organized, traditional, and hierarchical. Authority was related to age and remained exclusively in the hands of adults. Further, there tended not to be specific tasks for one or the other parent with regard to the affective and coercive aspects of child-rearing; the roles were rather diffuse. This was particularly the case for the relatively undifferentiated family farm and even the later family firm.

Freud's classical portrait of the father in the patriarchal Victorian family, especially his characterization of the father as the unrelenting, punitive, castrating representative of reality, implies, by contrast, a significant change in paternal and maternal functions, a change that must have resulted from vital, fundamental alterations in the family structure. Demonstrably and unequivocally, Freud dwelt far more on the father's coercive role than he did on the positive libidinal ties that exist between father and son. Therefore it becomes necessary to raise the question: what accounts for Freud's analysis of the father's relationship to the son, what can explain Freud's description of the family?

Because of the economic and political changes in society, the father became systematically differentiated from the household. He was forced into a different role. The decline of agricultural families, the rise of modern industrial enterprises that required a host of executive, administrative (white-collar), and professional roles, the differentiation of the family firm into the more functionally specific family and firm units drew the father away from the home—especially where relationships to the children were concerned. The father had to arrange occupational and social connections separate and distinct from the household.

The middle-class family, of course, had to adjust to this new situation. Under the circumstances the mother's role became functionally located in the routine maintenance of the home, particularly in the everyday upbringing of the children. The systematic, forced absence of the father precluded the possibility of his involvement in this way. To the greatest degree, the nurturant, affective ties had to be abandoned; to a lesser but still determining degree, even the coercive functions of the process had to be given over to the mother, particularly those involved in the earliest stages of child-rearing. At the same time, however, the father provided the family with its only link to the crucial extrafamilial areas of life—economic resources, and political and social authority, and prestige. The father alone provided the tie between family and external world, a connection indispensable for the continued existence of the family unit.

It was on this latter basis that the father tried to maintain traditional familial forms of control over his children: he made the same demands as before for authority, respect, submission, and loyalty. But the demands could no longer be morally justified; the father did not play a nurturant role, he had an entirely different (instrumental) function

in relation to his children. The identifications and attachments that had attended the former affectual exchange
were broken, and the father's demands appeared oppressive. The need to repress hostile sentiments lapsed, and the
guilt resulting from the expression of aggressive feelings
and thoughts, though never entirely overcome, was sufficiently diminished that the son could express the fantasied
desire for independence.

The son's demand for parity was facilitated by another development that followed upon the preceding social
change. It became necessary to develop systematically the
characteristics of personal autonomy in the son, so that he
might be able to compete effectively in the abstract economic and political markets. The imposition of high standards of autonomous achievement and the ability to meet
these standards led to an insistence on the son's part that
he share in the prestige and the symbols of prestige bestowed
by the society. This demand reflected an enhanced sense of
self-esteem that was in part both the cause and the effect of
personal contribution. The son became competitive with
the father on many levels; at the very least he was responsible for his own well-being, and it was psychically and socially inconsistent for him to defer to traditional authority.

In sociological terms this was why Freud's work proved
ego-syntonic; in sociological terms, again, this is the essence
of oedipal conflict.[21] The father had become available at
last for conscious examination, and because he made illegitimate and unjustifiable demands he appeared now
as coercive and punitive. The sons could demand autonomy
because the father could no longer effectively reward submission or punish rebellion. Freud was himself involved
in such conflicts; what he personally wanted is clearly recorded in his thoughts on a dream he reported: "The
thought corresponding to it [the dream] consisted of a pas-
sionately agitated plea on behalf of my liberty to act as I

chose to act and to govern my life as seemed right to me and me alone."

The personal factor is crucial, of course, in any appreciation of Freud's work. We indicated earlier his conditions for the return of repressed materials, one being a recent occurrence of an experience or impression resembling the repressed so closely that it can awaken it. The recent experience reinforces the latent energy of the repressed, enabling it to emerge into consciousness.[22] One recognizes immediately the relevance of this process to Freud's discoveries. The "recent experience" in Freud's case was the death of his father, which brought up the oedipal question. This is quite evident, for example, in *The Interpretation of Dreams,* the first classic of psychoanalysis. Freud repeatedly used his own oedipal experiences to provide examples for the points he was making, and in the preface to the second edition of the book he wrote that the work was "a portion of my own self-analysis, my reaction to my father's death."[23]

But more important than the personal factor is the social one.[24] Freud escaped the threat of isolation and rejection; he did not become one more introspective intellectual or artist whose work is of only academic interest. His wish to achieve equality with authority, his wish to do his own work, to gain independence and acceptance, to be a discoverer, could escape personal repression and become codified, not only because of what he had become in personal, professional, and intellectual terms, but also because of favorable circumstances in the environment. The changes that had transpired in the family structure allowed Freud to be recognized and accepted by the culture—if not by his own middle-class society then at least by those societies that had survived the pressures of differentiation, England and the United States. Freud complained about the resistance to his work, but all revolutionaries complain about that. The fact is that psychoanalysis has become institutionalized;

it is a profession with its own regulations, institutes, journals, and practitioners, and, above all, with formal (legal) and informal acceptance in the West.

We have already indicated the means by which such consciousness is achieved: in the socialization process (whether on the political or the familial level), any object that stands in a superordinate relationship to ego is internalized, as a consequence of the network of dependencies on that object.* At the conscious and sociological level, when the reciprocal moral obligations are fulfilled, the relationship remains relatively stable and the subordinate interprets his subordination as appropriate. If the superordinate meets the moral demands of the situation he retains license to authority.

But when the superordinate abandons his nurturant role, for whatever structural reason, the subordinate is then enabled to express the other dimension of the dependence-independence fantasy: he can demand equal authority and inclusion. For "if the father ceases to be a 'good father' or a 'maternal father' who can give things to his sons there is no libidinal cathexis to bind the aggression inherent in the situation. It is therefore not at all 'remarkable' that the 'stronger oedipal complex' should exist where the struggle for prestige, power, and property is keener."[25] That is, the unconscious fantasy can become manifest and conscious, just as hostility can be expressed toward the formerly inviolate authority figure—and this holds for religious reformation, for political enlightenment, or for the demands of the sons for equality in the family, as expressed in psychoanalytic theory and therapy.[26]

These were the sociological bases for Freud's discoveries. However, it must be emphasized again that because Freud

---

*This means, of course, as stated earlier, that *patterns* of action and interaction in relation to the object are internalized, as well as the object as such.

could not surmount the structural problem he could not grasp the whole issue: on the psychic level, other areas not yet affected by structural change had to remain repressed. It was for this reason that Freud overestimated the extent to which his discovery was applicable. The oedipal conflict as the decisive problem in social development (in Freud's terms, in relation to art, morality, religion, social psychology) does not explain all that Freud thought it could explain.

Moreover, the discovery of oedipal conflict is not the most important part of Freud's thought. His greatest contribution was not the description of the father/son conflict but rather the discovery that not only are there hierarchical, authoritarian relations external to man, but that these relations also exist internal to man and can control behavior. The mind is not a simple thing, Freud wrote, "it is *a hierarchy of superordinated and subordinated agents,* a labyrinth of impulses striving independently of one another towards action corresponding with the multiplicity of instincts and of relations with the outer world, many of which are antagonistic to one another and incompatible."[27]

These hierarchical, authoritarian relations can dominate the conscious, rational part of man—hence Freud spoke consistently of the "tyranny of the unconscious." He had an authoritarian conception of internal processes and he conceived of psychoanalysis as at least the means of describing, if not of redressing, the imbalance. Initially Freud conceived man's ego to be under the domination of id, and psychoanalysis was therefore heralded as the instrument that could liberate the individual from the control of unconscious, instinctual forces. Later he recognized that the unconscious included not only id processes but ego and superego processes as well—and he concluded in particular that superego played a repressive, punitive, authoritarian role in relation to ego.

This discovery is in any case decisive—but it is especially important here because it is on this basis that Freud's discovery of unconscious processes can be explained. It is superego that prevents different fantasies from achieving conscious expression—i.e., the defensive processes may be a function of ego but it is the threat of superego punishment that leads ego to a defensive position, and this threat can be seen to be effective when punishment is understood to include the deprivation of rewards. As we know, no individual can tolerate an infinite diversity of fantasy. Therefore, knowledge of the oedipal problem (including attachments to both mother and father), which had to originate in a wish, could be achieved only if superego no longer needed to be feared on this score—not only because of punishment as such but because no rewards were forthcoming for the control of impulses. As long as the father played a nurturant role, knowledge of the oedipal conflict was kept submerged, because violation, even in thought, would lead to deprivation. When the father abandoned this function the fantasy became available, because superego, existing simply as a coercive function, was no longer effective in this area.

In other words, both father and mother are internalized on all levels—though not equally so on all levels—and the degree to which the internalization process is effective varies with respect to changed external circumstances. In Victorian families the mother was cathected *primarily* as gratification, the father primarily as ego-ideal and superego (as rewards for control and punishment for failure). When the father's role changed and the nurturant function was dropped, the promise of reward was gone, and what remained was the coercive aspect. Under this condition superego demands had substantially lost their legitimation in the area of paternal authority, and the demands could be pushed aside. This means not only that hostility could be expressed, but that fantasies hitherto repressed could become available—and it was on the basis of these fantasies that Freud inferred the existence of unconscious processes.

We do not mean to oversimplify the problem; it must be understood that Freud knew (intellectually) that unconscious processes existed as a logical possibility. He had also the evidence of external experiences with his patients and the evidence of his own internal life, and these together pointed him to the ultimate conclusion. But above all, Freud discovered the extent to which his own actions had been and could be *controlled* by what was repressed and the extent to which the behavior of his patients was still controlled by these materials, and from this he inferred the existence of unconscious processes. Quite simply, man does not exercise sufficient control over his own actions; there is an area of the mind that pushes him in an authoritarian manner, and since this area is not known to us consciously it must be a function of some part of the mind unknown to us—the unconscious.

Freud therefore expressed not only the demand for inclusion of the individual in the family, but also (and more significantly) the demand that ego control the processes of the mind. He wanted one more superordinate-subordinate relationship to be overcome—this time, one internal to man. Freud offered ego autonomy as a goal against the "tyrannical" unconscious; the ego, he said, must become master in its own house. What psychoanalysis expressed was the rights of the individual in the family, but also the rights of the ego *within* the individual. When Freud stated that psychoanalysis seeks "to educate the ego," he was making a demand for the reorganization of the bases of control as these exist *internal* to man. This was the psychological equivalent of the political statement that all men are equal before the law, or the religious statement that any man can read and interpret the Bible, or the economic statement that all men can compete in the marketplace without preference, favor, or interference. His demand for the liberation of ego can be seen as one step in a process that began with the Protestant Reformation.

Freud's genius lies in the fact that he focused on *two* dimensions of the changing value structure, while the middle class at large was involved with only one—the rights of the individual in the family. Freud's contribution was the recognition and description of the hierarchical authority relations in the mind that affect the individual's contact with the external world. He demonstrated that unconscious processes can dominate the mind to an unfortunate degree and that ego can and *should* achieve control. Freud wanted to give support to an ego-based check on authority within the personality.[28] It became clear to him that if man was to achieve independence he would have to abandon not only the external forms of authoritarian control but also its internal forms.

The wish for autonomy in the Enlightenment became conscious and codified only in the area of structural change, that is, in political institutions. Ego was confronted with the task of mediating between the wish and the environment, the greater or lesser extent of its success being reflected in the political theories suggested and the institutions actually created—representative institutions fulfilling the wish to the greatest degree, repressive institutions indicating a retreat to earlier patriarchal values. But in neither case could the critical attack encompass the repressed. The family, especially, was untouched, and the individual's relationship to the family remained incomprehensible; the network of affective attachments that bind the family remained repressed.

There were, as we have seen, idiosyncratic demands for

the destruction of the family, but the oedipal content of these was so threatening that all such notions were abandoned. More to the point than these Enlightenment ideas on the family are Rousseau's comments on the problem. Rousseau explicitly denied the possibility of a connection between family and state, claiming that the two forms of authority were too utterly different to have any mutual basis. He observed that political authority could be either elective or hereditary, but that in either case all the advantages of paternity were lost.[29] Historical experience, however, suggests precisely the opposite conclusion: even when authority was invested in a child, the symbols were effective enough to make a paternal kind of control work.

Rousseau also argued that children remain attached to the father only so long as they depend on him for their own preservation—when the need passes, "the natural bond is dissolved," and both parties "return equally to independence." If father and children then remain united, he continued, they do so voluntarily, not naturally, and the family is then maintained only by convention.[30] This point of view is so patently mistaken that it does not warrant discussion. Rousseau himself remained affectively tied to parental figures right to the end, and the ties can hardly be described as conventional.

No matter whether the changes in the revolutionary era ended in dependence or independence, whether the demands were realistic or not, there was distortion in the perception of internal life—for the most part, internal reality was simply denied. An introspective psychology was sociologically and psychologically impossible; it could not be inferred from changes on the political level. There was virtually no introspective knowledge in the Enlightenment (or the Revolution) because social conditions did not permit it, and reactively the pressures against acquiring such knowledge were even greater than would ordinarily be the case.

Later, when sons challenged paternal authority and made the demand for inclusion in the family decision-making processes, ego again had to mediate the wish—and again there were tolerant demands for independence or regressions to the values of dependence (for example, as in Freud and Kafka, respectively). But there was also a lucid appreciation of the basis upon which paternal authority rested—and after this, of unconscious life. *Moreover, and most important, this insight could not itself encompass the repressed, in particular the relationship of mother to children.*[31]

This point of comparison between extents of introspective knowledge in the Enlightenment and in the first decades of the twentieth century requires amplification and clarification. The kind of knowledge that Freud and his generation made available, and indeed central to an analysis of man and society, was virtually absent in the Enlightenment. To the extent that such knowledge did exist, it never became vital and never interfered with the eighteenth-century interpretation of man and politics. It will help to compare one of the writers of the introspective generation—Kafka—to the man who, by reputation, was the outstanding introspective thinker of the Enlightenment era—Rousseau. The comparison will demonstrate that much of what was available to Kafka and his time was patently lacking in the Enlightenment.

That Kafka and his art present unusual difficulties is immediately evident in the extraordinary range of critical interpretation of his work. Psychoanalytically oriented writers themselves have suggested that Kafka's literature is the product of a normal mind with unusual artistic gifts, the work of a neurotic, or an expression of schizophrenic tendencies.[32] Without having to choose on this level (it is impossible to resolve this problem here, since it involves the question of the relationship of creativity to "normalcy"), it is possible to note that Kafka's writings contain palpable evidence of anxieties connected to the problem of dependence-independence, success, and the ability to work as an autonomous person.

Kafka, in fact, exhibited the destructive effects of anxieties that stemmed from the need or desire to become independent. He had to survive immense struggles before he could succeed at what he wanted to do. In the midst of the psychological crisis that came to a head in 1912, in the so-called "breakthrough" to consistent artistic genius, Kafka wrote in his *Diaries* (December 16, 1911): "In periods of transition such as I have undergone the last few weeks, and of which the present moment is more marked, I am often seized with a sad but calm astonishment at my lack of feeling. I am separated from everything by a space to whose limits I can't even force my way out."[33]

Kafka had no choice but to meet the anxieties head on and turn them to advantage, and in this he succeeded through literature. He was used by the anxieties, but he used them too: "It's an outbreak," he wrote once, "and it passes and partly has passed, but the powers that call it forth are trembling within me all the time, before and after—indeed, my life, my existence consists of the subterranean threat. If it ceases I also cease, it's my way of participating in life. . . ."[34]

It is not necessary that we indicate in detail at this point the psychoanalytic sources of these anxieties, but we can note their importance to the present inquiry by examining briefly Kafka's story "The Verdict." In this story we can identify quickly some of his concerns, and on the basis of this knowledge we can explicate symbols that he continuously returned to, so that we have a point of departure for observing the nature and content of his introspective quest.

The protagonist of "The Verdict," Georg Bendemann, writes a letter to a friend in Russia, but he has misgivings about announcing to the friend his engagement and impending marriage; he also feels that he must conceal his business success from this friend. If he were to hear that Georg is doing well and that he has become engaged, his friend "would be hurt, perhaps he would envy me and certainly he'd be discontented without being able to do anything about his discontent. . . ." That is, Georg is successful but he feels too guilty to take pleasure in it. His friend, by contrast, is a failure, and Georg obviously feels him to be too fragile and full of envy to bear anyone's good fortune; somehow Georg feels that his good luck is damaging to this other man. In the end, however, Georg decides to tell his friend about the engagement, though he adds defensively that the friend is not thereby diminished; rather, he should see his position as actually improved—for in Georg's fiancée the friend gains a "genuine friend of the opposite sex."

When Georg finishes the letter he goes with it to his father, to seek approval for what he has done. The father's room is as dark as Georg's is sunny; the room reminds one of the past, and even as Kafka indicates a defect of vision in the old man, even as the father complains that he can't handle things any more, that his memory is failing, Georg thinks, "my father is still a giant of a man." The fact is that as long as Georg's mother was alive, the father prevented him from expressing any independent initiative. But since her death—since the removal of the object that defined the father as authority—the father has become less aggressive, and his business has been taken over by the son and greatly improved, with even more promise for the future. Objectively, Georg has assumed the authority and power.

Georg talks to his father about his friend in Russia, but the old man's response leads Georg to think about his father rather than his friend. The father asks "strangely" if Georg really has this friend in St. Petersburg, and Georg (who, concerned with the other fellow's failure and envy, might just as well have been thinking about his father) is embarrassed. Forgetting his friend, he begins to protest how important his father is to him and to the business; he suddenly becomes very solicitous of the old man. The father again asks if there actually is such a friend in Russia, and now it no longer matters whether the old man's memory is really fading or not. The questions have subtly altered the objective situation by involving the past—Georg cannot separate his father from his friend, and begins to feel guilty about his father. And now, although Georg had not discussed his father's future with his fiancée, and although both had taken it "silently for granted" that the old man would stay on alone in the house, Georg suddenly decides that he will keep his father with him when he marries.

At this point Georg puts his father to bed, and the father asks twice if he is well covered up, to which Georg replies: "Don't worry, you're well covered up." With this reply the old man throws off the blankets, "with a strength that sent them all flying in a moment and sprang erect in bed. Only one hand lightly touched the ceiling to steady him." Georg's father has used the word "cover" to accuse the son of wanting him dead. Now the father appears to Georg to be far from dead, and he threatens that "even if this is the last strength I have, it's enough for you, too much for you."

The tables are effectively turned, but in a specific way. As long as Georg considered himself successful the father appeared weak. But the old man manages to activate Georg's guilt, and in so doing restores a past, subjective, but determinative relationship; invoking the past strengthens the father and weakens Georg. There is no room in this internal world for two men: there is room only for a man and a boy, one adult and one child. Georg can literally pick his father up and put him to bed, as he would a child; but when the old man shows his remaining strength, Georg's wish is substantiated—his father is still a giant of a man, and Georg is reduced from his successful, autonomous status to that of a child. As one grows in stature, the other shrinks: perceptions of strength, height, vitality vary with psychological states, and have nothing to do with objective reality.

Georg's father says one thing after another calculated to destroy his son's self-esteem. The friend in Russia would have been a true son, but not Georg (the friend in Russia was weak and unsuccessful). What is more, Georg has the temerity to transgress in the primary area, and the father therefore accuses him ("then my fine son makes up his mind to get married"). The father again declares his special relationship to the mother, and remarks, too, that he has an excellent connection with Georg's friend and has all of Georg's customers in his pocket. The final blow to Georg's independence is his father's threat and boast that he could sweep Georg's bride from his side, and Georg, now reduced, shamefully exposed, is sentenced by his father, for his violations, to death by drowning—and Georg runs out of the house and commits suicide by drowning.

For Georg to heed the verdict required that he see himself exactly as his father saw him. In other words, Georg wished for equality but did not feel rightfully deserving of it. To obtain a sphere of independence, autonomy, and authority meant to establish a new basis of association between himself and his father, to transgress the psychological-moral basis upon which the association already existed. Because the desire was overt, Georg had to answer for the guilt: he followed the command for self-destruction.

What is evident in this story is the connection between autonomy and transgression, the insecurity of identity, the lack of self-esteem, the uncertainty of substance, the incapacity for self-evaluation and for evaluation of the environment, the failure of the defenses to counter the self-destructive tendencies, and the essential but ambivalent wish on the part of the son to be independent and dependent, to be equal and subordinate. These are anxieties and wishes to which Kafka compulsively returned both in his stories and in his self-evaluation.

These fears and wishes and the inability to take any stand against their recurrent appearance—epitomized in the uncertainty of internal substance, which raised in turn the question of his relationship to reality—were explored by Kafka, for example, in the theme of emptiness. Kafka's character in "Conversations with a Supplicant" reports that "there has never been a time in which I have been convinced within myself that I am alive." Kafka's bachelor is continually starved; he has his pain but no second thing in the world to support him.[35] Gregor Samsa ("The Metamorphosis") is empty ("The food came out again just as it went in"), the Hunger Artist is empty ("Because I have to fast, I can't help it—Because I couldn't find the food I liked"). And, of course, Kafka was empty: "am entirely empty and insensible, the passing trolley has more live feeling";[36] "To die would mean nothing else than to surrender a nothing to the nothing";[37] "I am senselessly empty";[38] "There were times when I had nothing inside me except reproaches driven by rage";[39] "Cold and empty," "an empty vessel."[40]

Emptiness suggests a lack of inner substance, a fear that one is nothing, has no value. But it also suggests a feared loss of or withdrawal from reality, characteristically complemented in Kafka by symbols of being caged, trapped, or unable to escape and, conversely, by escaping (perceiving reality) or by viewing the world (reality) from a window.[41]

The ape in "Report to an Academy" awakes inside a cage: "I had no way out." The mouse in "A Little Fable" regrets that "I am in the last chamber already and there in the corner stands the trap that I must run into." The dog in "Investigations of a Dog" is driven into a "labyrinth of wooden bars which rose round the place." "He" is in a barred cage and feels "imprisoned on this earth." Gregor Samsa is caged in his room, and the Hunger Artist performs in a cage. As for Kafka, "the truth that lies closest, however, is only this, that you are beating your head against the wall of a windowless and doorless cell."[42]

The complementary theme in Kafka's work is "out of here," "away from here," and, as a spiritual destination, "Away-From-Here."[43] The ape finally devises a way out, the dog dislodges himself from the tangle of bars, and Gregor Samsa ventures out of his room when bemused by his sister's violin-playing: "He felt as if the way were opening before him to the unknown nourishment he craved." The Hunger Artist, too, would fill himself up if he could find the right food, and then he too could abandon his cage.

One always faces the possibility of distorting the integrity of an artist's work by systematically or schematically presenting the meaning of symbols. Nevertheless, given the overdetermined quality of the symbols, it is necessary for our purposes to abstract one meaning in particular: what Kafka feared was the loss of reality, and the trap he faced was the uncontrollable necessity of having continually to confront fantasies and wishes that were the source of extraordinary anxiety; to escape meant to secure control over these fantasies and wishes. The tension in Kafka's life, as reflected in his work, was bred by the constant doubt that he could succeed in this struggle. The process of having to deal with and refine fantasies and wishes is what we have called introspection, and Kafka's forced introspection was the source both of his despair and of his greatness as an artist. It is this introspection that "will suffer no idea to sink tranquilly to rest but must pursue each one into consciousness, only itself to become an idea, in turn to be pursued by renewed introspection."[44]

The irony of Kafka's life was that his talent, the sole justification for abiding an abominable world, was linked to introspection, which made the world what it was for him. That is why he praised and hated this power at the same time. He found introspection to be the most arduous path to knowledge—"Again pulled through this terrible, long, narrow crack; it can only be forced through in a dream; on purpose and awake, one could certainly never do it."[45] He found also that introspection leads to solitude, which increases still further the pressure to look inward: "The strongest likelihood is that it may lead to madness; there is nothing more to say, the pursuit goes right through me and rends me asunder."[46]

On the basis of these experiences Kafka learned a great deal about what came to be called analytic psychology. He discovered for himself, among other things, the unconscious motivation of behavior ("I can swim like the others, only I have a better memory than the others, I have not forgotten my former inability to swim. But since I have not forgotten it, my ability to swim is of no avail and I cannot swim after all");[47] the relationship of past to present and future ("We others, we, indeed, are held in our past and future. . . . Whatever advantage the future has in size, the past compensates for in weight, and at their end the two are indeed no longer distinguishable");[48] the subjective nature of perception and perceptual distortion ("In one and the same human being there are cognitions that, however utterly dissimilar they are, yet have one and the same object, so that one can only conclude that there are different subjects in one and the same being");[49] the human flight from death ("For healthy people, life is only an unconscious and unavowed flight from the consciousness that one day one must die");[50] repression and sublimation ("Life is a constant distraction that does not even allow for the reflection as to what it distracts from");[51] and, of course, he had considerable insight into his relationship with his father, as well as into the world of dreams.

Kafka's experience with the unconscious was as direct as it could be and still be kept under control. It was also destructive: he was staggered by the content of his wishes and fantasies, his self-destructive tendencies representing the surest criterion of that judgment. "Eternal youth is impossible," he wrote, for "even if there were no other obstacles, introspection would make it impossible."[52] In any event, when Kafka's introspective experience is compared to Rousseau's it becomes clear how vastly different the results were. Rousseau, in fact, did not have the insight, his knowledge of such things did not even approach Kafka's, and he could not make use of what he actually did understand.

We have already observed that Rousseau's ability to work in the capacity of social critic and political theorist was relatively short-lived, that after 1762 he tended for the most part to indulge himself in defenses of his goodness and in the solitary, withdrawn pleasures he could find in nature. When Rousseau was forced to surrender his identity, his attachment to a concern for society was largely broken, and he became increasingly fixed in the present, in a search for untrammeled pleasure, a posture that grew more pronounced with time and one that contradicted the purpose of introspective examination. "Without great remorse for the past," he wrote, "free from all anxiety regarding the future, my dominant feeling was one of enjoying the present."[53]

This feeling is remarkably expressed in Rousseau's last work, *The Rêveries,* and accounts for its singular quality. *The Rêveries,* like *The Confessions,* was consciously dedicated to introspective examination; it was to be a record of his isolated walks, when his head could be entirely free and he could allow his thoughts to wander where they would, "without resistance and without trouble." He said he wanted to find the cause of all that he felt; he wanted to consecrate his last days to self-examination.[54]

What one finds in *The Rêveries,* however, is not introspection as Kafka understood it, but a deliberate attempt to abandon, at the expense of reality, any part of the environment that might cause conflict.[55] Since reality could not fulfill Rousseau's wishes, he saw them being fulfilled in his lonely, solitary world; he hallucinated objects of gratification in the absence of real objects. Pleasurable ideas were accompanied by vivid, ecstatic feelings of fulfillment, the world was transformed by excluding from it what was painful: "there, the sound of waves and the agitation of the water, fixing my senses and driving every other agitation from my soul, plunged it into a delicious reverie."[56] He lost himself in "delicious intoxication," feeling "ecstasies, inexpressible ravishments, in mingling myself with the system of beings, so to speak, in identifying myself with the whole of nature."[57] It was in this way that he withdrew to concentrate on the immediate moment, so that "without registering its duration and without any trace of succession, without any other feeling of privation or enjoyment, pleasure or pain, desire or fear," he could experience "immediate existence alone."[58]

Rousseau examined the past, too, in his introspective moods, but essentially only in order to justify his actions, to find those things in the past that confirmed his self-image and enhanced his threatened self-esteem. Thus, in

The Confessions, The Dialogues,[59] and *The Rêveries,* he repeatedly returned to his view of himself as a most decent and sociable man, one who was as just, good, and virtuous as any man could be. However, in order to maintain these feelings about himself he had to distort a quantity of information to the contrary, as reported, for example, in *The Confessions.* The problem of his children, whom he had abandoned to a foundling home, was especially troublesome.[60]

In his own defense Rousseau explained that although he had done many things that might be considered wicked, he had not undertaken any of them with malicious intent. He had to deny to these things any moral significance, in order to keep his self-image intact. But at the same time he was bound to miss the salient point of the introspective quest, a realization of the sources of human behavior; Rousseau never did deal effectively with the question of personal motivation.

This is not to deny in Rousseau an awareness of the existence of internal life; this awareness was derived from his memories and from evidence already available in the culture (e.g., the writings of Montaigne). At an earlier period, in his *Confessions,* he was able to describe the pleasures of the masochistic experience, the fear of displeasing others and of being separated from them, the expiation of guilt involved in the process of confession; he also perceived a relationship between childhood and adult life, and he was aware on some level of the emotional basis of thought and action.[61] But after *The Confessions* his control over this kind of material progressively diminished, and at no time was he able to relate this kind of information to man's internal condition.

Rousseau understood that there were difficulties involved in the attempt to describe one's inner life, that the writer of autobiographical statements could be guilty of the worst kinds of distortion. Still, he was absolutely convinced of the unique quality of his work[62] and of the real success of his introspective efforts. "No man has hitherto done what I am preparing to do," he wrote about *The Confessions,* "and I doubt whether any other will do as much after me." In his later years, however, anxieties prompted by guilt became so great that all of his energies were mobilized to protect his self-image, to withhold as much as possible from consciousness. This was why Rousseau became fixed in the present, and why he could not muster the strength for the kind of work he would rather have done. All his powers were concentrated on repression, *thus away from introspection.*[63]

Rousseau's great insights occurred in the area of political and social relations. He had little perception of relationships on other levels; in personal terms, for example, he tended to idealize the family, especially his relationship with his own father—he could not see himself as an object with regard to figures in his past, or with regard to his own internal dynamics. He was never able to regard his anxieties as caused by anything but malevolent forces in the external world. Thus, when he tried to show how man could become responsible for himself and become an effective, autonomous actor, he addressed himself to political spheres and not to the family.

In this sense, Rousseau was very much the product of his own generation. There could be no systematic insight into psychic and familial processes until authority provided the internalizations necessary for autonomous activity among males on these levels. Where these internalizations are not possible, and where authority cannot be exposed to critical examination, this kind of insight is generally suppressed. Thus, such instances of introspective awareness as can be pointed to in the Enlightenment era, or in any other period prior to the institutionalization of modern industrial structures, originated as personal rather than social experiences, and remained so.[64]

In sociological terms, the Enlightenment and other democratizing movements are related to Freud and his work primarily in the sense that without these earlier movements and the changes initiated by them, what Freud did would be inconceivable. This relationship of structural change to Freud's work can be identified particularly by the singular direction taken by psychoanalytic theory: the emphasis on father/son relationships. Other connections on the level of psychoanalytic awareness not yet affected by social change remained repressed, for Freud's discoveries were limited by social processes more basic than those described by psychoanalytic theory itself.[65]

6

The Introspective Revolution:
Limitations of Insight

P SYCHOANALYTIC THEORY was accepted as legitimate
insight into personal and familial problems to the greatest
degree in England and the United States, those societies
in which the family had been most affected by the industrial process and in which personal autonomy in the family was most readily taken to be appropriate behavior. This
social acceptance immediately marks the introspective era
as distinctive.[1] There is a second factor that separates this
era from any previous one: the conscious capacity of a generation of writers to rationalize thoughts that had hitherto
been expressed only in symbolic form. Writers were now
able to think about the past, recover memories, critically
examine sacred figures, and infer from all this the existence
of various psychic processes; the knowledge thus acquired
very evidently influenced the form and content of the
literature.

The question of time, for example, was critical for all these writers—Proust, Joyce, Kafka, Richardson, Woolf, and others. All of them realized the importance of the problem of time without reference to Freud or, for that matter, to a writer like Bergson. The introspective novelists exploited their sense of the subjective, nonsequential nature of time; they knew that the mind leaps the intervals that separate past from present event, and they worked into their literature the sense of the simultaneity of past and present. Virginia Woolf noted that the "extraordinary discrepancy between time on the clock and time in the mind is less well known than it should be and deserves fuller investigation." Jules Romain observed that time seemed to be something quite arbitrary and elastic; he found it difficult to believe that it was a dependable entity, "and clocks seemed to him fallacious mechanisms for measuring it." Proust wrote that "this dimension of time, of which I had a presentiment in Cambray church, I would try to make continually perceptible in a transcription of the world which would have to be very different from that provided by our misleading senses." And Kafka wrote: "The clocks are not in unison, the inner one runs crazily on at a devilish or demonic or in any case inhuman pace, the outer one limps along at its usual speed. What else can happen but that the two worlds split apart, or at least clash in a fearful manner."[2]

The notions of unconscious processes expressed by the novelists and psychologists are not necessarily consistent, but they can in any case be understood in terms of each other. Freud's notion of the absence of time in the unconscious, for example, and Proust's reflection that "a single minute released from the chronological order of time has recreated in us the human being similarly released" lead to the same conclusion: the choice of individual reaction to events cannot be a function of chance but must depend upon past experience, on the memory of some analogous event. Although the past as object is gone, it remains as memory, and in that form is decisive for thought and action; events must be lifted from the scheme of temporal succession in order to be understood.[3]

The two characteristics that distinguish the introspective era—the social acceptance of introspection and the recurrence of specific introspective content—resulted from the particular conditions under which introspective thought was organized. It is therefore important to understand not only what these writers were able to learn but also what they were not able to learn. The analysis of the environment was again limited to the extent that insight is affected by external circumstances.

It was possible for certain repressions to lapse—the father, and struggles between father and son, became available to consciousness. From this followed inferences on unconscious life and on the relationship of past to present and future. But there was no equivalent insight into the female or, more specifically, into the maternal world. The oedipal mother exists in the literature, of course, but she was not available for the same kind of intense critical examination as was being devoted to other dimensions of internal conflict. Moreover, the pre-oedipal mother, shown by post-Freudian psychoanalytic theory to be just as important as these other dimensions, hardly appears in a controlled way at all.*

---

* "Pre-oedipal" characterizes the period antedating the appearance of the oedipal figure as a determinative source for identifications and internalizations, a span of time in the individual's life when the father's role is minimal and the mother carries the greatest burden in the socialization of children of both sexes.

The work of the two contemporary writers we have already examined, Freud and Kafka, represents a convenient focus for an examination of the implications of this inability to perceive the mother.[4] What links Freud's work to Kafka's is, of course, the emphatic stress on unconscious motivation, as well as the preoccupation with paternal authority and the conflicts of fathers and sons. But what links them also is the tendency to overevaluate paternal authority, to exaggerate the father's power while at the same time allowing the maternal influence to suffer serious neglect.

Kafka and Freud embody in personal and intellectual terms the content of the oedipal struggles they described. Both men wanted to achieve autonomy and acceptance, and both had to struggle against the weight of their experienced paternal past in order to work and to succeed. Kafka's struggle remained, in a sense, on a personal level. Freud's became social in that his point of view was organized in a theory and institutionalized in a profession; he may be understood as having codified the demands of the individual for autonomy on the personal and familial levels. This was never a part of Kafka's purpose; Kafka's concern was to create a literature. But to a considerable degree this literature was a result of the conflicts he experienced within his family, and it is on this basis that parallels between Freud's work and Kafka's can be examined and some light can be shed on the work of a generation.

The key document in any appreciation of Kafka's position in relation to Freud and his contemporaries is his well-known "Letter to His Father," a remarkable exercise in filial remorse and hostility. Kafka's "Letter" (it ran to some one hundred pages) was supposed to clarify his position with respect to his father; it was in fact an act of aggression and would have been so interpreted by his father.[5] His "Letter" has already been recognized as a literary work and as an index of Kafka's psychological insight into the conflicts of fathers and sons. However, it is also significant for its sociological implications. Kafka's "Letter" is an excellent description on an individual level of the sociological conditions that account for the lapse of repression and the release of aggression and insight with respect to the paternal figure. What Kafka wrote about here are the effects of the withdrawal of the father from the family into concerns only peripherally associated with the affective life of the family —the father's continued demands for loyalty and submission in spite of the break in affective relations, the appearance of the father in the middle-class family as a punitive, castrating figure, and the ability of the individual to reflect upon and understand his position in relation to his father once the father's nurturant role in the family has been given up.

It is hardly conceivable that such a document could have been produced prior to the economic and political revolutions of the eighteenth and nineteenth centuries. It is equally hard to conceive of this kind of aggression being directed at that point in time against the mother for failure to fulfill nurturant functions (in a pre-oedipal sense) with regard to the son or daughter. However, because Kafka's father was already withdrawn from the family, recognition of his failures and weaknesses was no longer repressed; rather, Kafka probed, exploited, and attacked them. In particular his father was reproached for being unavailable, remote, and inaccessible—and not the least reason for this was that Kafka's father was "completely tied to the business, scarcely able to be with me even once a day."

Kafka pictured his father as unloving, punitive, and tyrannical, lording it over everyone, leaving in his wake nothing but hostility. The most searing impressions of his young years were of a father who could come at any time "almost for no reason at all" and punish him. Being related to this man meant having to participate in a "terrible trial"—the father sat as judge but was himself unjust; not only that, he was as weak and deluded as the people he dominated.[6]

Because of the way Kafka presented his problem and the way he solved the conflicts involved, it is necessary to approach his work in personal as well as sociological terms. The solution to the personal conflict helped structure Kafka's literature. Primary in Kafka was his ambivalence: on the one hand he wanted love and acceptance from his father on the basis of independence and parity; on the other hand, because he was frightened by his own wishes, he wanted to remain passive, deferential, and subordinate. The conflict implied in such contradictory wishes dominated Kafka's life, and he managed a solution in one area only—literature. Writing became the vehicle for rebellion and the only justification for tolerating the anxieties he experienced in his struggles for personal autonomy.

It cost Kafka a great deal to write; he found it always extremely difficult to take any step that might define him as independent of and equivalent to his father. According to Kafka's own insight this was particularly true with regard to women—especially where marriage was the issue. To Kafka, independence in these areas meant transgression, threats to his father's preferred position that gave rise to feelings he found hard to tolerate. Insofar as Kafka was able to describe the trap he was in, the categories of action (and inaction) are familiar and consistent: "Marriage is certainly the pledge of the most acute form of self-liberation and independence. I should have a family, the highest thing that one can achieve in my opinion and so, too, the highest thing you have achieved. I should be your equal." However, "when I make up my mind to marry I can no longer sleep; my head burns day and night, life can no longer be called life, I stagger about in despair."[7]

Kafka could not challenge parental authority, but the bitterness that issued from the failure was more tolerable than the anxiety that arose from any possibility of success.[8] Kafka described himself as for the most part a dependent creature, but one with "an infinite yearning for independence." He failed to achieve that independence, however, because, as he said, he could not revolt against (what he considered to be) nature.

Thus Kafka's literature is keyed to the universal theme of authority and guilt, and his description of his own frustrations reminds us of his artistic work. Trying to explain his position to his father, Kafka wrote that the world was divided for him into three parts: "One in which I, the slave, lived under laws that had been invented only for me and which I could, I did not know why, never completely comply with; then a second world, which was infinitely remote from mine, in which you lived, concerned with government, with the issuing of orders and with annoyance about their not being obeyed; and finally a third world where everybody lived happily and free from orders and from having to obey."[9]

It is this picture of authority, particularly the aloofness and remoteness of authority, that gives Kafka's work its special quality. Authority is removed, isolated from people, indifferent to personal, individual needs, ambitions, or desires. Authority neither provides nor protects in any affective way, it knows and cares about no one in particular, yet it makes demands for obedience, loyalty, and submission as if it did provide and protect. Since authority no longer has legitimation for the demands it makes, withdrawal should be possible and rebellion justified. But in Kafka's world the characters wish the facts to be different;

they wish that authority were otherwise, but they do not rebel. Rather, they accept the assumptions of authority and they accept authority's view of them as their own view of themselves—and they are trapped. "They were given the choice of becoming kings or kings' messengers. As is the way with children, they all wanted to be messengers. That is why there are only messengers, racing through the world and, since there are no kings, calling out to each other the messages that have now become meaningless. They would gladly put an end to their miserable life, but they do not dare to do so because of their oath of loyalty."[10]

This point of view affords insight into Kafka's literature: it makes clear what Kafka meant when he wrote to his father that "my writing was all about you."[11] The substance of Kafka's work is always in the end a reaffirmation to himself and to his father that he really was submissive, that he did not seek independence, that he was an obedient son who accepted his obligations to authority even when these were not warranted. Thus, the content of Kafka's work may be understood both as an expression of and a reaction to the wish for independence.[12]

Kafka's vision of the dire consequences of independence (within the family, but, by extension, from all authority) was prompted by his desire to remain passive. His was a typical pattern of response to this problem, one manifested ultimately in all pluralized societies. Kafka's resolution of anxiety with respect to the family parallels Rousseau's with respect to political authority. In both cases the analysis of authority and the ability to act autonomously were obstructed by the inability to tolerate personal freedom. Neither writer was able to appraise objectively, for all people, what authority was like or how freedom from authority could be achieved and maintained.

In spite of Kafka's having approached the problem with

a vast sense of despair and from the standpoint of his own solutions, his work reveals a great deal of insight into the paternal world. There is, however, no equivalent insight into the female or maternal world. Kafka had little talent for describing women or relationships to women. They appear in his work relatively infrequently; when they do appear they are endowed with great redemptive or destructive power, but they are not treated with the insightful scrutiny that Kafka applies to the paternal world.[13]

As we have noted, this disparity of insight was true of the introspective writers in general, including Freud. From the time Freud described to his friend Fliess a dream of his that fulfilled the wish "to pin down a father as the originator of neurosis" (1897)[14] to the time *Moses and Monotheism* (1938) appeared, Freud stressed without deviation a masculine, paternal view of the world. We need only follow Freud's use of language to see how pervasive this view is. According to Freud, social organization, religion, and morality all have the same origins; all were acquired by man phylogenetically, as a result of the primal murder of the father. Society is based on complicity in the common crime and on the need to preclude the repetition of such an event; religion and morality are based on the need to prevent the eruption of libidinal and aggressive wishes. In Freud's classical portrayal of the totem murder the ambivalent feelings of the sons for the father proved decisive: tenderness turned into remorse for the deed, which in turn provided the motivation for the cultural restoration of paternal authority.[15]

This cultural process is repeated in the life of each individual; ontogenetically, moral restraint is derived from the mastering of the oedipal conflict. The son is ambivalent in his feelings for his father, "who embodies every unwillingly tolerated social restraint."[16] Nevertheless, because of the positive aspects of ambivalence[17] the son inevitably grants the father a continued existence in his internal world. In the solution to the oedipal conflict the father's authority is integrated in ego, where it forms the nucleus of super-ego, securing the male child against the return of libidinal cathexes directed toward the forbidden mother and per-petuating the paternal (cultural) prohibitions against transgression.

This process is biologically and psychologically guaran-teed—specifically, the threat of castration directed against the gratification of libidinal urges forces the son to abandon the oedipal project. The son's submission to the castration threat is the critical step in the formation of ego and super-ego; it is the dread of castration that comprises the nucleus around which the subsequent fear of conscience is organ-ized. It is under the assault of paternal reality[18] that the psychic apparatus is modified, that original tendencies are deflected into "safe," culturally approved channels. It is the father who stands for reality, who represents to the son the principles of restraint, denial, and authority.

The outcome of oedipal conflict is the internalization of paternal authority. The means by which individuals are constrained to heed the moral mandates of culture is the construction within the individual of a paternal barrier against unrestrained gratification. In Freud's view, how-ever, this resolution of oedipal conflict—and thus the grip on morality and ethics—is much more stable and successful in the male than in the female. Cultural contribution and development is a masculine function; historically and com-paratively, the female represents sensory gratification, the male represents abstract achievement.[19]

From the standpoint of the sociology of knowledge, Freud, Kafka, and the other writers addressed themselves in this way to paternal culture because at the time autonomy was possible only for the male. As we have noted, the paternal role became identified with the economic and political order, separate from the household and the nurturant processes. Because it was necessary to enter economic and political orders in modern terms, the father had to forfeit his "sacred" status—he could rather safely be exposed to aggression or to aggressive examination. The mother, on the other hand, the remaining nurturant figure in the family, could not be treated aggressively, and insight into relationships to her was blocked. This was very evidently the case in the more pluralized economic structures in England and the United States.

The fact that the father had to become, in a sense, the familial representative to society, providing the link between family and society with respect to financial resources, future prospects, and prestige, had important implications for the socialization of the children. To a great extent the father was forced to withdraw from the early phases of child-rearing, entering into the training of the children, for the most part, when they were considerably advanced, when it was necessary for them to take a step away from dependence on the mother in order to achieve a new level of autonomy. The father's influence came to be felt by the children primarily in relation to the socialization processes connected with the oedipal phase—i.e., in relation to the first sexually differentiated obligatory social roles.

This had immediate and significant consequences for father/son relations. It was the father's responsibility to inculcate in the son the standards of behavior required for successful accommodation to a highly competitive, individualistic, and mobile economic and social order. This meant, above all, interference with all possibilities of retreat to passive, dependent gratifications. There would be an end to permissiveness, to sentimental or sensual attachments to the dependent past or to the mother.

The sons, therefore, were exhorted to develop self-control and self-discipline, to be self-observant, and to fear the loss of control stemming from emotional response. They were told that emotional expression, sentimentality, and sensuality were harmful (feminine) and that if they did not exercise self-control they would never become men. At home and at school the sons were urged to be industrious, calculating, and self-contained. The sons observed the controlled behavior of the parents, they identified with the active, competitive father, and they accepted the necessary restraints. It was thus possible for males to view personal feelings, even within the family, as obstacles to the achievement of the most important social goals. Masculine virtue resided in the deliberate, aim-conscious rejection of pleasurable experiences and in "reasonable" behavior.

Thus, because the father was identified primarily with all the "unwillingly tolerated social restraints," and because he could not be loving except in terms of these rigorous demands, he could appear both as the unrelenting representative of the social order and as an object toward whom hostility could be expressed. But at the same time, because of the father's rigorous demands, the sons were able to participate competitively in the new industrial complex. The constant, vigilant self-scrutiny and rationalization of emotion that individuals learned to accept allowed personal goals to be approached in a more systematic and conscious way.[20]

These deliberate preparations for autonomous initiative were directed only toward the sons. Except in individual instances, the daughter was treated quite differently. She was to remain subordinate and dependent, both inside and outside the family. Her satisfactions were supposed to derive from the home and from domestic concerns—or, at best, from appearing in society in a way that would reflect masculine success. The respectable female did not seek equality in familial, political, or occupational processes. This was as much a factor of compliance as it was of male discrimination.[21]

It is from this standpoint that Freud's emphasis can be understood. His portrayal of the hero's rebellion, of the critical events in the life of the individual and the community as oedipal products resulting from conflicts between father and sons, reflected the middle-class background within which his work developed. This conclusion is underscored by the fact that his discovery of oedipal conflict and the mode of its resolution centered on the relationship of the male child to his father, just as the information on infantile sexuality was obtained from the study of men, and the theory deduced from it initially concerned male children. Freud himself pointed this out.[22]

Freud's perception of roles in the contemporary family was precisely that the male could achieve independence, but that an equivalent, productive liberation of the female was not possible. He saw quite accurately that the daughter could not organize the energy for a break in the way that the son could. This reinforced his stress on the decisive nature of oedipal conflict and allowed him to continue thinking along the lines of father and son. Thus, Freud noted that "a boy is far more inclined to feel hostile impulses towards his father than towards his mother and has a far more intense desire to get free from *him* than from *her*. In this respect the imagination of girls is apt to show itself much weaker."[23]

This was a fair rendering of the lines of authority and withdrawal from authority in the contemporary family. The son was anxious to escape the domination of the father and he was capable of doing it; there was no similar desire to escape the mother. The daughter, however, manifested a generalized inability to challenge authority; she could not critically examine, nor could she attack, either mother or father.

Freud could never adequately demonstrate why the daughter showed so much less initiative than the son in the matter of withdrawing from either parent, nor could he explain effectively enough why the son was less anxious to withdraw from the mother than from the father. His explanation of the daughter's relative immobility followed anatomical lines, including, of course, the fantasies and anxieties that accompany the most significant of anatomical differences: because the female has already been deprived of the penis the incentive for abandoning the oedipal position is weaker, and she tends to remain on an affective level, concerned with the wish to be loved and the fear of the loss of love.[24] The principal factor leading to the development of autonomous initiative—the resolution of the oedipal complex—is, as we know, much less successful in the girl than in the boy.[25]

This anatomical interpretation of the difference between male and female superego did not withstand subsequent (post-Freudian) investigation; as a more complex picture of the family emerged, the emphases in psychoanalytic theory shifted. The stress was put on object relations, rather than psychosexual development, and, in particular, the critical role of the pre-oedipal mother was explored. Beyond Freud's relatively simplistic anatomical suggestion, contemporary psychoanalysis "would put at least as much emphasis on early object relations in this respect. We would also consider carefully how the difference between the sexes with respect to internalization is one of kind rather than, or as well as, one of degree; that is, we would ask on which level of organization, with what admixture of gratification and renunciation, and how stably these internalizations take place in each sex."[26]

Although psychoanalytic investigators have had excellent success in developing insight into object relations and the pre-oedipal mother, there is typically one element missing: the literature contains no hint of the sociological origins and the limited historical duration of this pre-oedipal figure. The pre-oedipal mother in the terms presently employed in the psychoanalytic literature has existed only in the modern family structure (for our purposes, approximately from the 1850's through the 1950's). There is no history of this pre-oedipal mother prior to the organization of highly industrialized, technical societies; i.e., in the pre-modern family there was no sharply differentiated or extended pre-oedipal period in the sense of the psychic absence of the father and the singular domination of the mother in the early socialization process. Before the changes imposed by the economic revolution, the father entered the child's life at a much earlier stage than the present pre-oedipal concepts will allow, and he played a much more important role in the development of the children on what may be called primary levels.

It is only with the advent of the modern family that the mother has developed singularly intensive affectual relations to the children, and it is only with this in mind that the relationships of parents to children can be explained in a comprehensive way. That is, as a result of the changes in the economic order the lines of discipline and control in the family also changed. Initially, the father continued to represent authority in the family, but as the parental roles differentiated, the mother also developed as a source of restraint and control—with one critical difference between the two. Because the mother became the *primary* loving and protective figure she also became the *focus of compliant obedience* and commitment to the highest level of generalized cultural values. This was true for children of both sexes: in the pre-oedipal phase the children formed a sexually undifferentiated union with the mother based primarily on love and dependence.[27]

It is in the pre-oedipal phase that the child develops the primary personality structures—in particular, two structural components, ego and what may be called primary ego-ideal.* Ego develops as the center of conscious control and also as the locus of the child's conception of and orientation to self as subject and object. Primary ego-ideal, for the most part an unconscious structure, develops as a general conception of and orientation to self and others that is not directed toward external reality as such but toward the achievement of cultural values internalized from primary objects. Together, these two structures form that part of the personality that gives the individual his most generalized standards of aspiration and commitment.

The way in which ego and primary ego-ideal are structured will determine the way in which an individual will

---

* The concept of ego-ideal has had an unsettled and ambiguous place in psychoanalytic theory, for the most part because of the different ways Freud defined and described it in one place or another. "Since the publication of *The Ego and the Id* (1923) the predominant usage of the term has been as a synonym for the superego, although in relatively recent years a number of attempts have been made to differentiate the ego-ideal from the superego . . . to regard it either as a separate mental structure or as a descriptive term referring to some, but not all, of the functions of superego. Most of the recent formulations have been concerned with the need to distinguish between the benevolent and critical aspects of the superego . . . or with the differences between the ontogenetic development of ideals on the one hand and the conscience on the other." Here ego-ideal comes closest to what is usually conceived of as the precursor of superego, originating in the oral stage and being developed through the end of the anal stage. Joseph Sandler, *et al.*, "The Ego Ideal and the Ideal Self," *Ps. St. Chi.*, XVIII (1963) , 140. This article explains the history of the concept ego-ideal, the various uses of the concept, and especially Freud's several uses of the term. Also see, for example, Jeanne Lampl -de Groot, "Ego Ideal and Superego," *Ps. St. Chi.*, XVII (1962), 94-106.

use personal energy for social ends. The goals that one strives for, the ends that one aspires to, are defined as a result of primary identifications. One moves toward socially defined goals in order to maintain a constant sense of love and security, a sense that is acquired initially from objects cathected at the primary level. This is what "compliant obedience" means: the child will act unconsciously in the direction of fulfilling certain commitments consistent with the demands of the primary object(s). The psychological structures formed in the pre-oedipal period, therefore, direct the individual to the achievement of the deepest levels of reward. In the pre-modern family, when the primary period was characterized by the internalization of both parental figures, the deepest levels of reward were the love of father and mother. Given the continuing development of the modern family, this has come to mean particularly the mother's love.

The attachment between children and parents is built on these primary dependencies. It is because of these mechanisms that parental figures can direct the child toward growth and development as these are defined by the culture. In the modern family, for example, sexual identification is prompted by the mother, and her prompting is effective because at the close of the primary period, when sexual differentiation becomes a factor, it is the mother who has almost exclusive control over the child's willingness to perform. The mother in the modern family is therefore crucial in developing motivated behavior and in instituting sex-role identifications for children of both sexes.

This does not mean that the oedipal phase has lost its significance; on the contrary, the period is critical for several reasons. As we have noted, the father enters the socialization process in a definitive way at this point, and it is at this secondary level that children become oriented to sexually defined roles through identification with the appropriate figure in such a way that the earlier diffuse commitments now acquire specific content. At the same time, both father and mother take on additional important sexual meaning: the father becomes a generalized sexual object for the girl, as the mother does for the boy.

The implications of these changes for development in the oedipal period are different for male and female children. For the female the shift from pre-oedipal to oedipal stages has these consequences: the mother is internalized in ego and primary ego-ideal as a loving and coercive figure for whom the child strives unconsciously to fulfill social goals. The mother is also internalized in superego as loving and coercive—as sexual role model and loving object and as generalized negative sanction for sexually defined behavior. Moreover, because the father is for the girl a critical sexual object of identification, he is also internalized as a loving figure, as well as a representative of cultural sanctions.

At the close of the oedipal period, therefore, this "thread" of continued identification with the mother, which runs through the pre-oedipal and oedipal phases, and the internalization of both mother and father in the loving and coercive superego leave the female child with relatively undifferentiated ontogenetic and superego structures. Females cannot manage the break with the family efficiently because this network of affectual commitments is for them more complicated and inclusive than it is for males.

To the extent that the son is also dependent upon, identifies with, and internalizes the mother, she is no more available to him for critical examination than she is to the daughter. However, the relationship to the father is quite different, in the two ways we have indicated: the father has had to withdraw from his pre-oedipal role, and he cannot appear to the son in the oedipal phase as primarily a receptive, accepting, loving object. In fact, both the extent and the quality of affectual and coercive exchanges between fathers and sons has progressively diminished since the father's entry into the economic-occupational order in modern terms. Indeed, the son has come to be rewarded for demonstrations of initiative, independence, and willingness to compete—both in general and specifically with respect to the father. As a result of these various factors the son emerges from the oedipal phase with a more differentiated ontogenetic and superego structure. Objects and actions related to affective expression, competition, coercion, and neutrality are more clearly defined for the son. For these reasons the male child found it easier to withdraw and compete in social and psychological terms—and still finds it so today.[28]

For the daughter, then, remaining deferential and dependent has typically earned important rewards; on the other hand, the effort to compete or strive systematically for independence, whether directly or symbolically, has tended to create an intolerable level of anxiety. Now it is possible to see why the daughter showed "less imagination" in competing aggressively for occupational and political positions, why the daughter could appear to Freud to be less capable of culturally decisive superego development.[29] It is also possible to see why the son was (and is) less insistent on breaking with the mother than with the father; his choice is not alone (nor perhaps even primarily) because of the oedipal attachments (the mother as sexual object) but also because of the pre-oedipal attachments, which Freud was not able to observe.[30]

The problem for Freud was that he found it too difficult to work in this area. He did formulate the pre-oedipal concept, as well as the notion of separation anxiety,[31] and both of these are indispensable for an investigation of the mother and mother-child unit. But these concepts did not appear in Freud's work until quite late, and he never was able to appreciate their full significance. On the contrary, he acknowledged that this first attachment to the mother was really too difficult for him to investigate—in his experience these attachments were too thoroughly repressed.[32]

Freud's comments on primary narcissism, his attempt to deal with a question of Romain Rolland's on the origins of religious feeling, are interesting in this connection. Rolland had wondered whether the attachment to religion could not be traced back to that stage in human life when there is no subject-object dichotomy, when the infant-mother union is one whole, when the infant is unambivalently one with the world. Freud answered that he could trace the religious feeling only as far back as the feeling of helplessness in the child—that is, to the child's longing for a father's protection. Freud observed that though there could be something lying beneath the child's feeling of helplessness, for the present it would remain wrapped in obscurity, since he found it too difficult to work with such intangible qualities. The passages in which these thoughts appear can be and have been taken as evidence of Freud's resistance to this critical aspect of analytic theory.[33]

For a long time, therefore, the extent to which the mother is instrumental and perhaps even decisive for individual growth was not recognized by psychoanalytic theory. There is no doubt that this is the case.[34] However, increased understanding of the degree to which the child's original physical dependence upon the mother is paralleled by his psychological dependence on her, in addition to the recognition of the traumatic effects of separation, eventually led to a change in emphasis precisely in that direction Freud had found "so grey with age and shadowy and impossible to re-vivify"—the infant's relationship to the mother, particular-ly in the earliest years.

This shift in emphasis from the pregenital organization of the libido to object relations, ego formation, and the mother's role is strikingly evident no matter where one turns in the recent post-Freudian literature.[35] It is possible now to find the most direct statements on the primacy of the early mothering experience in individual develop-ment,[36] just as one can find the most serious admonitions against "one-sided" interpretations leading to "a matri-archal conception of the ego and superego."[37] Whether this recent emphasis on the mother is exaggerated or not is be-side the point. The very appearance of the pre-oedipal moth-er as a central and decisive figure in theory was, from a sociological point of view, inconceivable forty or even thirty years ago.[38]

Psychoanalytic writers have tried to explain this theo-retical shift in emphasis in terms of Freud's initial focus on psychosexual development and conflict in relation to clinical evidence derived from certain pathological types. For example, it has been pointed out that Freud deliberate-ly chose clinical experiences with obsessional neurotics as the basis for his psychological theories because in this illness all mental processes and conflicts are internalized and object relations are only weakly cathected, and thus the relationship of child to mother as object would not be perceived.

In addition, it would follow from this that Freud's earlier emphasis was on the way the individual was threatened by instincts on one side and by society on the other. Even when Freud's interests shifted to the ego—because of the kind of evidence available to him—the individual would still be seen as developing partly in submission to and partly in protest against the hostile environment. Since theory followed the data, Freud could not work out the positive aspects of social organization with respect to individual growth. He could not observe those factors in the family and society that support normal adaptations to reality. For this reason, again, the relationship of mother to child would not have been clear to him.[39]

However, this kind of explanation proceeds too rationally; it ascribes to Freud a level of conscious control that he did not have, and it releases him from the very determinants of behavior that he insisted upon, particularly resistance and repression. Freud was unable to perceive the relationship of mother to child for the reason he gave: it was all too shadowy, too remote, too difficult for him to grasp.

There is no doubt that Freud's work was periodically hampered in this way. For example, he was reluctant to accept the instinct of aggression as an original, independent motivating force. In 1909 ("Little Hans"), he wrote that he could not bring himself to concede to such an assumption; he could not imagine aggression to be equivalent to the familiar forces of sex and self-preservation. By 1931, however ("Civilization and Its Discontents"), he had completely reversed himself, wondering now how he could have overlooked the universality of non-erotic aggression. He ascribed this abiding oversight to his own resistance.[40]

Freud also had difficulty with the problem of infantile sexuality. According to Ernest Jones, for a period of some five years Freud regarded children as the innocent objects of incestuous desires, and only very slowly, "no doubt against considerable resistance," came to recognize the sexual life of children. For as long as possible he restricted sexuality to a later age, and "to the end of his life he chose

to regard the first year of infancy as a dark mystery en-
shrouding dimly apprehensible excitations rather than active impulses and fantasies."[41]

In the early days of the development of psychoanalytic
theory, when Freud was working on the nature of oedipal
conflict, he wrote to Fliess that he had the reassuring feeling that he would be able to find what he needed for his
work in his own internal resources, his own "cupboard."[42]
That is, connections were preconsciously available and he
was confident that he could call them up. But he was never
able to do this with the pre-oedipal mother; this figure
remained subject to repression.

Freud therefore was open to the kind of revision we
have been describing. The mother played a role in Freud's
scheme only in terms of oedipal conflict, and he would consider only the positive libidinal ties between mother and
son.[43] Thus he learned relatively little about the pre-oedipal
mother, the oral stage, the infant's hostility to the mother,
the effects of maternal rejection on the infant, or the relationship of the mother to ego, ego-ideal, and superego
development in general. In contrast, the most recent developments in psychoanalytic theory point consistently to
the fact that the strivings of the oral stage are no less significant for the individual or the group than are the events
of the later phallic stage.

On this basis, even the ground Freud felt most sure of
is being challenged—i.e., the patriarchal nature of religion, the oedipal origins of the hero, and the consistent
interpretation of decisive events (whether for the individual
or the group) as oedipal products. For Freud, the origins
of art, religion, morals, and social sense and the problems
of social psychology all converge on one concrete point—
man's ambivalent relations with his father. However, wheth-

er one follows the arguments presented here or those developing generally in the psychoanalytic literature, one sees
that this interpretation appears less and less tenable.[44]

This is particularly the case for the family. Prior to the
recent changes imposed on the family there was relatively
little functional differentiation in the obligations of authority figures, and these figures played a more protective
"maternal" role than was later to be the case.[45] That is,
the parents (taken as a psychic unit) and the father entered
the child's object world at a much earlier time than they
would subsequently and thus, along with the mother, appeared as sources of love and dependency. The child drew
support during the earlier periods of life from several relationships, rather than just one.[46]

Such relations as these would be difficult to verify historically. Still, it seems fair to say that in the pre-modern
period the unit of action was the family and not the individual, and child-rearing was a family project and not
related to specific, sexually differentiated roles.[47] The internalization of the parents as a collective unit in the pre-
oedipal period and the continuation of such object relations through the oedipal phase meant that the children
of traditional families, like the female in the modern one,
developed a less complex and less differentiated superego
structure. From the standpoint of personality this would
explain why an individual could remain a child to his family throughout life.

The pre-modern family structure did not provide models
for autonomous ego behavior with regard to parental figures, nor was it possible for superego to achieve the abstract
quality that allows for the implementation of personal
morality and the relaxation of external controls. Authority
was maintained in the family, as it was on all institutional

levels in traditional structures, on the basis of passive compliance with dictates. The control was tolerated because of the rewards provided by the nurturant figures.[48]

This pattern was disrupted in the family because of the demands of the newly developed industrial system, and the sons, at least, were able to achieve a measure of independence. Still, the withdrawal from traditional authority in the family could occur only in relation to potentially satisfying patterns of passivity and dependence. This had rather typical implications for behavior, and the kinds of reactions that followed underscore the universal nature of the struggles for autonomy against traditional figures no matter what the institutional level of activity. The forms of response were the same as those noted with regard to political conflict, including the positive features of self-control and emotional constraint, but including also the negative, regressive features following from the fact that competitive strivings against internalized authority must be bound up with guilt and anxiety and that the overt demand for independence can only be made at the expense of the loss of love and protection, or even the active hostility of the violated authority.

One form of reaction to the consequent pressure of conflict within the family was a withdrawal from autonomous initiative to dependence, a regression to passivity. This is what Kafka experienced and what he had to fight so strenuously against. As noted, however, Kafka could succeed only to a degree. Even Freud felt this kind of tension—very late in life Freud described an earlier experience of his own that showed how ambitious strivings led to inner conflict: "there was something about it that was wrong, that from earliest times had been forbidden. It was something to do with a child's criticism of his father, with the underevaluation which took the place of the overevaluation of earlier childhood. It seems as though the essence of success was to have got further than one's father, and as though to excel one's father was still something forbidden."[49]

Another response to conflict was the organization of a rigid, unyielding superego, the acceptance of "autonomous" behavioral mandates as a superego function not accessible to ego control. Thus the typical attributes of the "rugged" individual: every form of sensual or sentimental indulgence appears as a threat to control and is therefore despised as weakness; physical and mental hardships are viewed as so many tests of manliness and are not only accepted but even insisted upon. One cannot wish for love and protection because this would mean, on the one hand, submission to the father in the face of the desire for autonomy and, on the other, a return to a previous stage of dependence upon the mother—hence, the assertive, compulsive masculinity, and the rejection of the female along with severe injunctions against emotional effusion.[50]

These two responses have had a great effect on modern consciousness and represent important elements in the stereotypical pictures of the harmfulness of "bourgeois" existence. No doubt the system of controls in the modern family accounts for a great number of psychically inhibited and handicapped individuals (and for the acceptance of more than forty kinds of psychotherapy). But this is not all that emerged from the family. Adaptive, self-reliant, autonomous activity and an emphasis on systematic, practical effort were substituted for traditional passivity. The sons were socialized to the rigors of autonomous endeavor.[51]

It is in relation to resolving the anxieties associated with independent activity that the father's role has had important implications for personal development not stressed by Freud. The paternal threat that Freud identified was not alone an aggressive gesture. It also represented interference with pre-oedipal gratifications and a retreat to the maternal world. The father's demands for emotional constraint, abstract discipline, and systematic effort had the effect of stimulating ego development and the acceptance of the realities of autonomous existence. For modern Western man the prohibition of attachments to the dependent phases of the personal past was and is an adaptive force in the socialization process.[52]

We noted above that it became possible for the sons to compete with the father on the basis of this socialization process in occupational, political, and familial terms. However, it should be noted in addition that as the differentiation process has unfolded, the degree of autonomy and especially the degree of inclusion in familial processes has tended to increase. This is exemplified in the demand for and the granting of wider and more inclusive rights of participation and access to resources at *earlier* periods in the child's life. The degree of inclusion varies with age—it is not yet very extensive in the oedipal period and at that point inclusion still depends on criteria for achievement established within the family. But in the post-oedipal period, with the beginning of school and the assumption of other obligations external to the family, inclusion becomes more significant and is related rather to universal social standards. Since children *must* participate in activities external to the family, and since they are judged on adult grounds of competence and merit, it has become necessary to accede to demands for a degree of influence over family decisions, access to the symbols of prestige, and the legitimation of the kind of self-esteem that derives from successful autonomous behavior.

Of course, this extension of rights in the family is qualified by notions of safety, levels of expertise, and ability to acquire resources from external agencies, as well as age

—but still the rights are there. In modern social structures full familial "citizenship" is accorded the child at birth, and as the child grows older he is integrated at his insistence at higher levels in familial processes. The child is consulted on different problems, his wishes and aspirations are recognized as legitimate, and he is conceived of (in the post-Freudian world) as having the same kinds of feelings, hopes, and experiences as adults.

It is in the light of these considerations that certain similarities may be noted between the political and familial movements to autonomy. Both institutional dimensions became more specialized (in that the expressive was differentiated from the instrumental), and both were able to exploit bases of power internal to the structure. In the political sphere this meant rather general distribution of power; thus the right to vote, available to all citizens, became the typical means of exchange. In the family this distribution came to mean that all members could influence family decisions and gain access to at least some resources regardless of age.[53]

However, as we have noted, the parallels between the two institutions are not precise, and important differences also exist. The organization of abstract representative political institutions has meant, for example, that political authority could be repudiated without the experience of an intolerable level of guilt.[54] No equivalent mechanism has been developed for the family, and power in the family is dealt with in different terms. Moreover, the democratization of political institutions, including the elimination or lessening of hierarchical influences, has entailed an expansion of the base of the structure. Society was opened eventually to include all adult members, and this led to and facilitated the decline in affectual responses and attachments. On the other hand, the democratization of the family, including the declining importance of extended kinship and the abandonment of its hierarchical aspects, has entailed a narrowing of the institutional base. The family structure came to include a smaller number of individuals and these individuals became more dependent upon each other for the fulfillment of needs and functions that might formerly have been satisfied by more remote kin, or even by persons outside the kin structure.[55]

These variations in structural change also help to account for a situation that was alluded to very briefly in the first chapter. The failure to maintain the new values of autonomy and inclusion on the political level has led historically to a reliance on force and coercion to achieve stated goals. However, such failure on the familial level has led more typically to a reliance on love and permissiveness—that is, to a shift away from the rigorous paternal requirements for performance and toward a maternal acceptance of behavior regardless of merit.[56]

7

Universal Reactions to Modernization

AUTHORITY IN traditional societies rested, by both law and custom, exclusively in the hands of clearly identifiable figures. Those not included in the authority structure accepted and acted upon a "passive-dependent" posture. The figures and standards that regulated behavior and defined the legitimacy of objects and actions were identified with and internalized. The result was a reciprocal understanding of obligations and rewards, wherein personal orientations were consistent with the organization of power.

When this relationship of subject to authority is given conscious expression it can be stated as "I love the one I would like to be, and therefore I obey." On the basis of this affective commitment, and the coincident evaluative commitments, subordination and powerlessness were justified. For most people, the models for ego endeavor did not include autonomous initiative, and for centuries there were no systematic demands for personal and social autonomy. Traditional societies could not have maintained control without this kind of compliance.*

The pattern was disrupted, however, when structural changes forced violations of one of the important conditions that had legitimated the closed hierarchical organization of authority, thus enabling the individual to assume responsibility for himself; in response to this process the very nature of authority was changed. Relationships to authority on successive institutional levels came to be organized differently, and could be expressed on the level of consciousness as "I would like to become like the one I admire and envy." The figures and standards that could then be identified with and internalized deliberately encouraged patterns of autonomy and initiative, and people were thus enabled to move closer to what was already true for them in affectual and evaluative terms.

It is important that we emphasize the social as well as the psychological aspects of the different movements that changed the form and content of authority. These revolutionary changes should not be viewed in classical psychoanalytic terms simply as typical instances of recurrent revolt of sons against fathers, a form of revolt that is compulsively followed by a self-imposed surrender to domination by au-

* The focus of this chapter is on the institutionalization of new patterns of action at the level of personality, patterns that are legitimated by changing cultural values in the modernization process. We shall make only a few suggestions about patterns of action at the social level. It can be legitimately assumed, however, that there is a significant degree of congruence between personal and social systems. If autonomy, individual initiative, and rational calculation become systematic features of personality, there ought to follow institutional structures through which these personality factors can be expressed. If the personality mandates exist and the institutions do not, conflict will follow, and ultimately either the institutional structures will be organized or there will be regression on the personal level.

thority, by a re-imposition of patriarchal control. These movements, that is, do not simply represent successive attacks on oedipal authority as defined by Freud. On the contrary, oedipal authority did not exist in traditional systems, and it was only on the basis of the revolutionary separation of paternal from maternal functions, and the creation of exclusively masculine and secular structures, that an oedipal form of authority could be institutionalized. The revolutions that ushered in the modern era were intended to organize oedipal structures.

Historically, the typical results of identification with oedipal authority—self-control, active mastery, aim-conscious self-denial, the withdrawal of affect, and so on—figured significantly in the institutionalization at the social level of various kinds of normative standards that allowed for the implementation of autonomy and inclusion within different institutional frameworks. A number of factors contributed to the process, of course, but particular stress was laid on personal capacities based on these psychological characteristics, and it was the general acceptance of the moral appropriateness of these capacities that led to more tolerant social and personal controls over behavior.[1]

These several personality traits, and the kind of social organization that might be related to them, were first comprehensively described by Weber in *The Protestant Ethic and the Spirit of Capitalism*. According to Weber, these traits became available in society when certain mandates of ascetic Protestantism were institutionalized in social and psychological structures. Although the acceptance of these mandates led to a great sense of personal anxiety for those involved, their fulfillment came to appeal to the highest level of individual aspiration. Thus, insistence upon intense worldly activity and methodical work, deliberate regulation of conduct, and (because rational and affectual styles are exclusive of each other and institutionalized in markedly different areas) withdrawal of emotion from certain objects became for Weber exceedingly important bases for action in modern society.[2]

The effects of the acceptance of these standards were felt particularly when the commitment to the formal religious mandates began to wane; that is, while individuals tended to withdraw from the original ethical justification, the standards for behavior were retained, and these were peculiarly suited to capitalist endeavor as Weber defined it. From the standpoint of the individual actor, the most important demands were to bring order into conduct, to supervise and control one's own actions according to a specific set of rational standards, and to create a specific kind of social system by hard and continuous physical and mental exertion.

In order to act consistently in these terms it was necessary above all to maintain emotional control; in Weber's words, the habits of diligence, thrift, sobriety, and prudence would "enable a man to maintain and act upon his constant motives . . . against the emotions." Acceptance of this code of conduct led to economic and social practices quite different from those of traditional societies—accumulation based on self-denial, gratification based on self-regulated inhibition of desire. Failure to measure up to the standards of self-control and active mastery led to a sense of moral unworthiness and fear of the loss of self-esteem in one's own eyes and in the eyes of the community. These two systems of control were sufficient to ensure constant self-observation, and thus to ensure dedicated, methodical activity.[3]

The repudiation of emotional and spontaneous elements in religion and culture and the containment of interpersonal emotional connections constituted the principal means by which economic and other forms of activity could assume an impersonal, objective, and activist character. As

Weber noted, Protestant doctrine freed men from traditional restrictions against the accumulation of wealth even while it insisted upon an active, rational use of that accumulation—rational in the sense that the use of wealth is planned and impulsive wishes are self-consciously suppressed.[4]

It was on the basis of deliberate personal cultivation and social approval of these character traits that Weber distinguished modern from pre-modern activity.[5] Thus, he identified Benjamin Franklin as a prototype of the modern rational entrepreneur and compared him to a more traditional actor, Jacob Fugger. For Weber, Fugger represented individual, idiosyncratic activity, an example of personal daring based on a morally neutral position. But Franklin stood for an ethos, a codified ethical standard for personal conduct that was morally and socially appropriate for a whole society, not just for unique and random individuals.[6]

Franklin, of course, did dwell at length, both privately and publicly, upon the virtues of calculated and controlled activity; he insisted upon personal commitments to honesty, frugality, and industry, just as he condemned idleness and extravagance. He admonished men to be steady, settled, and careful in their work, to be prudential even in the smallest matters, to be conscious of time, and to avoid the consolations of vice. To Weber this constituted the expression of virtue that derived from proficiency in a calling, the "most characteristic" aspect of the social ethic of capitalist culture.[7]

But we must clarify the sense in which Franklin's maxims and his personal conduct are to be understood. His demand for effective, disciplined, "rational" effort had both a positive and a negative aspect; the exercise of self-control was intended both as an implementation of the new values of autonomy and as an avoidance of traditional passivity and submission, the latter identified typically by the inability to contain impulsive behavior, by the desire for sensual pleasures, or by the need to indulge in wishful (passive) contemplation.

Weber understood that it was important to insist upon certain kinds of behavior in order to prevent possible withdrawals to traditional value orientations; thus he noted that "the campaign against the temptations of the flesh, and the dependence on external things was . . . not a struggle against rational acquisition, but against the irrational use of wealth." From the ascetic point of view, therefore, it was necessary to be suspicious of "spontaneous expressions of undisciplined impulses" or of "idle talk, of superfluities, and of vain ostentation."[8] But Weber did not see the extent to which this attitude represents the negative and analytically distinct (if for practical purposes inseparable) aspect of the process of implementing new values: it was necessary to adopt this behavior in order to guard against real and active wishes for the abdication of control, the realization of which would lead to the loss of autonomy and independence.

Thus Franklin counseled that in economic life the first vice was debt: in debt the individual loses control over his own person and resources, for his creditor has the authority to deprive him of his liberty or sell him as a servant. The borrower becomes a slave of the lender; when you borrow *"you give to another power over your liberty."* One would not tolerate sumptuary legislation on the part of government; why stand for it in economic life? Franklin urged men to preserve their freedom and maintain their independence by hard work and abstinence: "Be *industrious* and *free;* be *frugal* and *free*."[9]

The accumulation of wealth through systematic effort was important because it was both the expression of and orientation to new values (personal autonomy and inclusion) and because it was a denial of passive dependence. Property became a criterion of independence because the acquisition of it was an affirmation of personal control. Such a standard focused on achievement and success, allowing one to participate in decision-making on a basis not of birth or blood but of merit. At bottom, however, the manifest disgust with failure reflected a fear of weakness, a fear of regression to the abiding wish for love and protection, and it was because of this fear that in the initial phases of economic, political, and familial change all those who were deemed unfit or unable to dispose themselves were not allowed to participate in the social order on any level of parity. Workers, women, and children, for example, were excluded, and were, moreover, expected to accept a subordinate position in a partially hierarchical class structure in which inclusion, status, and rewards were reserved for "men."

It was Weber's contention that Western societies manifested, in a manner unique among societies, a process of rationalization that affected such areas as economy, politics, law, and education, and that this could occur only insofar as there was an elimination of "magical elements" from thought processes—that is, insofar as the sacred was differentiated from the secular or the emotional differentiated from the intellectual. To Weber, this separation seemed to result from the diffusion of ascetic Protestant principles. However, the behavioral traits he described recurred not only at different times and at various institutional levels, but also in areas not particularly affected by Protestantism. Moreover, such behavior always served the same extra-religious purpose—to protect the sense of control over one's own psychic and physical resources and the sense of the right and the ability to dispose oneself autonomously, without interference from restrictive agents.[10] These mandates, in other words, stemmed from a process more general than the diffusion of Protestant principles. Specifically, they derived from the attack upon traditional authority: Protestantism was but one such occasion.[11]

In particular, the implementation of demands for autonomy had the invariable effect of isolating thought from its affective origins and of containing emotional commitments. These reactions prevented the sense of hostile violation from becoming conscious at the same time that they allowed for gratifications to be derived from the fulfillment of wishes for mastery and control. This is why the codification of the wish to be free and the attack on traditional authority—no matter what the time, society, or institutional level—have always been characterized by doctrines of self-discipline, self-denial, systematic, practical activity, objectivity, and rationality. Such doctrines are in fact psychological techniques for the maintenance of personal control.

The demand for emotional constraint occurred even in the family, though the withdrawal of emotion can never be as complete here as it can on other institutional levels. There must always be some significant level of affectual exchange between parents and children, because it is primarily on this basis that socialization is accomplished. The need to maintain relatively high levels of affectual exchange in the family does not, however, deny the fact that a substantial rationalization of emotion took place in the post-industrial era. It would be a mistake to stress the "associational" nature of the family and not take into account the factor of diminished emotional content.

That such a development might follow from the modernization process was already somewhat clear to Weber, who identified the tension created when "rational asceticism" conflicted with the desire for erotic attachments. Weber noted in this connection that "inner-worldly and rational asceticism can accept only the rationally regulated marriage." The ascetic values in marriage, as in economics, politics, law, and religion, reduced the extent of emotional expression and led to a more disciplined intimacy. A rather novel category of behavior was introduced into marriage, and the nature of the family was affected by the stress on mutual indebtedness and conscious responsibility in addition to libidinal ties.[12]

This tendency has been strengthened and extended in the modern era; parents are generally situated in a plurality of systems of action, and the desire to bring this multiple involvement under control forces them to lead themselves and their children away from impulsive activity toward disciplined activity. The proliferation of obligations not only inhibits the investment of erotic and affectual expression on the part of the father toward the family, but even the mother "has to have strong enough superego and other non-nurturant motives to be able . . . to renounce the erotic components of her attachment to her children as they come to the oedipal period." In this sense, erotic love in general and affectual commitments among members of the family in particular are brought to a degree under rational control and made to articulate with the other institutional dimensions of the society.[13]

Emotional expression within the family has always been legitimate, of course, to a considerable extent in the pre-oedipal phase with regard to children of both sexes and to some extent in the oedipal phase with regard to the female. But great pressure was and is exerted on the family to socialize the male children to the adult world of competitive autonomy, and indeed the parents cannot treat male children otherwise without damaging their potential for competition in economic and political spheres of activity. Thus, the normative standards characteristically associated with autonomy were also insisted upon in the family.[14]

In terms of both the positive and the negative aspects of personality mandates for control and constraint, it can be observed that whatever the personal, social, and temporal differences that separate men like Franklin, Rousseau, and Freud, the content of the message is basically the same, though it may be directed to three or four institutional dimensions: a degree of self-control, active mastery, and rationality is required for man to be independent; the inability to exercise control, the need to give in to impulse, to indulge sensual gratifications, or to be emotionally incontinent fosters dependent relations. In this sense the different movements toward autonomy have always represented in the first instance a process of detachment from dependence upon a kind of pre-oedipal authority and an identification with and internalization of oedipal authority.

Nineteenth-century Russia is an excellent example of a society not affected by Protestant mandates in which the insistence upon self-control, emotional constraint, and systematic, practical activity was intrinsically connected to demands for autonomy and inclusion. What these qualities meant to the men interested in rescuing Russia from a despotism that depended upon continued adherence to traditional roles and attitudes is singularly illuminated by the constant reference to a perfect model of passivity and dependence, a literary character, Oblomov, created in the late 1850's by the novelist Ivan Goncharov.[15] With remarkable psychological acumen Goncharov drew a portrait of a powerless, dependent object moved about by circumstances, totally incapable of sustained activity, nourished solely by wishes and dreams, and completely unable to deal in any practical way with the everyday world. Oblomov sacrificed any possible autonomy for the security of an existence based on infantile connections to objects that had nurtured and protected him. Constantly seeking a love and support that required the surrender of initiative, Oblomov was typically sentimental, self-indulgent, and ineffective.

From the days of the nihilist critics of the 1850's and 1860's—from Chernyshevskii, Dobroliubov, and Pisarev, to Lenin and the Bolsheviks—the psychological obstacles to change were referred to over and again in the terms established by Goncharov. What the radical activists so often saw themselves contending against was not only—sometimes not even primarily—the machinery of the autocracy, but the passive, impulsive, emotionally indulgent, and inert character of the people. Dobroliubov, who immediately used the novel as the basis for a famous critical essay attacking the contemporary Russian society, gave this malaise the name by which it continued to be known—Oblomovism.[16]

In his essay Dobroliubov pointed out that Oblomov "always remains the slave of another's will and never rises to the level of exhibiting the least bit of independence. . . . He is the slave of his serf Zakhar and it is hard to say which of them submits more to the power of the other." Oblomov is childish and impotent—he cannot "seriously, *actively* want anything," and because he cannot exercise self-control he must suffer the consequences and be controlled by others.[17] In practical affairs the man is helpless; he indulges fantasies of activity, movement, and change, but he never actually does anything, for the devotion to passive wishing precludes any kind of action. Oblomov's solution to life's difficulties is to give himself over to others because he cannot contend and achieve on his own.

The Russian Oblomovs, the intellectuals and people of gentry background generally, are all like this, according to Dobroliubov—they are characterized by "indolence, idleness, and utter uselessness." They are unable to resist the forces of their hostile environment, and their bondage is assured in the end by their having no capacity for work. Quoting Goncharov, Dobroliubov characterized the Oblomovs' conception of life: "They conceived of it as an ideal of repose and inaction, disturbed at times by various unpleasant accidents. . . . They tolerated work as a punishment imposed on our ancestors, but they could not love it, and they always shirked it whenever possible, deeming this permissible and right."[18]

Dobroliubov could not believe that Goncharov's insights stemmed solely from his unique artistic talent; rather, the novelist's ideas must have emerged from actual social conditions, from Russian life. In the same sociological vein, Dobroliubov ascribed Oblomov's fate to his class background: because Oblomov was a member of the gentry he was overprotected and prevented from realizing his powers in any self-motivated way. As a child he had always been in the care of nurses in whose interest it was to deny him independent action of any kind, and as an adult he always had serfs available to do his bidding. Oblomov's parents were much too fearful for the well-being of their son, and it became altogether easy for him to indulge in passive fancies rather than in active labor.[19]

But here Dobroliubov was mistaken: his hatred of the gentry-dominated society distorted his insight. Oblomovism was not confined to any one class; it was at the dead center of Russian existence. Lenin, who had considerably more practical experience with the difficulties of urging people to action, attested to this fact, complaining that three revolutions had transpired since Oblomov first came to be recognized, and such people still abounded, interfering with useful and practical activity. The Oblomovs had remained, and Lenin found them not only among landlords and peasants, but among intellectuals, workers, and Communists as well.[20]

Of course, it was one thing for opponents of the regime to deride the passivity and dependence that attended enduring compliance with traditional values, but it was quite another to aim deliberately at creation of a "Protestant" ethic in order to effect change, or to imagine that change could be effected only in these terms. Yet this is what happened, and that the psychological basis for change would have to take this form was already clearly stated in Goncharov's novel in the person of Oblomov's friend, Stolz, who was precisely the kind of practical, organized, hard-working man of affairs that Weber later described.

Stolz "lived on a fixed plan and tried to account for every day as for every dollar, keeping unremitting watch over his time, his labor, and the amount of mental and emotional energy he expended. It seemed as though he controlled his joys and sorrows like the movements of his hands and feet." Stolz was never timidly submissive, but always took the responsibility for his own actions, and felt a great sense of self-esteem when he isolated some weakness in his own behavior and was then able to correct it. Stolz rationally calculated the possibilities for action, and although people berated him for his self-control, claiming that passion justified everything, he held firm to his distaste for tempestuous demonstrations and his awareness of the potentially destructive consequences of such expression. He admired persistence above all other qualities; the more people argued with him, the more stubborn he became, and if he erred it was always on the side of "puritanical fanaticism."

In particular, Stolz feared imagination, "that two-faced companion, friend on one side and foe on the other—friend insofar as one distrusts it, and enemy if one goes trustfully to sleep to the sound of its own sweet murmur." He feared daydreaming, preferring to deal with the objective world: "All that could not be practically verified was for him an optical illusion. . . . He obstinately stopped at the threshold of a mystery showing neither childish belief nor fatuous doubt, but waiting for the formulation of a law that would provide the key to it."[21]

It is clear that Goncharov and Weber understood active, competitive, calculated behavior in virtually the same terms; not only are the qualities similar but so is the language. To be sure, Stolz acquired these characteristics to some extent from his partially German background. But Goncharov promised that Russia would soon produce such actors of its own, and indeed, not only did such models for behavior recur as an ideal in subsequent activist literature— most notably in N. G. Chernyshevskii's *What Is to Be Done?* (1864)[22]—but these qualities were deliberately encouraged by various radical groups. On the level of personal behavior, and more often in reference to political objects and actions than to economic ones, different radical groups typically sought to rationalize conduct, control emotion, and maintain active mastery in the same way we have reported for other times and places.

The separation of political activity from personal feelings was, to a significant degree, an explicit aspiration among radical groups,[23] the norms of conduct demanding withdrawal from emotional commitments and control over spontaneity in action. We shall not attempt a detailed discussion of the development of these standards of conduct or of the extent of their acceptance, but it will be relevant here to recall some aspects of Lenin's position, since his commitments again effectively reflect and epitomize the content of the ethic, particularly with regard to his insistence upon conscious, controlled behavior and the rejection of any kind of spontaneous, impulsive activity.

This position led to the primacy of Lenin's party in matters of political activity. Left to its own resources the proletariat would never achieve rational control or true consciousness; on its own the proletariat would impulsively choose immediate rewards against the sacrifices and denial required by the indispensable and infinitely more exacting goal.[24] It was necessary to oppose this tendency toward spontaneity with a rational, calculated, "conscious" organization that would provide the requisite external restraint and discipline. Lenin demanded, therefore, the avoidance of "subservience to 'spontaneity,' " which meant to him an emotional adaptation to immediate tasks, the inefficient use of personal energies, the absorption of the individual in subjective sentiment, and the use of the present moment for selfish gratification. The aim was to achieve a steady orientation to action that excluded the polar responses of apathy or excessive agitation; conscious action meant self-denying conformity with the dictates of reason.

It was in these terms that Lenin urged the systematic adaptation of several related personal and social modes of behavior. He insisted upon the formation of a strictly centralized party characterized by formal rules, by the development of objective criteria for action, and by a commitment to empirical fact as opposed to personal sentiment. According to Lenin this posture would protect the Bolsheviks "from shameful stagnation and waste of strength" and from the "willfulness and the caprices" of individual actors. What he sought, finally, was the adoption of a businesslike attitude to socialism, the combination of American practicality with a revolutionary purpose, the submission of oneself to conscious aim, and to action in conformity with a plan and a system.[25]

The fact that Lenin's movement ultimately recreated an undifferentiated authority structure should not obscure its basic commitment, whether to the delineated personality traits or, given the Marxist orientation, to the principles of personal freedom and inclusion. We pointed out earlier that if the pressures stemming from the demands for differentiation prove intolerable, different kinds of regressive reaction may follow, even when the values have been internalized. Individuals may indeed disavow the responsibility for choosing from among various alternatives that may otherwise be deemed appropriate. In seeking such a passive solution to conflict the individuals will require external authority to tell them what they are, rather than defining this for themselves. It is also possible that individuals will be forced to deny the moral appropriateness of choice as such, thus leading to rigid adherence to specific patterns of action. In either case, ego is not allowed to assume control over activity.

In psychic terms, the latter factor, especially, prevented at least temporarily the successful realization of democratic values in Russia. Important social-structural factors were also involved, of course. In part, chaotic conditions in the external world militated against any kind of tolerant solution; in part also, the arbitrary exercise of punitive authority followed because the Revolution had for various reasons been urged forward in the absence of appropriate (psychic and social) structural conditions. The continued conscious and unconscious adherence to traditional modes of response that rendered political or familial diversity intolerable (for most of the leaders as well as for most of the people) required that new standards of behavior in the all-important area of production also be strictly controlled by external agents. In general, these commitments to the old society were still viable, which was why the reorganization of undifferentiated authority on all levels proved possible in the first place. The few who resisted the formation of a closed society had little support and were quickly dealt with.[26]

The kind of rigid behavior manifested by Lenin and his

followers is to be distinguished from the exclusive and even ruthlessly exploitative elements in the relatively successful movements toward autonomy—movements successful in the sense that unconscious commitments to the past did not cripple the desire to implement values or to organize the market structures through which these values could achieve practical expression. In such cases both the positive and the negative aspects of the behavioral mandates were operative; the insistence upon "masculine" activity directed to some useful end had a dual motivation, and many of the worst features of modern social change were derived from the negative aspect of this dual process.

The problem here is that the behavioral demands involved in value change are initially internalized in superego —self-control, self-observation, and emotional continence, for example, are evaluative functions. To some degree these functions can come under conscious control (by ego and superego), and to the extent that this happens more tolerant attitudes will prevail. In fact, in those instances in which the processes of value change have led to personal freedom and wider inclusion there is an evident development of such control over the behavioral mandates and over the different institutions within which these are expressed. For functional reasons there may have been various standards that served as the basis for inclusion in one or another institutional area, but a vital part of every instance of value change that has resulted in greater inclusion has been the extension of conscious control. Increasingly complex and differentiated social structures remain viable only on the basis of concomitantly differentiated psychic structures.

But for as long as these behavioral factors remain unconscious superego functions (as long as control is threatened excessively by internal as well as external forces), the values will be implemented in a harsh and punitive way with regard to self and others. It was this superego quality that led in Western societies to varying but always significant degrees of exclusion in political life, to exaggerated and compulsive insistence upon work, duty, and discipline in economic life, and to familiar forms of oedipal conflict and personal regression in familial and private life. But these and the other regressive solutions to the pressures of change do not deny the essential fact that the personality traits we have described are universal reactions to demands for autonomy and inclusion.

From the standpoint of psychic structure, in particular, the important development historically has been the strengthening of ego—against impulse and the desire for immediate gratifications, but also, and more important for recent social developments, against restrictive and punitive superego. This process can be identified in the most pluralized societies by the relaxation of external controls, by the increasing flexibility of social mandates, and by the development of what has been called personal morality. The moral codes of traditional societies—or of modern, technically advanced authoritarian societies—tend to be rigidly defined, and the aim is to create an absolute unity between public morality and personal behavior. As societies differentiate, however, the unity must give way: the number of possible legitimate behaviors, objects, and interests increases so that except in the most general sense there can be no direct correspondence between public morality and private actions. Superego becomes more complex but less rigid, and morality becomes more generalized and focused more in the individual than in the social structure.

In other words, where complex alternatives are available in a society it becomes necessary for the individual to direct his own existence without traditional supports, i.e., without class, ethnic, or kinship ties. The individual must choose his personal goals from a wide scope of *legitimate* ends and select from among suitable alternatives the means for achieving these ends; he must make the most efficient use of personal energy within the framework of a highly complex system. The ability to act in this manner depends upon the development of ego strength and control, so that in this sense the internal as well as the external world is rationalized. The focus of control shifts from external authority and unconscious superego to the individual and ego.[27]

In modern pluralized societies, therefore, psychic and social structures are more differentiated than ever before, and they are under constant pressure to become even more so. At the social level, institutions as yet relatively unaffected by the various movements to autonomy come under attack, while groups of people that have been traditionally excluded demand the right to participate in institutions historically open to others. These attacks engender resistance to further innovative change because of a persistent gap between internalized standards and the need and the desire for change. Thus, for example, under the impetus of progressive democratization, women (and, for certain purposes, even children) may be allowed to participate (or may insist on participating) in different aspects of social structure. Moreover, for various reasons, in the process of change the emphasis may fall more on the inclusive aspect of the values than on autonomy. Where this is the case the old demands for adherence to behavioral manifestations of "manliness" become blocks to further movement. Psychic factors that may once have been extremely effective in socializing individuals to the rigors of competitive autonomy become aspects of symptomatic behavior.

At the personal level, the more the range of legitimate moral choices increases, the more internal pressure the individual must accept. The result of this continuing process of differentiation is that there is no longer any one right way to do a prescribed number of things—there are any number of ways to do a great number of things. The individual is committed to act, but because the most important criteria for the evaluation of objects and actions are competence and merit, and because these standards remain the basis for the distribution of rewards and status, the need to perform is constant, and it is difficult to arrange or to seek static periods or safe, passive positions. For the greatest part the personal struggle continues through life to the end.[28]

The prospect of unremitting social and personal struggle has been consistently identified by critics of Western bourgeois society as the principal feature of a barren civilization that has moved ahead substantially in industrial-technical development, but only at the prohibitive cost of a harmful and unceasing activism and a high incidence of aggressive behavior. The apparently unending process of rationalization at the expense of esthetic, ethical, and emotional sensibilities, the need to be self-disciplined in order to meet the demands of a competitive structure, and the need to organize and expend most of one's energies for extrinsic economic and social ends are the factors that have typically led to this conclusion.

This criticism of modern society has focused particularly on the economic-technical spheres of activity, on the nature of the bureaucratic-industrial organization that forces men to work with machines in a process over which they have no control and which serves some abstract purpose of gain not really related to them. The system is such that men are deprived of any sense of well-being or accomplishment, and the anxiety identified with this social structure presumably stems from the dissatisfaction that must follow the need to be passively related to this mechanistic order.

To a considerable degree, this standpoint derives from Marx's original attack on the capitalist system. Marx observed that the basis of bourgeois society was a ruthless egoism, an unfeeling rationalization of all aspects of life and especially of the work process, a rationalization that turned personal worth into mere exchange value and man himself into a commodity. As Marx expressed it many times, the only thing that brings men together in this form of social organization is the self-interest of each and the prospect of personal gain. He abhorred the capitalist system because it required that every man treat every other man only as the means to some calculated economic end.

Marx viewed capitalism as a necessary phase of social development but he had no tolerance for it—he was in fact, more tolerant of pre-bourgeois social forms because within these systems men were at least related directly to other men, if in a dependent way, and they still had some control over the work process and the product and were able to derive at least some small esthetic or artistic satisfaction from their work. But the revolutionary bourgeoisie destroyed the more primitive organization of production and the old patriarchal relationships based on it, as well as the sentiment and custom that existed in these traditional societies. Now each man was isolated, separated not only from other men but from the best qualities within himself. The triumph of the bourgeoisie was the realization of a completely Hobbesian world characterized by "avarice and the war between the avaricious, competition." The totally ego-oriented middle-class rationality that ended in the war of all against all made bourgeois society intolerable. In response to this conclusion, and on the basis of his interpretation of social process and class conflict, Marx envisioned the inevitability of a world without this kind of struggle, without aggression.[29]

The terms of this criticism, at least in the West, were eventually expanded to subsume bureaucratic-industrial structures as such, which came to be identified as destructive of human potential whether organized in a capitalistic way or not. But the writers in this sociological tradition still expressed a particular disappointment with Western societies. Thus, Weber noted that the ascetic morality he had described was instrumental in the rationalization of social structures and processes and in the organization of the industrial-technical system. But instead of providing men with ethical and psychological satisfactions, the system had become an "iron cage"; it had turned out to be merely more efficient. Modern man was bound to "the technical and economic conditions of machine production which today determine the lives of all individuals born into the mechanism . . . with irresistible force." The Puritans wanted to work in a calling; now men were forced to do so. Stripped of its religious and ethical bases the compulsive insistence upon methodical labor had become oppressive.[30]

However, the notion that the social relations of highly pluralized middle-class Western societies reflect basically the economic organization of these societies, and that the principles of personal freedom based on abstract legal and political structures are but techniques that bolster this economic organization has obscured the nature of the changes typically identified with the middle class, and has thereby distorted perception of the direction that modernization processes tend to follow. Even the more inclusive critique of modern societies that focuses on industrial, technical, and bureaucratic processes, no matter in what social form they appear, has been too narrowly conceived. Empirically speaking, it is not the work process, the economic order, bureaucratization, or any combination of these factors as such that has been the long-term source for discontent and social action. The more consistent pressure for social action has been prompted by the demands for autonomy and inclusion on all institutional levels and by the conflict arising from opposing wishes to extend or to limit the bases of inclusion in society. Moreover, the progressive differentiation of society leads to the development of generalized moral standards that force the individual to interpret, evaluate, and choose from a variety of acceptable courses of action. This need to make choices on the basis of personal morality, the pressures deriving from the desire to accept or reject different levels of autonomous activity, and the struggle for inclusion— these are in fact the general sources for persistent feelings of discontent.

The organization of institutional (market) structures within which the highly complex and demanding autonomous activities could be sustained—on the necessary basis of self-discipline, rationality, and the withdrawal of affect— legitimated the public expression of a high degree of aggressive behavior. The need to display constantly a compulsive, "masculine" activity and the ability to define others as incapable of this activity provided the psychic basis for exploitative relationships. This negative consequence, however, has overshadowed the positive contribution of the movements toward autonomy, which was to separate the individual from authority (from passive, submissive commitments to important figures of the past), so that objects and actions could be evaluated with some degree of independent control. This is the crucial test of all revolutionary activity, for freedom has no meaning if it is not the freedom to choose the objects that one is to be related to, and this becomes possible only after dependent connections to authority are severed.*

The classical critics of Western society were disturbed by the progressive rationalization of culture, and they could discern no means within the system by which the aggressive content might be softened. Many of these critics channeled the consequent feelings either into pessimistic resignation to the given trend or into the wish that further revolutionary interference with social process might end aggression

* Marx considered capitalism to be a necessary phase of social evolution for a number of reasons, one being the capitalists' ability to create and organize the highest and most complex forms of production. He also wrote, in the famous preface to *The Critique of Political Economy*, that no social order ever disappears before *all* of its productive potential has been exploited. But if all that the bourgeoisie contributed in a positive sense to social evolution was the productive base, and if, at the same time, they fostered aggression and exploitation, then why wait for capitalism to play itself out? In other words, what is so *necessary* about capitalism after all? Marx had no satisfactory answer for that question, and Lenin, for example, arrived at his own conclusions: socialists, also, can organize rational, technical, industrial societies. Neither Marx nor Lenin perceived the positive psychic and cultural contributions of middle class society, principally the vital break the middle class made with authority on all levels of activity. The break was made by separating men from authority and by creating, through the development of abstract relationships, a situation whereby authority could be dealt with in some independent way. The attempt to deal with the problems of aggression, conflict, and exploitation on the basis of authoritarian control over economic and political institutions was bound to end with regressive social forms because the identifications and internalizations necessary for the support of autonomous activity did not exist, and control over a chaotic internal and external situation of revolutionary change could only be achieved by the systematic use of violence. Further, authority relationships had still to be predicated on the traditional passivity, dependence, and subordination. However, any evolution toward higher levels of social existence must be based on the termination of traditional commitments to authority and, above all, this is what the middle class achieved in the modern era.

and anxiety. However, the inability to perceive unconscious contents prevented any real insight into the positive aspects of the rationalization of psychic and social structures. These aspects are related to the implicit awareness that emotional gratification is linked to dependence and that rational control of affect is linked to independence and autonomy. The middle classes in the West took advantage of a series of structural situations that permitted the termination of passivity and subordination, and they tried to create the psychic and social structures that would bolster and sustain their wish for freedom. The middle class made the decisive break with authority in religion, politics, economics, and the family. This break—not the productive facilities they established nor their commitment to rationality as such— was their signal contribution.*

For a time it seemed that the termination of these de-

---

* It can be inferred from our frame of reference that relationships to authority have evolved from a pre-oedipal emphasis on passivity and dependence to an oedipal emphasis on competitive autonomy— a position that is based to a significant degree on the rational control of affect. It is also possible to infer that as social structure changes these relationships to authority will continue to evolve, and it seems consistent to suppose that they will evolve in a "fraternal" direction with less emphasis on aggressive competition and more emphasis on affectual commitments. Indeed, we indicated in the notes to Chapter Six (note 51, page 297) that authority relations appear to us to be assuming a rather collegial form in the United States.

However, we must also note that certain efforts to effect changes in authority relationships at present in the United States and else-where reflect more a desire to escape the anxieties of autonomous activity than a desire to achieve some new level of independence from authority. It seems to us that these efforts are aimed at a return to the consolations of maternal concern and control and therefore represent a step backward, not a step forward. See Gerald M. Platt and Fred Weinstein, "Alienation and the Problem of Social Action," in *The Phenomenon of Sociology: A Reader in the Sociology of Sociology*, ed., E. A. Tiryakian (New York, forthcoming, 1969).

pendent connections in political and economic spheres would lead to independent mastery of the environment. But when the differentiation process touched upon the family and it became possible to observe to a degree the scope and content of internal, unconscious processes, the possibility for control over all aspects of social existence could no longer be so optimistically conceived. It could be immediately inferred from this discovery that without conscious control over familial and psychic structures, control over the environment was not going to follow. Thus, the development of psychoanalytic theory was crucial, not only because it demonstrated the existence of unconscious motivations and the extent to which these could be instrumental in controlling behavior, but also because it helped to clarify the extent to which the family is involved in social process as a mediating agent between psychic and social structures.[31]

Because the family is responsible for the socialization of individuals, intrafamilial relationships become important for society. This function was less critical when economic, political, and religious institutions shared in the guidance and protection of subjects. But when the social and personal goal is autonomy, and support is withdrawn from external structures, the family processes become decisive. The issue here is not simply one of sublimation of libidinal and aggressive energies, that is, of the withdrawal of affect from the family on the basis of necessary, multiple inclusion in processes external to the family. Rather, it is a question of value orientations, of whether the family will work to prevent the individual from becoming fixed in its orbit and of whether, through close articulation with social structure, it will provide the internalizations and identifications necessary both for independent activity outside the family and for tolerance of the diversity and complexity that is characteristic of pluralized societies.[32]

The divergence between family structure and the rest of the social system cannot, of course, be sharp. But the latitude in styles can be sufficient to account for regressive solutions to the problems imposed by the dominant values. Thus, if there is persistent and excessive affectual exchange and expression of emotion, particularly through the oedipal phase, and if rewards are offered for submission rather than independence, then the individual cannot withdraw from authority within the family or, subsequently, learn to deal with authority on other levels. Excessive coercion, on the other hand, leads to a tendency to accept the principle of autonomy as a "sacred" end rather than as a rational means for the achievement of some other end, as well as a desire to circumscribe the range of choices available to self and others. The latter alternative seems to have been characteristic of the family system that produced the "rugged individual," a response that fostered autonomous activity but also led to a significant degree of symptomatic behavior. Within the terms we have been discussing, the maximum goal of the socialization process is to foster in the individual a perception of self as a separate, independent actor without great guilt or anxiety, and to establish rewards for autonomous activities that are external to the family. Socialization so conceived leads to a willingness to perform in morally appropriate contexts and to an ability to examine critically the different aspects of authority.

The pervasive emphasis on the economic-technical bases of social relations has led to faulty interpretations of the social system, especially in the sense that the importance of familial and psychic structures has been seriously and consistently undervalued. This neglect becomes even more significant when we consider that the tendency for social structures is to become more complex and differentiated, to proliferate rather than to diminish the extent of conscious and unconscious attachments, and to broaden the range of personal choices that individuals must make. It is imperative that the family unit retain its importance with respect to other levels of the social system, for the initial commitments to values and to society at large must be established on a profoundly emotional basis, and this is best achieved at the earliest and simplest level of interaction, the relationship of mother to child. Indeed, it may be that the psychic basis for the ability to withstand the pressures stemming from the complexity of existence can derive only from the socialization of children in the family, a process that fosters, at the most primary levels, the internalization of commitments to work and to individual attainment, as well as to ethical and moral mandates tending to constrain and limit the possibilities for action, so that neither impulse nor rationality can completely dominate.

It remains a fundamental error of utopians to imagine that the just or decent society must or will be a simple one, to hope that social structures will not inevitably lead to some degree of anxiety, or to assume that psychic support for the tolerance of social demands will follow virtually automatically from some planned reorganization of productive and distributive networks. Moreover, those critics of modern societies who view complexity as some kind of deception, repudiate superego- and ego-oriented abstract and instrumental relationships, and insist that an end to separation and a re-establishment of expressive attachments on all levels are both necessary and possible—those critics misconstrue what can be achieved, given the present level of control over psychic and social structures. The desire to organize a "community" beyond the possibility for struggle or the existence of aggression is not an objectively based aspiration and is not indicative of what is available for the future; rather, it is a wish that relates to the past—the dependent past. We have, in fact, little knowledge of or control over object relations, or, more specifically, over unconscious materials, and it is difficult to say what combination of psychic and social structural conditions would be likely to produce significant degrees of such knowledge and control. But without these conditions, the hoped-for expressive commitments cannot lead to increased personal freedom; they must tend rather to the re-establishment of subordinate relationships based on the uncritical acceptance of nurturant and protective figures. Marx, the source of so much of this thinking, emphasized over and over again that the theoretical (we would say wishful) reform of society according to the ideals of intellectuals, in the absence of control over or conscious knowledge of the appropriate structural conditions, must result in utopian conclusions. Marx's error was not in stating the principle but in allowing himself to be too impressed with his own estimates of the ultimate content of structural factors and the necessary direction of social change.

Thus, modern revolutionary movements that have intervened in economic and political processes on the assumptions that (1) the dominant source of anxiety and aggression lies in the productive sphere of endeavor, and that (2) control over the economic and political machinery would lead to control over human nature, have failed to realize their primary goal, which was precisely a fundamental change in individual motivation. The "planned" authoritarian control over economic and political processes has not led to conscious control over psychic and social structures, and the planners find it difficult to encourage critical views of the system or to accept independent activity in society. Of course, the commitment to universal education and to scientific proficiency and industrial expansion, as well as to democratic values on the cultural level, has led to psychic and social differentiation in various areas, and the societies so constituted now experience public criticism from the inside. The criticism, however, is invariably levied by individuals who have succeeded in the society, or who are in a position to do so (i.e., from the "middle class"), and it takes the traditional form—demands for autonomy, inclusion in aspects of decision-making, the separation of the individual from authority, and the right to be treated in a predictable way according to abstract laws. These societies, then, face the problems that have historically confronted Western societies, problems resulting from wishes for greater or lesser inclusion and autonomy on *all* levels of social activity. From the standpoint of anxiety, guilt, and aggressive behavior, control over the economy for the purpose of ensuring the most inclusive distribution of goods—a course that now appears to be common to all advanced social systems—will have less of an effect than any of the classical thinkers anticipated.[33] The anxieties deriving from complexity and pluralization will remain, and will be resolved successfully only on the basis of personal autonomy expressed within appropriate institutional structures.

Notes

Notes

INTRODUCTION

1. We have no intention of elaborating upon the nature, content, and process of "market" structures at this point. We shall make use of the concept in a general way; we invoke it simply because of its utility in describing institutionalized mechanisms of interchange between two or more differentiated groups. See Talcott Parsons, "On the Concept of Political Power," *Proc. American Philosophical Society*, CVII (1963), 232-62; "On the Concept of Influence," with rejoinder to comments, *Public Opinion Quarterly*, XXVII (1963), 37-92. With regard to the historical origins of these market relationships and their development in theory see C. B. Macpherson, *The Political Theory of Possessive Individualism* (New York, 1962).

2. This is less true of Weber than of Marx—there are, of course, quite sophisticated psychological constructs in Weber, e.g., charisma. But we refer here specifically to a psychology of

the unconscious and to relationships between this construct and social structure.

3. T. H. Marshall, in his essays on *Class, Citizenship, and Social Development* (New York, 1964), touches upon some of the same problems regarding inclusion and its historical development. Marshall outlines three phases of citizenship: civil, political, and social. The first concerns individual rights: freedom of speech, press, and assembly, equality before the law, the right to own property, etc. The second (political) is more directly related to inclusion in political decision-making and takes the form of universal suffrage. The third (social) entails the rights of welfare, security, education, and so on. All three phases are temporally related, the first to the eighteenth century, coeval with the emergence of the bourgeoisie, the second to the nineteenth, and the third to the twentieth. However, Marshall's three aspects of citizenship represent quantitative upgrading of autonomy and inclusion rather than qualitative changes in morality. The breakthrough was in fact the legitimation of membership in the political community in the first place. The phases that Marshall outlines constitute no more than the intensification of a trend begun in the eighteenth century.

4. With regard to Parsons's work on social change see Talcott Parsons, "Some Considerations on the Theory of Social Change," *Rural Sociology*, XXVI (1961), 219-39; Parsons, "An Outline of the Social System," in *Theories of Society*, eds. T. Parsons, E. Shils, K. D. Naegele, J. R. Pitts (New York, 1961), I, 70-79; Parsons, *Structure and Process in Modern Societies: A Collection of Essays* (Glencoe, Ill., 1960); Kasper D. Naegele, Introduction to "Social Change," Part Five of *Theories of Society*, II, 1207-22. See also Neil Joseph Smelser, *Social Change in the Industrial Revolution* (Chicago, 1959); Robert N. Bellah, *Tokugawa Religion* (Glencoe, Ill., 1957).

For theoretical and empirical statements on value change see Talcott Parsons, "An Outline of the Social System," in *Theories of Society;* Parsons, Introduction to "Culture and the

Social System," Part Four of *Theories of Society,* II, 963-93; Parsons, *Societies: Evolutionary and Comparative Perspectives* (Englewood Cliffs, N.J., 1966); Parsons, "Full Citizenship for the Negro American?" *Daedalus,* XCIV (1965), 1009-54.

In addition, see the following by Talcott Parsons: *The Structure of Social Action* (New York, 1937); *The Social System* (Glencoe, Ill., 1951); *Working Papers in the Theory of Action,* with Robert F. Bales and Edward A. Shils (Glencoe, Ill., 1956); "Systems Analysis: Social Systems," in the *International Encyclopedia of the Social Sciences,* ed. David L. Sills (New York, 1968, 17 vols.), vol. 15, 458-73.

5. In order to test the process of internalization directly it would be necessary to .prove the existence of memory traces of learned patterns, and up to now this has been physiologically impossible. Nor is internalization the only mechanism of social control; there are others operating at other social levels. Finally, it is not theoretically necessary to accept the alternatives of internalization or the war of all against all. George Herbert Mead, for example, was able to formulate an extensive theory of order, stability, and concerted action in other terms. He put great emphasis on shared meanings in communication (symbols) and on the social pressures put on the individual through collective societal attitudes toward ego and ego's attitudes towards self.

6. Erik H. Erikson, *Childhood and Society* (New York, 1963, 2nd ed.); Erikson, *Young Man Luther: A Study in Psychoanalysis and History* (New York, 1962); Norman O. Brown, *Life Against Death: The Psychoanalytical Meaning of History* (New York, 1959); L. S. Feuer, *The Scientific Intellectual: The Psychological Origins of Modern Science* (New York, 1963); Herbert Marcuse, *Eros and Civilization* (New York, 1962).

7. Freud, *"Repression,"* XIV, 150.

8. See, for example, Ernst Kris, *Psychoanalytic Explorations in Art* (New York, 1964).

9. This, of course, is opposed to Freud's own view of the matter. Freud was convinced that his work depended upon him exclusively, in a singular and personal way. Moreover, Freud's

followers have tended to perpetuate this image of the founder of psychoanalysis as the unique exception to otherwise universal laws. But for psychoanalytic and sociological reasons this is an untenable position. See Freud, *The Origins of Psychoanalysis: Letters to Wilhelm Fliess, Drafts and Notes: 1887-1902,* eds. M. Bonaparte, A. Freud, E. Kris, trans. Mosbacher and Strachey (New York, 1954), letters of 21 December 1899, 306, and 23 March 1900, 314 (hereafter cited as Freud, *The Origins of Psychoanalysis*). Also see on this problem, as an example, K. R. Eissler, "An Unknown Autobiographical Letter by Freud and a Short Comment," *The International Journal of Psycho-Analysis,* XXXII, pt. 4 (1951), 322-23. "The process of self analysis, at the point of human history when Freud conducted it, was, so to speak, against human nature; without prospect of reward, without an inner compulsion or impulsion, the ego seems out of its own resourcefulness to have evolved the firm intention to withstand an inner revulsion and to bear voluntarily and of its own accord that pain which is for several reasons the most difficult to bear."

10. According to Parsons and some of his students, Western society has traditionally manifested a tension between the cultural and social levels of action, a tension that stems first from the universally inclusive content of Christianity, and second from the rationality involved in the Protestant variant of Christian doctrine. Inclusion and rationality are, of course, vital factors in democratization. See, e.g., Talcott Parsons, *The System of Modern Societies* (Englewood Cliffs, N. J., forthcoming).

11. Robert N. Bellah, "Religious Evolution," *American Sociological Review,* XXIX (1964), 358-74; Talcott Parsons, "Evolutionary Universals in Society," *American Sociological Review,* XXIX (1964), 339-57.

12. On this problem see Talcott Parsons, "Some Problems of General Theory in Sociology," in *Theoretical Sociology: Perspectives and Developments,* eds. John C. McKinney and Edward A. Tiryakian (New York, forthcoming); Talcott Parsons

and R. F. Bales, *Family, Socialization and Interaction Process* (Glencoe, Ill., 1955); Neil J. Smelser, "Sociological History: The Industrial Revolution and the British Working-Class Family," in his *Essays in Sociological Explanation* (Englewood Cliffs, N.J., 1968); M. Zelditch, "Role Differentiation in the Nuclear Family: A Comparative Study," in *A Modern Introduction to the Family*, eds. Bell and Vogel, (Glencoe, Ill., 1960).

13. See Parsons on power and influence, works cited in note 1. Also see Parsons with Gerald M. Platt, "Considerations on the American Academic System," *Minerva*, VI (1968).

14. This frame of reference is, of course, manifestly opposed to the Marxist viewpoint on all levels. The differences may be quickly summarized: society constitutes a rather limited network of institutional structures, and, as society differentiates, no one of these structures is found to be more important than any other for stability or change; social change does not, therefore, reflect simply what is occurring on the level of the organization of production, as Marx would have it, but occurs, rather, in response to violations on *any* institutional level; the functions of change and conflict are related more readily to the factors we have indicated (inclusion, autonomy) than to the organization of productive forces and the social relations generated thereby.

To cite an important example, there is considerable evidence that a capitalist class in Marx's sense of the term did not exist in any substantial way in pre-revolutionary France, nor was such a development necessary for the kind of social change demanded by the Enlightenment writers or attempted during the Revolution. These events were political and social responses to *normatively* defined political and social situations of discontent. See George V. Taylor, "Noncapitalist Wealth and the French Revolution," *American Historical Review*, LXXII (1967), especially 490-94. See also the discussion that follows the article.

One aspect of Taylor's article is of particular relevance

here. Taylor argues that because the evidence seems to support no useful Marxist interpretation of the Enlightenment and the Revolution then there can be no useful *sociological* interpretation at all—as if the Marxist view of such processes were the only possible view. Thus, for Taylor, the Enlightenment turns out to be an interesting episode, not significantly related to the Revolution. "The revolutionary mentality was created by the crisis [of 1788-89]. It was, in fact, the writing of the *cahiers* that forced a crystallization of issues and their formulation in ideological terms. For the mass of the upper Third Estate, the schools of revolution were the electoral assemblies of 1789, not the salons and *sociétés de pensée* of the old regime." From this it follows that "the intention to smash the legal basis of nobility and, along with it, the whole system of language, symbols, images and formalities that reinforced the subservience of the lower groups, was a product of the revolutionary crisis, not a cause." That is, because it is now apparently wrong in the light of available evidence to argue in rather traditional fashion that the Revolution came about through "long years of economic change, class formation, and the gradual growth of class consciousness in a bourgeoisie that played a capitalist role," then value change must have been immediate and must have depended upon a particular crisis. But this is, sociologically and psychologically, an impossible position: it is one thing to move beyond Marxist conceptions; it is quite another to ignore valid sociological and psychological insight.

Involved in this problem, as well, is the fate of the concept "bourgeoisie": once the Marxist position is abandoned, the traditional definition (special relations to specific modes of production) must also be given up. But it is possible to redefine the concept, and the attempt should be made. There was in France a substantial group of monied, educated, skilled, and ambitious people who were essentially excluded from decision-making processes. These people we may refer to as "bourgeois," and what distinguished them was their ability to formulate and maintain a position of autonomy and inclusion, given certain qualifications with respect to the psychic factors of self-control, rationality, and emotional constraint. On the political level there was a demand among the bourgeoisie for a relatively open society characterized by abstract legal mechanisms and representative institutions. The existence of this demand is predicated on the existence of identifiable psychic factors. Moreover, equivalent bourgeois positions that can be seen on the economic, familial, and personal levels of action are based on these same psychic factors, and it is the recurrence and consistency of these factors that permit us to formulate a definition of the group "bourgeoisie." What these factors are will be indicated at length in later chapters.

The fact that the bourgeoisie did not manage an overt, consistent, public, "class-conscious" expression until 1788-89 is no indication that the attendant feelings did not exist before that time—obviously they did, and not only among middle-class types, but in the aristocracy as well. Had this not been so, the Enlightenment could not have occurred—that is, the whole range of circumstances involved in the Enlightenment, including aristocratic connivance at circumventing official censorship, the techniques developed for the distribution of Enlightenment writings, the wide audience undoubtedly enjoyed by the *philosophes,* the popularity accruing to them as individuals, in addition to what they were able to write, would not have been possible. The opposition to traditional values so evident in the work of the Enlightenment generation would have been an intolerable burden had there not already existed the feeling that the hierarchical and exclusive values of the old regime were oppressive. Therefore, in order to account for the direction ultimately taken by the Revolution—that is, the development of abstract political and legal mechanisms, representation, the opening of society to talent, and so on—it is necessary to assume both the existence of a "bourgeois" class and the concept of process through time.

1: *THE SOCIOLOGY OF VALUE CHANGE*

1. With regard to this formulation of values see Emile Durkheim, *The Elementary Form of Religious Life,* trans. Joseph W. Swain (Glencoe, Ill., 1954); Durkheim, *The Division of Labor in Society,* trans. George Simpson (New York, 1933); Talcott Parsons, "An Outline of the Social System," in *Theories of Society,* eds. T. Parsons, E. Shils, K. D. Naegele, J. R. Pitts (New York, 1961), 43-47.

2. This process is described by the general sociological construction known as "structural differentiation." In Smelser's terms, "when one social role or organization becomes archaic under changing historical circumstances, it differentiates . . . into *two* or *more* roles or organizations which function more effectively in the new historical circumstances. The new social units are structurally distinct from each other, but taken together are functionally equivalent to the original unit." Neil Joseph Smelser, *Social Change in the Industrial Revolution* (Chicago, 1959), 2. See also Smelser's more recent work on this topic: *Essays in Sociological Explanation* (Englewood Cliffs, N.J., 1968).

3. The advocates of change must determine whether the source of the perceived difficulties is in the structural organization or in the value system. But since values rank higher in the system of social control, structural arrangements are always questioned first: historically, the initial attempts to reduce tensions have always been made in the form of structural change, whether the institutions thus modified were actually responsible for the tension or not; it was and is the case that only after a series of such attempted structural adjustments has proved inadequate that the values of the system are brought into question. Descriptions of the natural history of revolution, which are in essence theories of value change, have followed a similar line of thought: each of these approaches has posed an extended period of time from the origin of discontent to the time of revolutionary change, but it is in the interim, of course, that structural rearrangements are attempted in order to allay the discontent. In general, it has been this rearrangement that the theorists have defined as the revolutionary process. However, it is also in this interim period that the source of strain is identified—whether the tension arises from struc-

tural dysfunction, from difficulty in acquiring resources, from difficulty in achieving the goals established by the system, or from the norms and values as such. Because the natural history of revolution theorists have not perceived (or at least have not honored) this distinction, they have had difficulty indicating why some situations of discontent have led to revolution (value change) while others have terminated prior to a revolutionary overthrow. See Lyford Paterson Edwards, *The Natural History of Revolution* (New York, 1965); George Sawyer Pettee, *The Process of Revolution* (New York, 1938); Crane Brinton, *The Anatomy of Revolution* (Magnolia, Mass., 1957); Herbert Blumer, "Collective Behavior," in *Principles of Sociology,* ed. Alfred McClung Lee (New York, 1939), 165-222; but also see, in this connection, Neil Joseph Smelser, *Theory of Collective Behavior* (New York, 1963).

4. A partial condition of this change in commitments is the "desacralization" of the previous social arrangements. See Edward A. Tiryakian, "A Model of Societal Change and its Lead Indicators," in *Theory and Method in the Study of Total Societies,* ed. Samuel Z. Klausner (Garden City, N. Y., 1967). The author defines change as follows: "Societal change involves a fundamental redefinition of the situation, i.e., a new basic religious/sacred reorientation which simultaneously involves a desacralization of the previous order." We should point out, however, that although desacralization must occur in order to violate the previous moral system, the critical consideration is the decline in obligation to the previous system. This decline leads to desacralization but also constitutes the parameter for action in the institutionalization of the desired state. Thus it is necessary to consider the desacralization a type of subcondition of "terminated obligations" to the extant morality. (The above quote is taken from an earlier version of Tiryakian's paper. The published version has been revised, but the position cited here remains the same.)

5. These ideas are adapted with necessary modifications from David Rapaport, *Organization and Pathology of Thought* (New York, 1951); and from Jacob A. Arlow and Charles Brenner, *Psychoanalytic Concepts and the Structural Theory* (New York, 1964).

6. A second level of this frame of reference relates to the simultaneous discharge of energy into the somatic structure.

Personal equilibrium cannot be recovered through symbolic processes alone, and part of the affectual (emotional) discharge is always into the motor and secretory systems. In purely technical terms this process is relevant to the present work, because the affectual "deposit" is very likely a prime source for the kinds of anxiety we shall describe later in relation to the work of certain innovators. However, this is a physiological aspect of psychoanalytic theory, and to carry it further would obviously be beyond the scope of the present work.

7. On this issue see Rapaport, *Organization and Pathology of Thought,* 689 et seq., and Arlow and Brenner, *Psychoanalytic Concepts and the Structural Theory,* 84-87.

8. Parsons writes, respectively: ". . . cognitive perceptions and conceptualization"; "cathexis attachment or aversion"; "the integration of cognitive and cathectic meanings of the object to form a system." Talcott Parsons, *Social Structure and Personality* (New York, 1964), 17-33.

9. Freud was moving toward this conception of superego; note this comment from Erikson: "Instead of accepting the oedipus trinity as an irreducible schema for man's irrational conduct we are striving for greater specificity by exploring the way in which social organization codetermines the structure of the family; for, as Freud said toward the end of his life . . . 'what is operating [in the superego] is not only the personal qualities of these parents but also everything that produced a determining effect upon them themselves, the tastes and standards of the social class in which they live and the characteristics and traditions of the race from which they spring.' " Erik H. Erikson, "Identity and the Life Cycle," *Psychological Issues* (New York, 1959), vol. 1, no. 1, monograph 1, 21. The quotation is from Freud, "An Outline of Psychoanalysis," XXIII.

10. "Symbolically generalized expressions of id-impulses" in psychoanalytic terms refers to objects of gratification, in their symbolic (image) expression, that are projected into thought. In Parsons's terms this notion constitutes the social expression of drives that mediates the drive manifestation. Further, Parsons considers the drive in its symbolic expression to be integrated and adapted into a social matrix that leads it to socially ordered action. Such a change in the formulation of the id concept is necessary if we are to make sociological sense out of Freud. Without a sociological dimension, Freud can be of little

consequence either for sociology or history; and though post-Freudians have tended in this direction, they have not gone nearly far enough.

11. Parsons, *Social Structure and Personality*.

12. The relevant literature indicates that fantasies arise only in the absence of objects of gratification. On this point see, for example, Hanna Segal, "Fantasy and Other Mental Processes" (Symposium on Fantasy), *The International Journal of Psycho-Analysis*, XLV (1964), 191-94.

13. That fantasy is nonlegitimate and non-institutionalized expression does not mean that the content of the fantasy, or some crucial aspect(s) of the content, was not available in the society prior to a refined codification. Indeed, the content may have been available in ideological doctrines that some segments of the society wished were normative mandates. It is the advocates of change who, given certain circumstances, organize various fantasy reactions into a unified ideological statement, and attempt further to institutionalize the content as political, religious, or even artistic or scientific standards of behavior.

14. "Moral indignation on the part of self and others" should be understood in several senses. Those who adhere to the new values express moral indignation toward those who continue to adhere to the old, and are at once self-indignant, since they themselves hold these values. On the same basis, those who oppose the new values also express moral indignation. All of these reactions are produced by the content of the fantasy, and all have implications for the analysis of the historical materials we shall review.

An important fifth criterion for distinguishing fantasy-based movements should also be cited: a period of considerable duration elapses between the recognition of the source of strain and the institution of new solutions. In the interim—because of the psychological difficulty of withdrawing from inherited values—the disaffected will try any number of other types of reorganization. When these attempts fail to produce results, the final step will be taken, by sizeable portions and important factions of the population. However, we shall have no opportunity to investigate this aspect of the problem here.

15. In that such a movement negated institutional structures and worked against any form of differentiation, by denying that differentiation was either possible or necessary, it repre-

sented a regressive development. Such movements are, in fact, based on the most archaic pre-oedipal wishes. See Gregory Rochlin, "The Dread of Abandonment," *Ps. St. Chi.,* XVI (1961), especially 452.

16. Talcott Parsons, "The Political Aspects of Social Structure and Process," in *Varieties of Political Theory,* ed. David Easton (Englewood Cliffs, N.J., 1966).

17. Reinhard Bendix, in *Nation Building and Citizenship: Studies of Four Changing Social Orders* (New York, 1966), 40 et seq., makes similar points on father/son symbolism in such traditional societies.

18. Edward A. Shils, "Centre and Periphery,", in *The Logic of Personal Knowledge: Essays Presented to Michael Polanyi* (London, 1961), 117-30.

19. Freud, "Formulations on Two Principles of Mental Functioning," XII, 218-26.

20. This is an important factor, because failure as such can be repressed as rapidly as anything else. Also see Susan Isaacs, "The Nature and Function of Phantasy," *The International Journal of Psycho-Analysis,* XXIX (1948), 73-97.

21. We have relied heavily on Jules Nydes's excellent essay, "The Paranoid-Masochistic Character," *Psychoanalytic Review,* L (1963), 215-51.

22. Wolfgang Lederer, "Dragons, Delinquents, and Destiny," *Psychological Issues* (New York, 1964), vol. IV, no. 3, monograph 15.

2: *THE FRENCH ENLIGHTENMENT*

1. Alexis de Tocqueville, *Democracy in America,* ed. and abridged Richard D. Heffner (New York, 1956), 113.

2. These internal influences that opened the way for withdrawal of affect from authority were complemented by certain external factors as well. There was, for example, a reliance on English attitudes and actions toward authority, and especially the presumed English equality in terms of authority. The fact that a Montesquieu or a Voltaire could distort the English experience in reporting it to his own country is clearly relevant, since the distortion took the direction of the wish. Further, legitimation was derived from scientific advances that were tak-

en to indicate a profound level of human capacity for organizing the environment; legal and political equality were in fact predicated on this newfound capacity. There was a tendency also to an exaggerated notion of the freedom and safety of intellectuals and reformers at the courts of Frederick and Catherine.

3. Within the framework of "traditional authority" Weber established three ideal-structural types of traditional organization: patriarchalism, patrimonialism, and feudalism. The fundamental difference among these types is the diffusion of authority from a central source to more peripheral groups (e.g., bureaucracies, nobility, and so on), in an evolutionary flow. Though he expressed the notion in different terms, Weber obviously felt that such changes take place in the authority structure at the social-system level and not at the cultural-value level. Weber clearly also assumed that the moral system legitimating the later, more developed types of authority structure was the same system that had legitimated the earlier types. Eighteenth-century France represented the political diffusion of authority that Weber spoke of. In these terms the problem facing the nation was twofold: France had a central authority figure who was not fulfilling and was unable to fulfill the moral mandates of his position; and France had evolved an elaborate *concrete* authority structure that was not supported by the values legitimating political authority in the society. Therefore, as noted, France had either to regress structurally, which was impossible, or change the values, which it tried to do. Max Weber, *The Theory of Social and Economic Organization*, eds. and trans. Talcott Parsons and A. M. Henderson (New York, 1947), 346 et seq.

4. It should perhaps be stressed that latent or preconscious aspiration among the bourgeoisie is an indispensable hypothesis for an understanding of the Revolutionary period. If one were to consider only the overt level of behavior—the bourgeois desire to live in the noble style, to strive for noble rank, to despise in the noble fashion certain otherwise productive occupations, and in general to use the nobility as a reference group—then one would be forced into the sociologically untenable position that bourgeois values changed in toto with regard to evaluative, affective, and status relationships in a matter of some ten

or twenty years. Values, however, are the *last* things to change. It is true that the aristocracy succeeded in exacerbating middle-class anger by denying the middle class access into the elite—or at least convincingly threatening to do so. But the most that can be claimed for specific instances, such as requiring all army officers to produce at least four quarterings of nobility (1781), is that they were triggering mechanisms, activating latent hostility and ideological support for hostility. Excellent summaries of the class problem can be found in Franklin Ford, *Robe and Sword* (Cambridge, Mass., 1953); and in Elinor Barber, *The Bourgeoisie in Eighteenth Century France* (Princeton, N.J., 1955).

The expression of bourgeois values during the Revolution —as promulgated by Sieyes, for example—could not have got the broad reception it did unless these values had been accepted on some level for a long time. What Sieyes wrote was the product not of recent disenchantment but of long-standing bourgeois competencies: "Look at the *available* classes in the Third Estate, and like everyone else I call 'available' those classes where some sort of affluence enables men to receive a liberal education, to train their minds and to take an interest in public affairs. Such classes have no interest other than that of the rest of the People. Judge whether they do not contain enough citizens who are educated, honest, and worthy in all respects to represent the nation properly." The Third Estate demanded the right to participate on a level of parity; in Sieyes's language, these people wanted to be *something*. Sieyes pointed out the corrupting nature of privilege and the value of competitive energy in the competent fulfillment of tasks; all the difficult tasks, he complained, are handled by the Third Estate, and without the privileged orders the more responsible posts would be infinitely better filled. Higher offices "ought to be the natural prize and reward for recognized ability and service. . . . Nothing would go well without the Third Estate; everything would go better without the other two. The Third Estate then contains everything that pertains to the nation while nobody outside the Third Estate can be considered as part of the nation. What is the Third Estate? Everything." Emmanuel Joseph Sieyes, *What is the Third Estate?*, trans. M. Blondel (London, 1963).

5. Quoted in Arthur M. Wilson, *Diderot: The Testing*

Years, 1713-1759 (New York, 1957), 142. Rousseau, of course, went beyond this position in democratic content; he insisted explicitly on the equal involvement of all people in the community. Rousseau is taken up separately in the following chapter.

6. D. Diderot, "Supplement to Bougainville's 'Voyage,'" in *Rameau's Nephew and Other Works*, trans. Jacques Barzun and Ralph H. Bowen (Garden City, N.Y., 1956), 238.

7. These were (at minimum): "Entire freedom of the person and his goods; to speak to the nation by means of one's pen; to be judged in criminal matters only by a jury formed of independent men; to be judged in any case only in accord with the precise terms of the law; to profess in peace whatever religion one wishes. . . ." Peter Gay, *Voltaire's Politics: The Poet as Realist* (Princeton, N.J., 1959), 31, 136-37, 154.

8. P. H. D. d'Holbach, *Système social* (London, 1773, 3 vols.), vol. II, 1-20, especially 12, 18, 34. Also *Système de la Nature* (London, 1771, 2 vols.), vol. I, 154. These conclusions drew in part from the consistent assumption that men become milder as they become more enlightened. See, for example, J. le R. d'Alembert, *Preliminary Discourse to the Encyclopedia of Diderot*, trans. R. N. Schwab (New York, 1953), 62.

9. Claude Helvétius, "De l'homme," *Oeuvres philosophiques* (London, 1791, 4 vols.), vol. III, 384-85, and vol. IV, 284-88.

10. The Enlightenment was perfectly willing to attack the other symbol, the Church. This is an important issue and will be raised again; for now we shall be content to acknowledge the insistent claims that democratic processes derive from the Christian tradition, while recalling that the *philosophes,* in their time, were conscious of only the rigid and exclusive content in religion. It was possible to conceive of monarchy and democratic organization as co-existing, but it was not possible to imagine them thus with religion also politically involved.

11. Sebastian Mercier, *L'an deux mille quatre cent quarante* (London, 1771), 27-29, 106, 180, 295-315, and especially 303, 305. Morelly, in his *Basiliade,* also created a perfectly harmonious society ruled by a benevolent king. Later, in *Code de la Nature,* Morelly created a representative system. See note 22 below.

12. The thought of incest appears, for example, in La Met-

trie's *L'homme machine,* in Morelly's *Basiliade,* and in Diderot's "Supplement," as noted above. It also appears on a conscious level in personal terms in Rousseau's *Confessions.* Here Rousseau described his relationship with Madame de Warens, who was to him "a tender mother, a beloved sister." Rousseau mentioned the melancholy and depression that attended his love, the "secret oppression of the heart," which he found difficult to overcome. "I felt," he wrote, "as if I had been guilty of incest." Jean-Jacques Rousseau, *Confessions,* ed. E. Rhys (New York, 1931, 2 vols.) vol. I, 179. (Hereafter, *Confessions,* volume and page. Translation altered slightly for the sake of readability.) There are other, perhaps less explicit instances, and, of course, there are the efforts of the Marquis de Sade.

13. Choderlos de Laclos, *Les liaisons dangereuses* (New York, 1961), 271, 292, 335-36, 369.

Martin Turnell—in *The Novel in France* (London, 1950), 66-75—has already discussed the relationship between the aristocracy's behavior and its tenuous social position. The aristocratic protagonists of Laclos's novel, the Vicomte de Valmont and the Marquise de Merteuil, took advantage of their position and of the time and the kind of society made available to them to organize seductions for the purpose of destroying the people involved. Sexual enjoyment in these encounters was secondary; the primary function was the accumulation of power and the expression of sadistic aggression.

Though Valmont and Merteuil would challenge anyone, they sought out particularly the innocent and the uncorrupted, since this kind of person bore the values of society—and what was required was a confrontation with society, the forcing of the moral order to combat. "You know Madame de Tourvel, her religious devotion, her conjugal love, her austere principles. That is what I am attacking; that is the enemy worthy of me; that is the end I mean to reach. . . ." Valmont's quarry was the principle, not the woman, i.e., society, not the individual.

Valmont was anxious to be esteemed, but being denied the traditional occupations of the aristocracy—military, manorial, or administrative—which either no longer had a place or could be fulfilled by any trained person in a rapidly differentiating society, he was forced to squeeze esteem, and a sense of self-worth, out of his antisocial activities on the symbolic level left to him—the sexual encounter. The language used to exult in amorous triumphs is the language of the hero; given the particularly sweet triumph that occupied Valmont's interest in the story, he boasted that he would be able to say to his rivals, "Behold my work, and seek a second example in the age"; and above all, in victory there was "glory."

By blending the language of the bedroom with that of the battlefield (Valmont's great conquest of Madame de Tourvel was "a complete victory, achieved by a hard campaign and decided by expert maneuvers"), Laclos appealed directly to the aristocratic anxiety. The same fear of obliteration that drove Valmont to reassert his authority on the symbolic level forced his class to redefine an identity in terms of race and blood, and to refurbish the untenable illusion that its members were peculiarly suited to command.

It must also be pointed out that ordinarily Valmont did not care about his victims; that is, on the conscious level he felt no particular emotional attachment. But he did come to care about Madame de Tourvel, whose virtue he destroyed just the same. Concerning his feelings in this case, Valmont remarked that he held fast to the notion of glory to save himself from the humiliating thought that he might depend in "any way upon the very slave I have myself enslaved; that I do not contain the plenitude of happiness within myself." This is a peculiarly aristocratic thought. It is true that the nobles had economic and political power over the classes subordinate to them; but psychologically, aristocratic status and security depended on the dependence of others. The aristocratic role was so structured that they could not see themselves as men unless others could be permanently defined as children. There was no room in this traditional, conservative, aristocratic culture for equivalent men. There was room only for men and subordinate, dependent "children," so that an aristocrat might wonder about the sufficiency of his internal substance. Valmont can be understood as representing the decline of his class even in the midst of its political resurgence.

14. Diderot, "Supplement," *Rameau's Nephew and Other Works,* 217-18.

15. Frank Manuel, "Toward a Psychological History of Utopia," *Daedalus,* XCIV (1965), 320.

16. Helvétius, "De l'esprit," *Oeuvres,* vol. I, 100, 192-211.

17. Marquis de Sade, "Philosophy in the Bedroom," *The Marquis de Sade*, trans. Richard Seaver and Austryn Wainhouse (New York, 1965), 319, 324-25.

18. The wish to terminate marriage and the family as institutions was heard consistently in the history of Russian radicalism, also. Khanykov, a member of the Petrashevsky circle, put it this way: "The family, I repeated from that time on, is oppression, the family is despotism, the exclusive rule of privileged groups, the broken harmony of the passions; the family is monopoly, the family is immorality, the family is depravity, the family is god the oppressor, this greedy villain crucifying his son for love, the church says, the church—that nest of rapacious scoundrels; the family is the exclusive possession, the egoistic distribution of wealth; the family is misery, the family is the broken health of humanity; the family is a miasma, an epidemic; the family is evil incarnate, and the state based on it is a poisoned organism, its destruction is near." Quoted in Nicholas Riasanovsky, "Fourierism in Russia: An Estimate of the Petraševcy," in *American Slavic and East European Review*, XII (1953), 295-96.

The wish was repeated in Bakunin: "The true and complete freedom of the people also requires the abolition of the laws of inheritance and the family, including church and civil marriage. . . ." Vladimir Burtsev, *Za sto let* (1800-1896) (London, 1897), 87-89.

Also note, for example, the revolutionary pamphlet of P. G. Zaichnevskii and P. M. Agiropulo, *Molodaia Rossia* (1862), which demanded "the abolition of marriage as a highly immoral phenomenon, and the abolition of the family, an institution that hinders the development of man." V. Bogucharskii, ed., *Materialy dlia istorii revoliutsionnogo dvizheniia v Rossii v 60kh godakh* (St. Petersburg, 1906), 56-63.

The demand was made by other actors in the movement as well. Although this call for the destruction of the family appears on the periphery of radical democratic ideology, it has never become central, for reasons we have indicated. But since the family is the dominant institution in the West that still imposes severe dependency relationships, the struggle for autonomy may one day force the issue into a central position in some form.

19. Helvétius: "De l'esprit," *Oeuvres,* vol. I, 47-52, 71-72, 138, 151, 205-6, 210, 213, 231, 295, 297-98, 317-22; vol. II, 7, 25-27, 64-65, 97, 99, 113, 165, 169, 173-74, 220, 255-56. "De l'homme," *Oeuvres,* vol. III, *passim.*

20. Holbach, *Système de la Nature,* vol. I, 4-5, 17, 50, 63, 65-66, 77, 80-81, 109, 124-26, 130 (on the notion that inequalities among men are a benefit to society; also *Système social,* vol. II, 41), 135, 154-61, and especially 158 (on government's and man's ability to manipulate the environment).

21. Cf. Freud: "Parental influence governs the child by offering proofs of love and by threatening punishments which are signs to the child of loss of love and are bound to be feared on their account. This realistic anxiety is the precursor of the later moral anxiety. So long as it is dominant there is no need to talk of superego and of a conscience. It is only subsequently that the secondary situation develops . . . where the external restraint is internalized and the superego takes the place of the parental agency and observes, directs and threatens the ego in exactly the same way as earlier the parents did with the child." Freud, "New Introductory Lectures on Psychoanalysis," XXII, 62.

According to Helvétius and Holbach, of course, there would never be a "secondary situation"; superego could never develop. Freud's view of superego has no social analogue; it is impossible to imagine any society, even the most primitive, without an internalized morality. The views of Helvétius and Holbach have no empirical substance in this connection.

22. Morelly, *Code de la Nature* (Paris, 1950), 171-72, 176, 207, 229, 244, 255-56, 285-328.

23. Helvétius: " . . . if words were precisely defined and their definitions arranged in a dictionary, all the propositions of morality, politics, and metaphysics would become as susceptible of demonstration as the truths of geometry."

24. Rousseau had a different view of man. See Chapter 3, below.

25. Helvétius: "De l'esprit," *Oeuvres,* vol. II, 433-34; see also, for example, Holbach, *Système de la Nature,* vol. I, 80.

26. The psychological frames of reference developed in the Enlightenment therefore anticipated a man like Sade — he could have been explained, for example, in terms óf an unfor-

tunate heredity, a bad organic structure that accounted for uncontrollable passions manifested in destructive self-interest. But limited by their assumptions, the men of the Enlightenment overlooked one whole dimension of aggression: they were prepared for the id fantasy, but they did not suspect the moralist himself as aggressor, armed with the superego fantasy of absolute moral ends.

27. See Edith Jacobson, "The Self and the Object World," *Ps. St. Chi.,* XV (1954), 123.

28. Mercier, 194-223, especially 216, 219; also 64-66 (on history).

29. Most of Voltaire was burned, because of his preoccupation with human frailty, but the whole of Rousseau was preserved. They burned Herodotus, Sappho, Anacreon, and "the vile" Aristophanes; they burned Livy, Ovid, and Horace, and reduced Seneca by one-fourth. Everything written against Christianity was burned because it was useless; Tacitus was preserved, but only those with strong dispositions were allowed to read him. The best of the remainder of the world's literature was reprinted and corrected according to the "true" principles of morality.

30. A.-N. de Condorcet, *Sketch for a Historical Picture of the Progress of the Human Mind,* trans. G. Barraclough (London, 1955), 173-202, especially 201-2. Italics added.

31. Diderot, "Rameau's Nephew," 51, 78; "D'Alembert's Dream," 106, 127-29, 168; "Supplement," 220, 228, in *Rameau's Nephew and Other Works.*

32. Diderot, "D'Alembert's Dream," 179; "Rameau's Nephew," 35, 38, 50.

33. Diderot, "D'Alembert's Dream," 117.

34. One wide-awake scientist had earlier arrived at these conclusions: La Mettrie had scandalized his contemporaries, and the philosophic generation was anxious to disown him. But Diderot was driven to precisely the same conclusions: there is no real basis for morality, hence no criteria for judging any man's behavior and no moral way to organize society. See Aram Vartanian, *La Mettrie's l'Homme Machine* (New York, 1960), 156, 167, 183-94 *passim.*

In Diderot, again, mind was but a special function of material body, and everything obeyed physical laws. The essential difference among men was in the brain itself, in terms of specialized nerve endings or other organic factors. Whether a man is "despotically" or "anarchically" organized is purely a function of the nervous system. Diderot, "D'Alembert's Dream," especially 153-56, 100, 102. Diderot also wrote: "Our habits are established so early that they are called natural, innate; but there is nothing natural or innate other than nerves, more flexible or more rigid, more or less mobile, more or less disposed to vibrate." Diderot had a conception of human nature developing in the environment, but a nature fixed so early and so permanently that it hardly differed from "inherited human nature."

35. See, for example, Diderot's *Jacques the Fatalist and His Master* (1773-1774), trans. J. Robert Loy (New York, 1962), especially 175.

36. Consistent with his physiological point of view, Diderot located moral sense in a physical organ, the diaphragm, and man was then moral or immoral according to a fortunate or unfortunate heredity. This was not altogether satisfying, since a wicked man still had no responsibility and could not be blamed for failure to conform to social standards. Nor could it explain another phenomenon we now know to exist, the "wicked" man with a strong moral sense. However, this addition to theory did help to solve certain problems. It accounted for observable forms of human behavior that could not be explained by self-interest. It was also good enough to overcome the real (intellectual) dilemma: namely, in Nietzsche's terms, because the disappearance of God deprives ideas of equality and justice of all justification, all is logically permitted. Diderot, for his own peace of mind, had to show that all was not permitted, at least not to most men. His notion of a moral sense and conscience served to abate the chronic frustration at being caught " . . . in a devil of a philosophy that my mind can't help accepting and my heart refuting."

3: *ROUSSEAU: THE AMBIVALENT DEMOCRAT*

1. There were very real and important differences between Rousseau and the other writers of the time that isolated him in significant ways from his contemporaries. The personal, in-

tellectual, and social points of conflict have been reported in a number of works on the period. See in particular William H. Blanchard, *Rousseau and the Spirit of Revolt, A Psychological Study* (Ann Arbor, 1967), which describes a number of Rousseau's conflicts, and does so in consistent psychoanalytic terms. There are similarities between Blanchard's work and the material presented here, but the differences are more important. In any event, our emphasis is upon Rousseau's democratic ideology, and in these terms, in spite of the difficulties he experienced, Rousseau very much belonged to his time. His ideas were more radical and often more sophisticated than others that were made available, but tended nonetheless in the same direction: the inclusion in the political process of those who had hitherto been excluded.

2. See the first of Rousseau's "Lettres Morales," to Mme. d'Houdetot in *Correspondance Générale de J.-J. Rousseau,* ed. Dufour and Plan (Paris, 1924-34, 20 vols.), III, 347. Rousseau really regarded his first forty years as of little consequence, but when he grew bitter over his work and the society that rejected him he reversed this assessment, claiming that the first forty years were his years of wisdom. *Correspondance,* letter 1092, 25 June 1761, VI, 162. Also see *Correspondance,* letter 1249, 12 January 1762, VII, 50. (Hereafter, *Correspondance,* letter number, date, volume, and page.)

3. *Correspondance,* 1249, 12 January 1762, VII, 50-51.

4. Jean-Jacques Rousseau, *Confessions,* ed. E. Rhys (New York, 1931, 2 vols.), II, 4 (hereafter, *Confessions,* volume and page).

5. *Confessions,* II, 3.

6. Rousseau, "A Discourse on the Moral Effects of the Arts and Sciences," in *The Social Contract and Discourses,* ed. G. D. H. Cole (New York, 1950), 144. All references to "The Social Contract" (hereafter, *Social Contract*), the "Discourse on the Arts and Sciences" (hereafter, *Arts and Sciences*), the "Discourse on the Origins of Inequality" (hereafter, *Inequality*), and the "Discourse on Political Economy" (hereafter, *Political Economy*), are to this edition.

7. That Rousseau did not aspire to achieve was, strictly speaking, not true; he was ambitious and he did try his hand

at several pursuits. However, he could succeed at nothing, and the content of the anxiety that prevented him from accomplishing anything worthwhile is well summarized by this statement. *Confessions,* II, 63, and also, for example, I, 199.

8. *Correspondance,* 1155, 24 October 1761, VI, 260; *Confessions,* II, 194.

9. *Confessions,* II, 7-8. Emphasis added.

10. *Confessions,* II, 13-14, 31, 53-54; *Correspondance,* 196, 28 November 1754, II, 135; *Correspondance,* 944, 11 December 1760, V, 290; *Correspondance,* 1261, 28 January 1762, VII, 76.

11. It was this sense of transgression and fear of separation that accounted for Rousseau's predilection for the *ménage à trois* in which he appeared either as the guilty, depressed transgressor or as the innocent, childlike, desexualized third. He arranged this kind of situation with Mme. de Warens and her lover Claude Anet, thought about it in connection with St. Lambert and Mme. d'Houdetot, and arranged precisely this fate for his character St. Preux *(La Nouvelle Héloïse).* For St. Preux, with whom Rousseau identified, it became a case of no sex, no transgression, but no autonomy either. *Confessions,* II, 66; II, 15, 53-54; on de Warens, I, 183-84, 179, 233; on St. Lambert, II, 125; on St. Preux, II, 80.

12. There is a good deal of distortion in Rousseau's *Confessions,* especially on this issue. Rousseau reinterpreted the past in the light of the contemporary anxiety (the plot to ruin him). The punishment, of course, was internal, but he could not understand that and thus had still to have a reason: it was not his aggression, therefore, that was to blame, but the envy and malice of others. See Jules Nydes, "The Paranoid-Masochistic Character," *The Psychoanalytic Review,* L (1963), 215-51; and Charles Kligerman, "The Character of Jean-Jacques Rousseau," *The Psychoanalytic Quarterly,* XX (1951), 237-51. Rousseau's compulsive insistence on poverty, incidentally, can be viewed from the same vantage point.

13. "I discovered that it was by no means as easy as one imagines to be poor and independent. I wanted to live by my profession; the public would not have it. They invented a thousand ways of indemnifying me for the time they made me lose.

. . . I know no slavery more cruel and degrading than that. . . ." *Confessions*, II, 74-75. Also see, for example, *Confessions*, II, 54, 107; *Correspondance*, 1261, 28 January 1762, VII, 76; *Correspondance*, 1260, 26 January 1762, VII, 70. For Rousseau on cities, see *La Nouvelle Héloïse* (Paris, 1960), 207-212 (hereafter *LNH*), and *Emile*, trans. B. Foxley (New York, 1914), 26 (hereafter, *Emile*).

14. *Confessions*, II, 76, 78. Rousseau observed, for example, that he had friends to whom he was attached "by the purest friendship and perfect esteem." Yet he resented these relationships and construed his friends' behavior in the worst possible light. These connections became oppressive to him because it appeared that the intent was to gain control of his behavior; it was therefore necessary for him to withdraw. "This obstinate desire to control me absolutely in all my fancies . . . became cruelly burdensome. . . ." As Rousseau looked back in his *Confessions* he was convinced that his friends had wanted to harm him in this manner. The "Coterie Holbachique," especially, became "afraid" that he would be happy and content in the country; this was the origin in his mind of certain "plots" to lure him back to the city. *Confessions*, II, 67; II, 14. Also, *Correspondance*, 1092, 25 June 1761, VI, 162; *Correspondance*, 944, 11 December 1760, V, 290; *Confessions*, II, 18.

15. *Confessions*, II, 77; *Correspondance*, 490, 25 March 1758, III, 314.

16. *Confessions*, II, 76; *Correspondance*, 499, Spring 1758, III, 328. Rousseau wrote once that it was wrong to surrender to the contemplative life, "for it is nothing but indolence of spirit, something to be condemned at every age. . . ."

It has been pointed out that Rousseau wavered between two ideal social situations, called by Judith Shklar "Sparta and the Age of Gold." The first defined life in the political community, the second "that of the quiet village," the opposite of the political unit, in which happiness and innocence stem "from one source only, unspoiled family love." The first model reflects the substance of Rousseau's work in political speculation, the second the substance of his "charming" reveries, *La Nouvelle Héloïse* and *Emile*. In the first instance Rousseau is truly the austere, tough-minded critic. In the second, he is already beginning more overtly to shade off into passivity and dependence, creating a world of harmony, without conflict but also without separate individuals. When Rousseau lost control over his critical faculties he followed the second path to its logical conclusion—the fulfillment of a wish for infantile unity with the environment, a world completely without aggression. This peaceful world recurred as a fantasied ideal in his novel, in the *Confessions*, in the *Rêveries*, and in at least one of his letters. In the *Rêveries* in particular he was driven to hallucinating gratificatory experiences, in a search for "pleasure without stain." Rousseau, *Les Rêveries du promeneur solitaire* (New York, 1961 Collection Internationale) (hereafter, *Rêveries*). In Rousseau's works the predisposition to dependency is very often implied; in the *Rêveries*, the extreme (passivity and the absence of ego control) completely dominates. See Charles Kligerman, "The Character of Jean-Jacques Rousseau," and Judith Shklar, "Rousseau's Two Models: Sparta and the Age of Gold," *Political Science Quarterly*, LXXXI (1966), 25-51. The theme was essentially this: "O Nature! O my mother! Here I am under your sole protection; here no cunning two-faced man can come between us. . . ." The theme was more or less elaborated upon in this fashion: "To seek out some wild spot in the woods, some deserted place where nothing showed the hand of men or announced servitude and domination, some hiding place where I could fancy myself the first to penetrate and where no bothersome third person could come to interpose himself between nature and myself." *Confessions*, II, 282; *Correspondance*, 1260, 26 January 1762, VII, 72. In *LNH*, 454, the theme reads the same; in *Rêveries*, 121-22, as follows: ". . . thinking that I was there in a refuge unknown to all the universe and where persecutors would not unearth me. A sentiment of pride soon mingled with this reverie. I compared myself to those great travelers who discover a deserted island, and I said to myself complacently, 'Without a doubt I am the first mortal who has penetrated here.' I looked on myself as almost another Columbus."

17. *Confessions*, II, 55, 59.

18. "Beguiled by the absurd hope of procuring the final triumph of reason and truth over prejudice and lies and of making men wise by showing them where their interest lay, ex-

cited by his [i.e., Rousseau's, for he is speaking of himself] vision of the future happiness of the human race and by the honor of contributing to it, he [Rousseau] discovered an idiom worthy of so great an enterprise." Rousseau, *Dialogues: Rousseau juge de Jean-Jacques* (Paris, 1962), 171. (Hereafter, *Dialogues*.) "I made short work of the petty lies of men; I dared to strip their nature to the bone, to follow the progress of time and of the things that have disfigured this nature, and comparing man as men have made him with natural man, I boldly revealed, in his so-called perfectibility the true source of his misery. My soul, exalted by these sublime contemplations, ascended to the Godhead and from there, seeing my fellow creatures following blindly the path of their prejudices, of their errors, their misfortunes and their crimes, I cried aloud to them with a feeble voice they could not hear: 'Fools who complain continually of nature, learn that all your ills come from yourselves.' " *Confessions*, II, 39. Rousseau claimed he had been sent by heaven to perfect its most noble work; he was the defender of God's cause and of the laws of truth.

19. Rousseau, *Politics and the Arts: Letter to M. d'Alembert on the Theatre,* trans. Alan Bloom (Glencoe, Ill., 1960), 23 (hereafter, *Politics and the Arts*); *Inequality*, 273. Later Rousseau withdrew the quality of "proof" from his assertions and posed the argument more accurately: "If my own views were absolutely proven I should be little disturbed by yours, but to speak sincerely, I myself am rather more persuaded than convinced; I believe but I do not know. . . ." *Correspondance*, 1092, 25 June 1761, VI, 161.

20. This anxiety over the loss of control was quite evident in Rousseau's personal life: wherever the limits and boundaries were not definitely drawn, he rushed into the gaps with fears and fantasies. Madame de Staël once summed up this propensity in terms of his relationships: "Sometimes he would leave you still loving you; but if you had said a single word that could displease him, he recalled it, examined it, exaggerated it, thought about it for a week, and ended up by quarreling with you."

This was an abiding source of pain for Rousseau, and though he could not control the cause, he certainly regretted the effect. He lamented his "cruel imagination which always anticipates misfortunes . . . ," his "melancholy imagination which always exaggerates misfortunes . . . ," his "cruel imagination which tortures itself incessantly in anticipating misfortunes which do not exist. . . ." *Confessions,* I, 200, 319; II, 139, 204, 225. On his feelings concerning his friends see *Confessions,* II, 61, 64, 165; *Correspondance,* for example, 1261, 8 January 1762, VII, 78; 1240, 4 January 1762, VII, 37. Note too his comments on his relations with Thérèse, *Confessions,* II, 74.

So long as Rousseau could manage some measure of control, he was able to step back and reflect to some degree on what he was doing. But when he lost control, everyone in his world became implicated against him, and there could no longer be communication. The result, for Rousseau, was to insist on complete exposure; he could not abide equivocation. See, for example, *Confessions,* II, 206. The inability to abide uncertainty became intellectualized as part of Rousseau's objective knowledge: "Doubt with regard to what we ought to know is a condition too violent for the human mind; it cannot long be endured; in spite of itself the mind decides one way or the other and it prefers to be deceived rather than believe nothing." "The Creed of a Savoyard Priest," in *Emile,* 228-78, especially 229-30 (hereafter, *Savoyard Priest*).

21. The problem of the motive for achievement has been discussed from Plato to Parsons; see, for example, A. W. Gouldner, *Enter Plato* (New York, 1965), 97. Rousseau wrote of a period in which the expansion of faculties kept "a just mean between the indolence of the primitive state and the petulant activity of our egoism . . ." and which must have been "the happiest and most stable of epochs." *Inequality,* 243-44.

22. *Correspondance,* 244, 10 September 1755, II, 207. Rousseau pointed out, for example, that the Abbé de St. Pierre was wrong to think that human reason would perfect itself, anticipating that each century would add to the enlightenment of those it followed. "He did not see that the human understanding always has but one and the same span, and a very limited one, and that it loses on the one hand just as much as it gains on the other, and that ever-new prejudices deprive us of as much of our acquired knowledge as our cultural reason can replace." *Correspondance,* 3423, 26 July 1767, XVII, 156.

23. Rousseau's "fanciful notions" are to be found in his

novel, *La Nouvelle Héloïse,* and in *Emile,* especially in the "Profession de Foi." The people who bear Rousseau's virtues in these works are not to be confused with his appreciation of political and social man. The novel, for example, was the product of a "charming and mad reverie." Rousseau wrote it as a function of his withdrawal from society into an internal world he could pleasurably control. *Confessions,* II, 77; *Correspondance,* 1260, 26 January 1762, VII, 72-73; *Correspondance,* 1240, 4 January 1762, VII, 36; *Correspondance,* 1249, 12 January 1762, VII, 50.

There is a consistency of language in Rousseau's work, centered particularly on the notions of duty, interest, and passion, that gives the whole body of work an appearance of unity. These two works, *La Nouvelle Héloïse* and *Emile,* however, cannot be reconciled with Rousseau's ideas on men as they are in society because he was far more ambivalent about possibilities in the "real" world than he was about possibilities in his intensely subjective, personal world—although it should be noted that even here he could not imagine any ultimate success. Still, in the fictional works, Rousseau tried to show instances of the triumph of virtue over the dangerous passions of love, vanity, pride, and corrupt self-interest. In doing so, he used the traits found in nature (self-love and compassion), to which he added the social faculties (reason and conscience), while leading his characters to the expression of virtue. They overcome passion, sacrifice interest to duty, and improve themselves through assisting others to achieve well-being—up to a point.

Primary among those human faculties by which these characters are able to realize a measure of virtue was conscience. Conscience, of course, is the critical concept in any theory of autonomy; it implies moral capacities on a personal level and is the necessary factor in self-discipline. In these works Rousseau wrote vigorously on the attributes of this human function. He even mentioned once the possibility of a "progress ordained by our primitive affections"—a progress that man could attain to when conscience and reason (by itself the least resource) combine with man's nature to guide his aspirations and actions. *Savoyard Priest,* 252, 253, 259. Ultimately, however, Rousseau could not believe that conscience could constrain human behavior. Further, his use of compassion in *Emile* and *La Nou-*

velle Héloïse, as the affective basis for right moral conduct (e.g., "le base de toutes les vertus est l'humanité"), is a clear example of why these works cannot be considered consistent with his political theory. In Rousseau's political works, compassion is not and cannot be the effective binding emotion in society.

24. That is, in the novel and in *Emile.* Emile and his wife leave their rural surroundings for Paris and are destroyed. And in his novel, Rousseau's heroine, the true bearer of Rousseau-istic virtue, ends more enamored of death than of continued life. Not the least consideration is the challenge to virtue and good order that life presents. Though she lives blamelessly as wife and mother, she can never overcome the passionate attachment to her first love, whose presence is a constant threat. And although this "involuntary sentiment" has been no prejudice to her virtue so far, "who could have answered for my future years? Perhaps if I lived another day I should be culpable." *LNH,* 728-29.

25. "Where all is necessary there is no liberty; without liberty, no morality in actions; without morality, where is virtue?" *Correspondance,* 2028, 4 March 1764, X, 340.

26. Rousseau could finally advise Emile only "to conquer his affections" because only then could he make reason and conscience effective. Until then Emile would have only the semblance of freedom, "the precarious liberty of the slave who has not yet received his orders." Emile must learn to forsake all things at the command of virtue in order to be independent. *Emile,* 408-410. Also see Rousseau's comment on this work in *Correspondance,* 2230, 13 October 1764, XI, 339.

27. *Savoyard Priest,* 241.

28. *Confessions,* I, 48.

29. It should be clear that in considering *The Social Contract* or other works of Rousseau we are not concerned with his ideas as pragmatic possibilities or as political theory. Rather we are interested in the expression of the wish for autonomy and inclusion and in the ambivalence provoked by the wish. There are certain palpable evidences of the values of control and authority, and these are the present concern.

The values of authority and control are immediately manifest in the situation Rousseau described in which men are just forming into a community appropriate for the expression of the general will. Man cannot possibly participate at once on an autonomous level. What is required is a legislator whose role is to design the political apparatus and supervise the struggles involved until the people are inured to the demands of independence. *Social Contract,* 40.

Rousseau also indicated that the liberty he prized was not possible everywhere; not all people were capable of managing it. He also elaborated certain criteria in *The Social Contract* upon which the desired autonomy would have to be based. *Social Contract,* 48-49. It should be understood that if these criteria are adhered to, then the contract is impossible to implement. Rousseau himself could indicate only one society to which the contract could refer: Corsica. One might assume that the preconditions Rousseau specified could result from a revolutionary interference with history. However, not only did Rousseau never discuss that possibility, and not only did he deny that he had revolution in mind, but he stated that liberty could not be recovered by revolution; in fact, it could not be recovered at all. He argued that it is the natural propensity of government to proceed from the many to the few. "If it took the backward course from the few to the many, it could be said that it was relaxed; but this inverse sequence is impossible." Given these facts, there are two statements made about Rousseau's work that can be seen in perspective: *The Social Contract* was not applicable in France, and Rousseau in fact preferred an elective aristocracy to democracy as a form of government. The point is this: Rousseau was interested in establishing the moral bases upon which any society could rest, regardless of the form of government it might adopt. A nation must either adopt the contract or become a tyrannical society based on dependent relationships. Rousseau considered the best form of government to be relative to time, place, and circumstances—and he considered elective aristocracy ultimately to be the best kind of administrative organization. However, there is only one possible *state*: one based on the social contract. The principles of the contract, therefore, were democratic, applicable to any society, and the form of government employed was of less consequence than the existence of the contract.

30. *Social Contract,* 13-14.

31. *Emile,* 7.

32. Rousseau considered the small political unit infinitely superior to the great one; we have quoted his description of these conditions above in relation to the city-state. *Social Contract*, 44-45; also see "Considérations sur le Gouvernement de Pologne," in C. E. Vaughan, *The Political Writings of Jean-Jacques Rousseau* (New York, 1962, 2 vols.), II, 442-43, 483 (hereafter, *Poland*). Obviously, the ideal situation considered in *The Social Contract* admits of more facile solutions to technical problems, especially those concerned with the crucial concept of the general will. Rousseau stated that he would explain how these advantages should be arranged in the large state, but the explanation was not forthcoming. In any case, as we have seen, the moral requirements apply to any state.

33. *Social Contract*, 23-24, 27, 30, 37, 50.

34. *Correspondance*, 3423, 26 July 1767, XVII, 156. Reason and truth, of course, are no argument against the passions. "Truth has almost never amounted to anything in the world because men act more from passion than they do from intelligence, and while they approve the good, they do evil." *Correspondance*, 2028, 4 March 1764, X, 340. Also see *LNH*, 292, 670; *Emile*, 408; and *Correspondance*, 3781, 15 January 1769, XIX, 58; 1347, 29 April 1762, VII, 203; 3423, 26 July 1767, XVII, 156.

35. *Inequality*, 227-29, 241; *Confessions*, II, 85. See Freud, for example, "Group Psychology and the Analysis of the Ego," XVIII, 140.

36. *LNH*, 351, 353.

37. *Correspondance*, 557, 13 October 1758, IV, 82; 1261, 28 January 1762, VII, 76; 1869, 18 July 1763, X, 39; *Social Contract*, 133-36. Man achieves great things only through the passions, and if a man is concerned only with salvation he will achieve nothing in the temporal order.

38. *Correspondance*, 1869, 18 July 1763, X, 39, 37.

39. *Politics and the Arts*, 57; *Correspondance*, 1261, 28 January 1762, VII, 76; *Poland*, 434. "Greek theater was all right for Greek culture, but not for the French." "One kills his father, marries his mother, and finds himself the brother of his children; another forces a son to slay his father; a third makes a father drink the blood of his son. We shudder at the very idea of the horrors with which the French stage is decked out

for the amusement of the gentlest and most humane people on earth." *Politics and the Arts,* 33.

40. *Correspondance,* 1795, 30 April 1763, IX, 265-66; *Emile,* 7; *Political Economy,* 295; also see *Social Contract,* 52. This attachment to the state was at least the intellectual origin of nationalism in Europe. The end of monarchy and church as institutions fostering and using emotional ties to bind the community left the state as the alternative focus for maintaining social attachments. Men would love the community "with that exquisite sentiment which every man living in isolation has for himself." The love of one's country would be the whole of one's existence, since alone man is nothing.

41. *Poland,* 428, 432-34. In this essay on Poland Rousseau said, for example, that education could be domestic and private but exercises must always be public and common: "for here it is not only a question of occupying them, of giving them a robust constitution . . . but of accustoming them at an early age to discipline, equality, fraternity, competition, to live under the eyes of their fellow citizens and to desire public approbation." In *Emile* and *La Nouvelle Héloïse* Rousseau declaimed endlessly on vanity, pride, rivalry, etc.

42. *Social Contract,* 127-28.

43. *Social Contract,* 18.

44. Rousseau wrote: "If people were rendering good for good it is clear as day that virtue would make the human race happy, but how can one find a real and worldly advantage in being good oneself amongst the wicked—this is the philosopher's stone which is still to be found." *Correspondance,* 1113, 12 August 1761, VI, 189.

4: *ROBESPIERRE: THE RETREAT TO AUTHORITY*

1. I.e., the "shopkeepers, retail merchants, traders, artisans, small manufacturers, hired laborers, porters, water-carriers, waiters in cafés, janitors in buildings, barbers, wig-makers, stonemasons, and makers of ladies' hats . . . the people of Paris without the frosting—and generally without the dregs, since the vagrant, the shiftless, and the delinquent did not become true *sans-culottes.*" R. R. Palmer, *The Age of the Democratic Revolution* (Princeton, N.J., 1959-64, 2 vols.), II, 47.

2. Some explanation of the term paranoia is in order: "It is perhaps significant of paranoid dynamics that, more than most categories, the adjective 'paranoid' is employed as an epithet to convey the impression that such a person is really quite offensively sick. Such usage tends to obscure the fact that paranoid traits may be quite mild, are almost universal, and are often found in persons whose ego strength may be otherwise quite sound. Frequently, in fact, paranoid attributes are mistakenly identified as ego strength because the capacity of the paranoid character to be oppositional is often confused . . . with healthy and courageous self-assertion." Jules Nydes, "The Paranoid-Masochistic Character," *The Psychoanalytic Review,* L (1963) , 217.

3. Saint-Just identified the problem precisely when he declared that "we must set ourselves to forming a public conscience." L. A. L. de Saint-Just, *Oeuvres Complètes,* ed. Charles Vellay (Paris, 1908, 2 vols.), II, 374-75. (Hereafter Saint-Just, *Oeuvres.)* (Also see I, 368.)

4. J. M. Thompson, *Robespierre* (New York, 1935, 2 vols.) , I, 56, 68, 77, 90, 99-100, 117, 129, 139, 167-68, 170-71. (Hereafter, Thompson, volume and page.) See also M. de Robespierre, *Textes Choisis,* ed. Jean Poperen (Paris, 1956, 3 vols.), I, 89-94. (Hereafter, Robespierre, *Textes,* volume and page.)

5. Robespierre, *Textes,* I, 99-117.

6. See, for example, Robespierre, *Textes,* II, 145-46; III, 163-64.

7. Robespierre once interrupted a speech being delivered to the Jacobins, denouncing religion, with these words: "I believe the society cannot hear this talk without danger. We must not attack the religious prejudices the people adore; time must mature this people and put them, little by little, above these prejudices."

8. Prior to his assumption of power, it was particularly in the milieu of the club that Robespierre exerted his supreme influence and that the effects of these qualities were most evident. At the Jacobin meetings the public came to hear truth and Robespierre gave them truth. He wanted and he got a passionate, not a reasonable response. "You cannot imagine," Desmoulins reported on one occasion, "the abandon, and the conviction of truth with which some passages of this speech [against

the war, January 2, 1792] were delivered; it brought tears into the eyes not only of the women in the gallery, but also of half the men in the hall." And J.-B. Louvet, describing the reception of a two-hour peroration, complained that "this was no longer applause, this was a compulsive stomping, this was a religious ecstasy, this was a holy furor." Pierre Bessand-Massenet, *Robespierre* (Paris, 1961), 29. Also, G. Walter, *Robespierre* (Paris, 1961, 2 vols.), I, 225; II, 340.

9. Robespierre did not at first take such an extreme view on the question of the king; the demand evolved, alongside his need to dominate. See Walter, *Robespierre*, I, 66-67; II, 35; I, 320-22, 324. Also Robespierre, *Textes,* I, 157 et seq.

10. Robespierre, *Textes,* II, 91-96, 66, 69-71. Saint-Just, *Oeuvres,* I, 368-70, 396; II, 7, 13, 21. It was pointed out, for example, that to bring Louis to trial would be to imply the possibility of his innocence; the Revolution could therefore end by being guilty. It would be a mistake to submit the Revolution itself to litigation.

11. Saint-Just, *Oeuvres,* I, 369.

12. This kind of factor is overdetermined, of course; still this one aspect should be noted again: because gratitude is linked to submission it becomes necessary to deny obligations in order to act. If there is nothing in the past to be grateful for, then one avoids the threat of passivity at the same time that aggression becomes justified. Among these other things, repression of this sort then leads radical innovators to feel that they are self-caused, that their position in history and their view of history are self-generated. Comte pointed this out in reference to Condorcet. If the past is as Condorcet described it, then advanced civilization becomes an effect without a cause. But the inconsistency here was lost on Condorcet, for he had repressed the past. See Charles Frankel, *The Faith of Reason* (New York, 1948), 143.

13. On the de-Christianization movement see A. Mathiez, *La Révolution et l'église* (Paris, 1910) and F.-A. Aulard, *Le Culte de la raison et le culte de l'être suprême* (Paris, 1892).

14. See George G. Andrews, "Making the Revolutionary Calendar," *The American Historical Review,* XXXVI (1931), 515-32.

15. Robespierre, *Textes,* III, 175.

16. Saint-Just, *Oeuvres,* II, 494.

17. See Saint-Just's poem "Organt," 1788. Saint-Just resented bitterly the disparity between what is said and what is done: folly was revered everywhere, but especially in France, where monks fornicated and heaven was sold by the square foot; folly took hold of ministers, magistrates, priests, and generals, and even the king had submitted and become brutal and mad. Saint-Just, desiring autonomy and doubting the human capacity to tolerate it, is a perfect example of the need for a highly structured, rigid, external world that can protect the individual from the fear of his own wishes and suppress the "wicked"—even as the goals are declared to be democratic.

18. Saint-Just, *Oeuvres,* I, 422. Saint-Just stated simply that "our aim is to create an order of things which establishes a universal tendency toward the good." Saint-Just, *Oeuvres,* II, 235.

19. "Power is so cruel and evil that if you release it from its inertia, without giving it a goal, it will march straight to oppression." Saint-Just wrote that he could give men laws, consistent with their nature and their hearts, that would end wickedness and corruption. Since "wickedness" was not natural to man, there was no reason why this could not be done. Saint-Just, *Oeuvres,* 1, 419-20; II, 492-93.

20. Saint-Just, *Oeuvres,* II, 495.

21. Saint-Just, *Oeuvres,* II, 493, 501.

22. On education, see Robespierre, *Textes,* II, 187-98; Saint-Just, *Oeuvres,* II, 516-19. On religion, see Robespierre, *Textes,* III, 155-80, especially 175-76; Saint-Just, *Oeuvres,* II, 524-25.

23. Robespierre and Saint-Just actually conceded little to reason. Robespierre pointed out that reason was only too often a sophist that pleaded the cause of the passions; and Saint-Just wrote, more dramatically, that all things must be brought before conscience, for the mind is a sophist that leads virtue to the scaffold. Robespierre, *Textes,* III, 168; Saint-Just, *Oeuvres,* II, 495.

24. Robespierre, *Textes,* III, 115.

25. In other words, the *sans-culottes* did not necessarily agree with the political and economic policies of Robespierre's faction either. It has been said that this was so because in hard

economic and political terms the *sans-culottes* were more radical. The problem is not that simple. The *sans-culottes* wanted to retain political power in their own hands rather than relinquish it to some representative body. However, their concern for political power derived largely from the need to ensure themselves of economic protection, and economically they reflected the values of the old regime. Their failure to produce leaders of stature could be laid to the ambivalence of their aspirations; they could not finally make up their minds whether to stand firm with the old or move on with the new, and they could not have it both ways. See the discussion in Barrington Moore, Jr., *Social Origins of Dictatorship and Democracy* (Boston, 1966), 83-87, especially 85 on Jacques Roux.

26. Robespierre, *Textes,* III, 99. Robespierre was therefore provoked when someone complained about this arrest or that execution, when someone pointed out that one or another act was illegal in terms of the constitution. Liberty, he pointed out more than once, could be seized from another power only by force, and whatever was necessary to defend it was right. The Revolution was above legality and it made its own laws.

27. Robespierre, *Textes,* III, 118; Saint-Just, *Oeuvres,* II, 83.

28. Robespierre, *Textes,* III, 112-13. "We wish . . . to fulfill the intentions of nature and the destiny of man, realize the promise of philosophy, and acquit providence of a long reign of crime and tyranny. That France . . . may . . . become a model to nations, a terror to oppressors, a consolation to the oppressed . . . and that, by sealing the work with our blood, we may at least witness the dawn of the bright day of universal happiness."

29. Robespierre, *Textes,* II, 99.

30. Robespierre, *Textes,* III, 119.

31. Danton and Robespierre could not begin to understand each other, and Danton had a facility for infuriating Robespierre. Danton remarked, for example, that virtue was what he did with his wife in bed every night. Robespierre responded to this by saying that he could not see how such an immoral fellow could defend the cause of liberty. Danton's demands for clemency and moderation in the midst of the Terror finally got him executed. As far as Robespierre was concerned

there were only two possibilities: the people or its enemies, i.e., patriots or counterrevolutionary hypocrites, and by his opposition Danton had become one of the latter, "an abettor," in fact, "of unjust opulence and aristocratic tyranny." "The patriotism of which they [the Dantonists] boast is neither absolute nor universal. . . . It has nothing in common with public virtue. . . ." Danton did point out along the way that "if reason does not come back to this nether earth, what we have seen is nothing compared to what we will see." Robespierre, *Textes,* III, 85, 94, 132, 141-50; II, 60-65; Saint-Just, *Oeuvres,* II, 232; Walter, *Robespierre,* I, 424.

32. The Law of 22 Prairial (June 10, 1794) denied prisoners the aid of counsel, awarded to the court the decision whether to hear witnesses or not, and allowed, as noted, only two possible sentences, acquittal or death. However, the rigid application of alternatives allowed Robespierre to free individuals who had already been apprehended by the police machinery of the Terror; they were freed if they met the moral requirements.

33. Robespierre would have liked to achieve complete control, but since this was impossible, and since the anxieties were internal, he lived with and imposed upon others a state of continual maximum tension. He was constantly fearful that the guilty would be encouraged by laxity and inertia, that if a man were to fall off guard he would be penetrated and contaminated, that the merest penetration of vice would lead to a flood that no one could control. Robespierre therefore lost the capacity to distinguish objective results from subjective intention, and thought from action. He advised, for example, not to judge opposition by differences in language, but by identity of results. So far as Robespierre was concerned there were no alternatives to his program: thus the foreign hypocrite (Cloots), who urged international war and called Paris the center of the globe, intended the same thing as the vile federalist who wanted to burn Paris to the ground. Robespierre, *Textes,* III, 124. In addition, see note 9 above.

34. For different reasons, of course, but to the same effect. Robespierre insisted, on the one hand, that "it is in the virtue and in the sovereignty of the people that one must find the source of opposition to the vices and despotism of govern-

ment," and, on the other hand, that the masses quit the political role and end their opposition to his government. He asserted that the people, disparate and fragmented, should not attempt to make decisions for society as a whole. The people, however, burdened as they were with the continued economic pressures, had no intention of abandoning their position. Five days before he was overthrown Robespierre warned that he was going to head off the possibility of the development of opposition in the Convention. No one there could mistake his meaning. Robespierre, *Textes*, III, 113-15; Saint-Just, *Oeuvres*, II, 236; Walter, *Robespierre*, II, 39, 66-67.

35. This judgment concerns his leadership in the Convention, at any rate. It must be pointed out, however, that the ultimate determinant of Robespierre's defeat was the refusal of the *sans-culottes* to support him in the streets. Their disenchantment stemmed from the fact that he would not or could not arrange an economic situation that would satisfy them. Perhaps no one could have arranged a satisfactory conclusion. It has been noted that Robespierre could not have given in to *sans-culotte* demands without offending the peasants, thereby jeopardizing his hold on power anyway. See Moore, *Social Origins of Dictatorship and Democracy*, 89-90.

36. See, for example, J. L. Talmon, *The Origins of Totalitarian Democracy* (New York, 1960).

37. Robespierre, *Textes*, II, 90, 135.

38. Alexis de Tocqueville, *The Old Regime and the French Revolution*, trans. Stuart Gilbert (New York, 1955), 144.

39. I.e., where the writer is critical of Robespierre. Robespierre has been defended as a consistent democrat who used the Terror and the other techniques of coercion to deal tactically with an immediate crisis.

40. This is what Robespierre brought to the situation; this is not, however, all that can be said. See notes pp. 42-43 Chap. 1.

41. See, for example, Robespierre's speech on the jury system. *Discours et rapports de Robespierre*, ed. Charles Vellay (Paris, 1908), 1-21.

42. Thus, at this point, it is hard to label Robespierre's economics as "bourgeois." He could no longer think except

in terms of absolute virtue and the possibility of organizing the environment in such a way that conditions for the expression of virtue would be created. Presumably, this would put an end to all special interest and, hence, to all exploitation. In any case, Robespierre held that the greatest service the legislator could render was to compel men to be virtuous—meaning by this that the formation of law could end corruption in politics (defined as interest and prejudice) and factionalism (the result of these vices) permanently. The economic situation would solve itself, once the political process was organized. See especially Robespierre's speech on religion and morals, *Textes*, III, 155-80; Walter, *Robespierre*, I, 327; II, 37.

43. Robespierre, *Textes*, II, 89, 144; I, 71-73; III, 115, 155-80. Also see *Correspondance de Maximilien et Augustin Robespierre*, ed. Georges Michon, Société des Etudes Robespierristes, (Paris, 1926), vol. 3, 183, 246, 279, 304.

44. Robespierre, *Textes*, I, 176; III, 122; Saint-Just, *Oeuvres*, II, 273, 311-26. Saint-Just: "All factions are therefore criminal because they tend to divide the people; all factions are therefore criminal because they neutralize the power of public virtue."

5: *THE INTROSPECTIVE REVOLUTION*

1. "We psychoanalysts were not the first and not the only ones to utter this call to introspection; but it seems to be our fate to give it its most forcible expression and to support it with empirical material which affects every individual. Hence arises the general revolt against our science. . . ." Freud, "Introductory Lectures on Psychoanalysis," part 1, XV, 285.

2. Heinz Hartmann, *Ego Psychology and the Problem of Adaptation*, trans. D. Rapaport (New York, 1958), 71.

3. Freud, "Repression," XIV, 150.

4. See also Freud, "A Note on the Unconscious in Psychoanalysis," XII, 260. "Thus an unconscious conception is one of which we are not aware, but the existence of which we are nevertheless ready to admit on account of other proofs or signs."

5. Hartmann, *Ego Psychology and the Problem of Adaptation*, 63.

6. Freud, "An Outline of Psychoanalysis," XXIII, 172, 191, 193.

7. It may happen, for example, that the repressed evades the defensive process and becomes (or remains) accessible to consciousness. Such material may then be isolated; i.e., affect may be withdrawn from the material, leaving it unconnected to anything psychically relevant.

8. Freud, "Moses and Monotheism," XXIII, 94-102, 127. Translation altered, emphasis added. (Hereafter, "Moses.") Also Kris, *Psychoanalytic Explorations in Art;* K. R. Eissler, "On the Metapsychology of the Preconscious," *Psychoanalytic Study of the Child,* XVII (1962), 9-41. (Hereafter, *Ps. St. Chi.,* volume and page.) See also Freud, V, 598.

See, for example, Kafka, who wrote that "there is no such thing as observation of the inner world, as there is of the outer world. . . . The inner world can only be experienced, not described." And also: "What is ridiculous in the physical world is possible in the spiritual world. *There* is no law of gravity. . . ." Franz Kafka, "The Eight Octavo Notebooks," *Dearest Father, Stories and Other Writings,* trans. E. Kaiser and E. Wilkins (New York, 1954), 65. (Hereafter, *Dearest Father.*) Translations sometimes altered for the sake of readability.

9. See Freud, "Creative Writers and Day-Dreaming," IX.

10. Sigmund Freud, *Letters of Sigmund Freud,* ed. Ernst Freud, trans. T. and J. Stern (New York, 1960). Letter to Arthur Schnitzler of May 8, 1906, p. 251. Also see May 14, 1922, pp. 339-40. "I have formed the impression that you know through intuition—or rather from detailed self-observation—everything that I have discovered by laborious work on other people." Also "Delusion and Dream in Jensen's 'Gradiva,' " IX, 43-44; "An Autobiographical Study," XX, 65. Psychoanalysis "can do nothing towards elucidating the nature of the artistic gift, nor can it explain the means by which the artist works. . . ."

11. Freud, "Repression," XIV, 149; "Creative Writers and Day-Dreaming," IX, 153; and Freud's preface to Reik's *Ritual: Psychoanalytic Studies,* XVII, 261. "By working it [the oepidal conflict] over with the greatest variety of modifications, distortions, and disguises, the dramatist seeks to deal with his own most personal relations to this emotional theme."

12. Freud described it once as requiring "the relaxation of watch upon the reason," and to amplify the point he quoted a letter of Schiller's in which the poet admonished his correspon-

dent to make use of, rather than be ashamed or frightened of, the "momentary and transient extravagances which are to be found in all truly creative minds and whose longer or shorter duration distinguishes the thinking artist from the dreamer." Freud, "The Interpretation of Dreams," IV, 102-3.

13. Nietzsche wrote that the introspective thinker "suffers from the inclination of his judgment as though from seasickness! . . . Indeed, there are a hundred good reasons for staying away from it [the domain of dangerous insights] *if one—can.*" Friedrich Nietzsche, *Beyond Good and Evil,* trans. M. Cowan (Chicago, 1955, Gateway ed.), 27. Freud, in "The Psychopathology of Everyday Life" (VI, 212-13, added in 1917), acknowledged Strindberg's talents in this direction, but he observed, too, that Strindberg's knowledge "was assisted by grave mental abnormality." On Strindberg, see also Theodore Lidz, "August Strindberg: A Study of the Relationship Between His Creativity and Schizophrenia," *The International Journal of Psycho-Analysis,* XLV (1964), 399-406.

14. Franz Kafka, *The Diaries of Franz Kafka,* ed. Max Brod, trans. Martin Greenberg (New York, 1949, 2 vols.), II, 114. (Hereafter, *Diaries,* volume and page.) The translations are sometimes altered for the sake of readability.

15. August Strindberg, *Letters of Strindberg to Harriett Bosse,* ed. Arvid Paulsen (New York, 1959), 52.

16. Feodor Dostoevsky, *The Insulted and the Injured,* trans. C. Garnett (London, 1915), 242.

17. Kafka, "Reflections," 47, and "Fragments," 285, in *Dearest Father.* Freud: "I had gained my first insight into the depths of the life of the human instincts; I had seen some things that were sobering and even, at first, frightening." Freud, "The Question of Lay Analysis," XX, 273.

18. "I do not want to stress the obvious, namely that analysis is to a large extent based on introspection, nor the difficulties which arise in an attempt to make an introspective psychology scientific in the usual sense of the term." Heinz Hartmann, *Essays in Ego Psychology* (New York, 1964), 310. Also Hartmann, "Comments on the Scientific Aspects of Psychoanalysis," *Ps. St. Chi.,* XIII (1958), 138.

19. Sigmund Freud, *The Origins of Psychoanalysis: Letters to Wilhelm Fliess, Drafts and Notes: 1887-1902,* eds. M. Bona-

parte, A. Freud, E. Kris, trans. Mosbacher and Strachey (New York, 1954), 206-24, especially 223, letter of 15 October 1897.

20. K. R. Eissler, "An Unknown Autobiographical Letter by Freud and a Short Comment," *The International Journal of Psycho-Analysis,* XXXII (1951), part 4, 323.

21. See Freud, "Family Romances," IX, 237; and "Sexuality in the Etiology of the Neuroses," III, 278. Bruce Mazlish has written an article, "Freud and Nietzsche," (*The Psychoanalytic Review,* vol. 55, no. 3, 1968, 360-375), in which he concludes that a revolution had occurred between the time that Nietzsche wrote and the time that Freud did, accounting for levels of insight and Freud's ability to develop his insight in a systematic, "scientific" way. Mazlish indicates in general that this was a move from intuitive philosophical insight to scientific control. However, we think that the more important distinction is the one between idiosyncratic insight manifest in earlier periods and insight organized in response to social structural changes and that the difference is a function specifically of systematic changes in the family—as evinced in the direction that psychoanalytic theory took: father and son conflict.

22. Freud: "A whole number of influences may be concerned, not all of which are necessarily known. A spontaneous development is also conceivable, on the analogy of what happens in some neuroses. What is certainly of decisive importance, however, is the awakening of the forgotten memory trace by a recent real repetition of the event." Freud, "Moses," XXIII, 97. With regard to authority, the event represents the experience of desertion or failure on the part of that authority.

23. Freud wrote about the book: "It was, I found, a portion of my own self-analysis, my reaction to my father's death—that is to say, to the most important event, the most poignant loss of a man's life. Having discovered that this was so, I felt unable to obliterate the traces of the experience." Freud, Preface to the 2nd edition of "The Interpretation of Dreams," IV, xxvi. Freud's self-analysis is very often evident in "The Interpretation of Dreams." For example: "Nor is it by any means a matter of choice that our first examples of absurdity in dreams are related to a dead father. . . . The authority wielded by a father provokes criticism from his children at an early age, and the severity of the demands he makes upon them leads them, for their own

relief, to keep their eyes open to any weakness of their father's; but the filial piety called up in our minds by the figure of a father, particularly after his death, tightens the censorship which prohibits any such criticism from being consciously expressed." Freud, "The Interpretation of Dreams," V, 435. The quotation is also interesting because of its conclusion. If the censorship is tightened so that criticism is blocked from consciousness, how did Freud manage? The discoveries characteristic of Freud's work originated in a cathected wish refined into an intellectual product. Social circumstances in the family allowed this to occur. According to Freud, "mental work is linked to some current impression, some provoking occasion in the present which has been able to arouse one of the subject's major wishes. From there it harks back to a memory of an earlier experience (usually an infantile one) in which this wish was fulfilled; and it now creates a situation relating to the future which represents a fulfillment of the wish. What it thus creates is a day-dream or phantasy, which carries about it traces of its origins from the occasion which provoked it and from the memory. Thus, past, present and future are strung together, as it were, on the thread of the wish that runs through them." Freud, "Creative Writers and Day-Dreaming," IX, 147-48. See also, for example, Joseph Sandler and Humberto Nagera, "Aspects of the Metapsychology of Fantasy," *Ps. St. Chi.,* XVIII (1963), 176, 191. Further, the fulfillment of the wish was briefly hampered because it was interpreted as a triumph over the father for the oedipal mother. Freud commented on this too, to this effect: in ambitious fantasies "we can discover in some corner or other the lady for whom the creator of the phantasy performs all his heroic deeds and at whose feet all his triumphs are laid." Freud, "Creative Writers and Day-Dreaming," IX, 147.

It was no coincidence, of course, that such themes as the relation of fantasy to creative thought and of father to son should have constantly preoccupied him. Freud's Count Thun dream, reported in "The Interpretation of Dreams," contains the whole problem in brief. The dream, as Erikson has noted, is a "total situation" relating father and political authority, social status and personal need, internal and external world. Erik H. Erikson, *Insight and Responsibility* (New York, 1964), 197. In analyzing his dream, Freud described certain aspects of hostility toward political authority that he believed were originally related to an earlier rebellious attitude toward his father. He then drew the appropriate conclusion: "A Prince is known as the father of his country; the father is the oldest, first, and for children, the only authority, and from his autocratic power the other social authorities have developed in the course of the history of human civilization—except in so far as the 'matriarchy' calls for a qualification of this assertion." Freud, "The Interpretation of Dreams," IV, 217, n. 1; "Introductory Lectures," XV, 153, 159. In addition, note Freud's definition of the hero as "someone who has had the courage to rebel against his father and has in the end victoriously overcome him." Freud, "Moses," XXIII, 12. Also see "The Interpretation of Dreams," V, 620. "Is the ethical significance of suppressed wishes to be made light of—wishes which, just as they lead to dreams, may some day lead to other things?"

Until Freud worked out the implications of this problem, he had to lean on Fliess, defer to him, and get approval for his work from him. It is remarkable that after the letter to Fliess in which Freud stated to his friend his interpretation of the oedipal conflict and of the Oedipus-Hamlet tragedies, he had to ask Fliess if he thought the ideas were sound. See Ernest Jones, *The Life and Work of Sigmund Freud* (New York, 1953, 3 vols.), I, 295. (Hereafter, *Freud,* volume and page.)

24. Freud had at least partial insight into this: "Even in our middle class families fathers are, as a rule, inclined to refuse their sons independence and the means necessary to secure it and thus to foster the growth of the germ of hostility which is inherent in their relations. . . . In our society today, fathers are apt to cling desperately to what is left of a now sadly antiquated *potestas partis familias.*" See Freud, "The Interpretation of Dreams," IV, 257; on the personal aspect, see "The Interpretation of Dreams," IV, 169ff, and V, 467.

25. Géza Róheim, quoted in *The Psychoanalytic Quarterly* IX (1940), 544, in a review of Abram Kardiner, *The Individual and His Society, The Psychodynamics of Primitive Social Organization* (New York, 1939), summarizes a discussion of Chapter 5, "The Analysis of Tanala Culture," 291-351, with especial attention to p. 331, to which the quotation refers.

26. The relationship of this construct to Weber's ideas on

modern character structure and the formation of modern institutions is dealt with at some length in Chapter VII, below. The relationship between this and Marx's thinking is indicated briefly in note 14 of the Introduction, and again briefly in Chapter VII.

27. Freud, "A Difficulty in the Path of Psychoanalysis," (1917), XVII, 135-44. Emphasis added.

28. It should be pointed out that psychoanalytic theory does not indicate the possibility or the need for total control of ego over the mind. Ego must be able to withdraw from its controlling, organizing functions in sex and sleep, when instinct takes over.

29. Rousseau, *Political Economy,* 287; *Origins of Inequality,* 256-57.

30. Rousseau, *Social Contract,* 4-5; see also Holbach, *Système social,* II, 17-18, 26.

31. See Chapter 6 for an elaboration of this point.

32. See, for example, F. B. Glaser, "The Case of Franz Kafka," *Psychoanalytic Review,* LI (1964), 99-121; Charles Neider, *The Frozen Sea* (New York, 1948); J. H. Seyppel, "The Animal Theme in Franz Kafka," *The American Imago,* XIII (1956), 69-93. In connection with these various psychoanalytic statements, and also in reference to our own remarks on Kafka, see in addition, John S. White, "Psyche and Tuberculosis: The Libido Organization of Franz Kafka," *The Psychoanalytic Study of Society,* IV (1967), 185-250.

33. Kafka, *Diaries,* I, 180, 173.

34. Franz Kafka, *Letters to Milena,* ed. Willy Haas, trans. Tania and James Stern (New York, 1953), 200-1.

35. Kafka, *Diaries,* I, 26.

36. *Ibid.,* 310.

37. *Ibid.,* 316.

38. *Ibid.,* 309.

39. *Ibid.,* 20.

40. Kafka, *Diaries,* II, 91, 76-77; see also II, 79.

41. There is an important connection in Kafka's work between food and reality and between the window and reality. Sometimes all three factors will appear together, as follows: "It is the food on which I thrive. Exquisite dishes, exquisitely cooked. From the windows of my house I see the porters carry-

ing the provisions, a long cavalcade, which often halts, and then each one clutches his basket to him to protect it from damage. And they gaze up at me too, amiably, some of them in delight." The window symbol, however, occurs by itself innumerable times in Kafka's work. For example: " 'What is it? What is it?' I exclaimed, still held down in bed by sleep, and stretched my arms upwards. Then I got up, still far from being conscious of the present, and, with the feeling that I must thrust aside various people who were in my way, made the necessary gestures, and so at last reached the open window." Or again: "Whoever leads a solitary life and yet now and then wants to attach himself somewhere, whoever, according to changes in the time of day, the weather, the state of his business and the like, suddenly wishes to see any arm at all to which he might cling— he will not be able to manage for long without a window looking on to the street. And if he is in the mood of not desiring anything and only goes to his window sill a tired man, with eyes turning from his public to heaven and back again, not wanting to look out and having thrown his head up a little, even then the horses below will draw him down into their train of wagons and tumult, and so at last into the human harmony." Of Kafka's five guiding principles on the road to hell, the first is this: "The worst lies outside the window."

The quotations given are from the following works: Kafka, "Fragments," *Dearest Father,* 264; "The Eight Octavo Notebooks," *Dearest Father,* 61; "Meditations," in *The Penal Colony, Stories and Other Short Pieces,* trans. Willa and Edwin Muir (New York, 1961), 39. For other references to the window see "Fragments," *Dearest Father,* 209-10, 216-17, 243, 266, 346, 350, 357-58, 364; and *Diaries,* I, 20-21, 27, 45, 48, 150, 159, 177, 198, 291, 294, 302, 305, and II, 23, 32-33, 45, 57, 62-63, 91, 146, 155, 157, 161, 172 ("the perpetual attraction of the window"), 221. The last quotation, that on the five guiding principles, is from II, 226. This list itself is only partial; see, for example, "The Metamorphosis."

42. Kafka, *Diaries,* II. 197, "I awoke to find myself imprisoned in a fenced enclosure which allowed no room for more than a step in either direction." *Diaries,* II, 157.

43. See Kafka, "Fragments," *Dearest Father,* 351.

44. Kafka, *Diaries,* II, 202.

45. *Ibid.,* II, 191.

46. *Ibid.,* II, 202.

47. Kafka, "Fragments," *Dearest Father,* 297.

48. Kafka, *Diaries,* I, 27.

49. Kafka, "Reflections," *Dearest Father,* 42.

50. G. Janouch, *Conversations with Kafka,* trans. C. Rees (New York, 1953), 102.

51. Kafka, "Fragments," *Dearest Father,* 299.

52. Kafka, *Diaries,* II, 227.

53. Rousseau, *Rêveries,* 150.

54. "I shall consecrate my last days to the study of myself and to prepare in advance the account which I shall not be slow to give of myself. Let me devote myself entirely to the sweetness of speaking with my own soul, because that is the only thing of which men cannot rob me." Rousseau, *Rêveries,* 62, 66.

55. "The pleasure of going into solitude . . . overlaps that of escaping from my persecutors; and having arrived in places where I do not see any trace of men, I breathe more at my ease, as in a retreat where hatred does not pursue me." Rousseau, *Rêveries,* 151.

56. *Ibid.,* 120.

57. *Ibid.,* 145.

58. *Ibid.,* 121-22. The painful event, however, has as ready access to consciousness as any other event. Rousseau, therefore, alone and with no one to reflect with or against, was forced to deal with recurring painful memories—the abandonment of his children and other things that disturbed his conscience. Rousseau, *Rêveries,* e.g., 171-72.

One of the thoughts that intruded into Rousseau's reveries concerned a theft he had once committed. In his youth Rousseau had been employed in the house of a Comtesse de Vercellis. When that lady died, Rousseau's employment was terminated, but he did not leave the house without a conflict. He had stolen a bit of ribbon and when he was asked where he had got the ribbon, instead of confessing his crime he said that a servant girl had stolen it and given it to him. In spite of all the girl's protestations, Rousseau would not tell the truth, and the girl was sacked. Rousseau, *Confessions,* I, 74-77. Rousseau bore the guilt for this episode for the rest of his life. It was reported in his *Confessions* and it recurred as a source of turmoil in the *Rêveries.* But in examining his motivation in the *Confessions* he wrote that "never was wickedness further from my thought than in that cruel moment. . . ." And in the *Rêveries* he organized a terribly elaborate, abstract statement on the problem of lying in order to repeat that ultimately he had never been malicious, even though some of his acts were bad. All this was taken care of by the defenses and by the intellectual consequence of the defenses (the definition of morality), so that his conscience, he said, had always kept to its first integrity ("I have not the germ of a harmful passion in my heart"), and his innocence would sustain him in his last, trying days. As long as he could convince himself that there was no moral significance involved in the things he had done, there could be no psychological significance either. Rousseau, *Rêveries,* see fourth promenade, 93-113. Rousseau summed up this theme in his *Rêveries* by observing that if, despite mature reflection, we still do the wrong thing, "we shall not in justice bear the suffering because we have not the guilt." Rousseau, *Rêveries,* 86.

59. In the *Dialogues* Rousseau again emphasized his goodness as a man and the value of his system as a true and correct critique of social institutions. He pleaded for the unity of his work and for the unity of his principles and his life. At the same time, he again identified the existence of a universal conspiracy against him. In his mind the true nature of the human heart had at last been explained; he had destroyed the pretensions encouraged by society, he had provided the necessary criteria for understanding the principles of justice, and he had organized his life consistent with those principles. Rousseau had pointed the way to human harmony by showing that nature had made man good but that society corrupted him, and for all this he was persecuted by those whose selfishness could not possibly be overcome by virtue. It is in this work that one can see the extent to which Rousseau ultimately lost the battle for control over consciousness and reason. He had mobilized his remaining conscious and logical forces in the service of a paranoid delusion, and he used logic to corroborate and sustain ideas that were determined by this delusion. The *Rêveries,* which followed the *Dialogues,* was by far the greater piece of literature, and showed a greater degree of control. Still, this work, too, manifests content similar to the above.

60. Rousseau, *Confessions,* I, 316; II, 8-10, 117. See also note 58. Rousseau, of course, also continually returned to the universal plot aimed at his destruction, a plot urged forward

ceaselessly and without change or exception, "the most singular and astonishing enterprise ever carried out."

61. See Freud, "Three Essays on Sexuality," VII, 193. "Ever since Jean-Jacques Rousseau's *Confessions,* it has been well known to all educationalists that the painful stimulation of the skin of the buttocks is one of the erotogenic roots of the passive instinct of cruelty." Also, "Introductory Lectures," XV, 337-38.

62. In the *Rêveries,* Rousseau remarked that he had come to realize that to know oneself was not so easy as he had thought in the *Confessions.*

63. See Voltaire, "On the Pensées of M. Pascal," *Philosophical Letters,* trans. E. Dilworth (New York, 1961), 119-45. This is probably the best example of this process in the Enlightenment era. One can find in Pascal recognizably "Freudian" insight into internal processes. Pascal, however, refused to concede to man any ego strength at all, so that his exaggerations of internal weakness and his special pleading for Christianity gave Voltaire the excuse to dismiss him *en bloc.* For example, Pascal pointed out that man was a double, full of astonishing contradictions. Voltaire wrote that "this so-called doubleness of man is an idea as absurd as it is metaphysical." The Enlightenment did not have much tolerance for this view of man, excluding Rousseau on virtually the same grounds.

64. Actually, Diderot was capable of this kind of insight too. Among the many superb suggestions to be found in Diderot's work and in his correspondence was, for example, this part of a letter to Sophie Volland, a conceptual description of what can be considered "free association," although the emotional basis for this kind of thinking is not explicitly noted and was probably not observed: "Conversation is a peculiar thing, especially when the company is a bit mixed. Note the circumlocutions that we've made; the dreams of a delirious man are not more whimsical. However, as there is nothing incoherent either in the head of a man who dreams or in the head of a madman, everything is also controlled in conversation; but it is sometimes very difficult to reconstruct the imperceptible links which have held together so many disparate ideas. One man throws out a word which he has detached from what has preceded and followed in his head; another man does the same and then it's every man for himself. A single physical qual-

ity can lead the mind, which is interested in it, to an infinite number of diverse things. Let's take a color, yellow, for example: gold is yellow, silk is yellow, bile is yellow, hay is yellow; how many threads would this thread not respond to; madmen, the dream world, the incoherence of conversation, all require the passage from one object to another through the mediation of a quality they hold in common."

Diderot also had an idea of repression, of the problems that derive from sexual repression. It was he who quipped, "if your little savage was left to himself and to his native blindness, he would in time join the infant's reasoning to the grown man's passion—he would strangle his father and sleep with his mother." Diderot described his conversational partner, Rameau's nephew, as childlike, as now and again losing control over what was inside him, and, in the "Supplement to Bougainville's 'Voyage,' " Diderot pointed out that society made too many demands on men, and that it was impossible to find anywhere a man who could be at the same time a believer, a citizen, and a man. Freud quoted this statement of Diderot's on the savage three times: in "Introductory Lectures," part 2, XVI, 337-38; at the end of part 2 of "The Outline of Psychoanalysis," XXIII, 192, n. 2; and in "The Expert Opinion in the Halsmann Case," XXI, 251. Also see *Lettres à Sophie Volland,* ed. A. Babelon (Paris: 1930, 3 vols.), I, 155; "Rameau's Nephew," 54, 78; "Supplement to Bougainville's 'Voyage,' " 208, 234.

Diderot had an idea that "our mental state is one thing; the account we give of it, either to ourselves or to others, is another." And he complained, just as Helvétius had complained, that no one would study himself, "nobody will have the courage to keep an exact account of all the thoughts of his mind, all the impulses of his heart." But, again like Helvétius, Diderot did not mean this in the sense of man having an independent psychic structure that accounted for unique combinations unaccountable for in terms of the physical and the organic. As a function of the effects of social process on thought, Diderot was left with a physiological psychology, and the possibility of an introspective psychology was not contemplated.

This is not to deny that a psychology of the unconscious is not itself organic or reducible to organic factors. But there is a level at which it has a social and individual content that is unique. In other words, a physiological psychology can never replace or supersede an introspective psychology. Individual and cultural interaction contributes a dimension that physiological psychology cannot handle. The expectation of reducing the mind to physiochemical functions is hopeless, and misses an aspect of reality. Fantasy cannot be resolved to the organic, especially when it becomes socially available and people act in terms of it.

Diderot, like Rousseau, had two sources for the kind of insight displayed: one was the availability in the culture of certain ideas (e.g., Diderot's relationship to Sterne); the other was Diderot's own memory and fantasies. That he could have come as close as he did to introspective awareness was related to his ability to remember the past, to regret and enjoy it; this, as we saw above (Chapter 2), led him to be cautious, the least inclined to grand, systematic statements about man's nature from a political point of view—i.e., his moderation allowed him to take a more tolerant view of internal as well as external reality. Again, though, it must be pointed out that this was primarily a personal, rather than a social, experience.

65. Sometimes the notion of the unconscious appears as The Unconscious, implying, in a sense, a particular quantity. From this follows the idea of a "progressive unfolding of the unconscious," implying again that at some point the possibility for complete consciousness will exist. Total consciousness is, for various psychic and social reasons, inconceivable to us. In any case, the unconscious should be understood dynamically; some materials do come under the control of ego, but other materials are undoubtedly lost or simply remain repressed.

6:   *THE INTROSPECTIVE REVOLUTION:*
     LIMITATIONS OF INSIGHT

1. Various factors have been cited as instrumental in the organization of psychoanalytic theory. For example, it has been pointed out that Freud had many sources to draw upon in organizing his theory; notions of hypnotic suggestion, dream symbolism, mythology, innate archaic mental heritage, unconscious motivation, and even more specific notions like hysteria, paranoia, and the problem of neurosis were all dealt with in

the nineteenth century. Political circumstances have also been pointed to, as well as such an amorphous notion as the "barrenness" of bourgeois civilization, which presumably turned the focus of the individual in upon the self. Again, though, it must be emphasized that political unrest or economic deprivation has always led away from introspection toward the greater denial of internal reality. There will be exceptions, of course, but these will be personal expressions; we have already indicated that what distinguishes Freud is his acceptance in society. The attempt to reduce tension is typically aimed at the institutional dimension provoking the tension, and the existence of economic or political problems has no meaning for introspective insight. Psychoanalytic theory and introspective literature dealt with personal and familial tensions, and an analysis of origins must begin with the relevant institutional problems—family and psychic structure.

2. Literary style and content that attempted to break down the sense of rational control and to approximate unconscious thought processes and behavior appeared before Freud. The work of writers like Proust, Kafka, and Lawrence appeared at the same time as Freud's but did not depend on him. Lawrence published *Sons and Lovers* in May, 1913; this won him a reputation as a novelist with excellent insight into the implications of the oedipal conflict. But the novel was written before Lawrence had any real knowledge of Freud and before Freud is mentioned in any of his correspondence.

Of all the introspective writers of this period, Freud was most familiar with the work of his Viennese contemporary, Arthur Schnitzler. Freud was very impressed with Schnitzler's insight into unconscious processes. No one can tell the extent to which Freud eventually influenced Schnitzler—but some of the dramatist's earlier efforts (e.g., "The Green Cockatoo," "Paracelsus") could easily have been done by Schnitzler without reference to Freud, though Schnitzler knew of him and his work. Schnitzler was familiar with the problem of unconscious motivation from his own professional (medical) background. In any case, the idea content was not limited to Viennese society; rather, it appeared in all the middle-class Western societies. On Freud and Schnitzler see Herbert I. Kupper and Hilda S. Rollman-Branch, "Freud and Schnitzler—(Doppelgänger)," *Journal of the American Psychoanalytic Association,* VII (1959), 109-26.

The attempts of literary people to portray unconscious processes before Freud, or at the same time as Freud but independent of him, and to treat the general perception of the subjective nature of time, have been amply documented. See, for example, H. Meyerhoff, *Time in Literature* (Berkeley, 1955); A. A. Mendilow, *Time and the Novel* (London, 1952); Melvin Friedman, *Stream of Consciousness: A Study in Literary Method* (New Haven, 1955); Shiv K. Kumar, *Bergson and the Stream of Consciousness Novel* (London, 1962). Also see Leon Edel, *The Psychological Novel, 1900-1950* (New York, 1955); and F. J. Hoffman, *Freudianism and the Literary Mind* (Baton Rouge, 1957, 2nd ed.). On the ideas that were available for Freud to draw upon, see L. L. Whyte, *The Unconscious Before Freud* (New York, 1960); also see I. Bry and A. H. Rifkin, "Freud and the History of Ideas: Primary Sources, 1886-1910," in *Psychoanalytic Education* (New York, 1962), 6-37.

3. On the references to time in Freud's work see the editor's introduction to "The Unconscious," XIV, 187. Also see, for example, Henri Bergson, *Matter and Memory,* trans. Paul and Palmer (London, 1911); Bergson, *The World of Dreams* (New York, 1958); also see H. Meyerhoff, *Time in Literature* (Berkeley, 1955).

4. Kafka knew about psychoanalysis but he did not have much respect for its potential—rather, he exhibited an artist's distaste for the ratiocinating mind that tries to penetrate the great mysteries of the world with reason and logic. "Anyone who has no more to say about this than psychoanalysis ought not to meddle with the subject." Franz Kafka, "Fragments," in *Dearest Father, Stories and Other Writings,* 247.

5. Kafka, "Letter to His Father," (hereafter, "Letter"), in *Dearest Father, Stories and Other Writings,* trans. Kaiser and Wilkins (New York, 1954) (hereafter, *Dearest Father*). It is interesting that Kafka gave the letter to his mother to deliver to his father, interesting because it is characteristic of Kafka to approach things by indirection—to explain himself in a letter, to intellectualize the content (i.e., to make literature of it), and to give the letter to his mother instead of his father, for

whom it was intended. Kafka's mother never delivered the
letter; she gave it back to the author "probably with a few com-
forting words." Max Brod, *The Biography of Franz Kafka*,
trans. G. H. Roberts (London, 1947), 16-17.

6. Kafka, "Letter," 142-43, 148, 151, 160-61, 167-68, 177.

7. Kafka, "Letter," 182-83, 188-89, 190-91, 192.

8. "But we being what we are, marrying is barred to me
through the fact that it is precisely your most intimate domain." Kafka, "Letter," 191.

9. Kafka, "Letter," 148.

10. Kafka, "Reflections . . ." *Dearest Father*, 39. "You are
free and that is why you are lost." Kafka, "Fragments," *Dearest Father*, 224.

11. Kafka, "Letter," 177.

12. See above, pp. 159-60.

13. Kafka, derogating the therapeutic claims of psychoanalysis, wrote that "all these so-called illnesses, however sad
they may look, are facts of belief, the distressed human being's
anchorage in some maternal ground or other. . . ." Kafka also
composed his own appreciation of primary narcissism, the
oceanic experience, the omnipotent union of self with a maternal world of gratification that exists unconsciously in the life
of every individual: "Expulsion from Paradise is in its main
significance eternal: still, although expulsion from Paradise is
final, and life in this world irrevocable, the eternal nature of
the occurrence (or, temporally expressed, the eternal repetition
of the occurrence) makes it nevertheless possible that not only
could we live continuously in Paradise, but that we are continuously there in actual fact, no matter whether we know it here
or not." (Translation altered.) "Fragments," *Dearest Father*,
300; "Reflections," *Dearest Father*, 41. There is also a good
deal in Kafka concerning his ambivalence with regard to wom-
en on the level of the oedipal conflict. The above quotations
constitute Kafka's most important statements in this area.

14. Freud, *The Origins of Psychoanalysis, Letters to Wilhelm Fliess*, 206. The citation refers to a letter of May 31, 1897;
also see the letter of April 28, 1897, 194.

15. Because no one of the sons could take the father's
place (though each of them wanted to), the bitterness that had
provoked the deed began to subside, while a longing for the

father grew. When the equality of the sons could no longer be maintained (because of cultural changes), the father ideal was revived in the form of gods, and with the institution of paternal deities society became patriarchal; the social order produced godlike kings who transferred the patriarchal system to the state. The price of having deposed the father and then having wished him restored was the domination of paternal authority over the sons. The material covered here is easily and readily available in Freud, "Totem and Taboo," XIII, 141-60; also see "Moses and Monotheism," XXIII. In this connection and in connection with this chapter generally, see Roy Schafer, "The Loving and Beloved Superego," *Ps. St. Chi.,* XV (1960), 163-88; and Hans W. Loewald, "Ego and Reality," *The International Journal of Psycho-Analysis,* XXXII (1951), 10-18.

16. "In the son's eyes his father embodies every unwillingly tolerated social restraint; his father prevents him from exercising his will, from early sexual pleasure and, where there is common property in the family, from enjoying it." "Introductory Lectures," XV, 205.

17. There exists love for the father as such, but in addition, because the little boy's hostility is much greater to his father than to his mother, the paternal image is reactively more idealized. At the same time the son can recognize social as well as physical differences between father and mother; the son identifies with the figure of strength. In all these ways, according to Freud, the paternal image is established in an enduring and authoritative manner. See Schafer, "The Loving and Beloved Superego," *Ps. St. Chi.,* XV (1960).

18. Religious feelings are understood to originate in an attempt to cope with external, hostile reality. The creation of the father god is an expression of the need for help and protection from the father in order to avoid the castrating reality that the father represents. The longing for the father, the seeking of his help and protection, is a defensive compromise effected so that one can come to terms with his superior, hostile power. Loewald, "Ego and Reality," 13.

19. "The male sex seems to have taken the lead in all these moral acquisitions, and they seem to have then been transmitted to women by cross-inheritance," Freud, "The Ego and the Id," XIX, 37. Also, for quite some time Freud simply con-

sidered that the male and female solutions to the oedipal conflict were symmetrical. Freud, "The Dissolution of the Oedipal Complex," XIX, 177-79. Ultimately (in essays written in 1925 and 1931), Freud radically altered his opinion on this issue. The process in the female then turned out to be far more complicated than he originally thought—but, as noted, it was a faulty process.

20. Peter T. Cominos, "Late-Victorian Sexual Respectability and the Social System," *International Review of Social History*, VIII (1963), 18-48, 216-50, especially 245-46. It is our opinion that Cominos drew the wrong conclusions from the data. The sons were able to break connections with the father, though not without anxiety. They were not able to break with the mother, but this was as much for pre-oedipal as oedipal reasons. If the solution were dysfunctional it might take two forms rather than one, as Cominos suggested. One form is the desire to use the female in a maternal way, seeking pre-oedipal gratification. The other is the denial of any such desire. Both solutions could lead to the type of male sexual attitudes described by Cominos. See above, pp. 192-93.

21. See, for example, J. A. and Olive Banks, *Feminism and Family Planning in Victorian England* (New York, 1964), 11-12, 29-41 (on female occupations), and 58-70 (on the female as the dependent symbol of masculine success).

The relative inability of the female to challenge authority immediately brings to mind the suffragette movement. The following can be said on this issue: the values of inclusion had already been established, and female demands in this area did not constitute value change but simply a wider scope of inclusion. There was hostility in Western societies to the notion of equality of participation for females, even in terms of their ability to vote. This hostility to the right of women to vote should be seen, though, in relation to the kind of threat that female participation presented: the man could not "see" the woman as competitor without identifying her as male or as "unmother-like" (mother-like" being the apparent absence of power, the presence of love). However, more important than the question of male resistance is this: considering that the values of inclusion and representation had been institutionalized for a considerable time, why did it take the female so long to organize and press for these demands? A consistent, viable, dependent posture cannot ultimately be explained in terms of discrimination and hostility. The continuation of such super- and subordinate relationships, which are in some sense rewarding and productive, *must* depend on some form of compliance. In this connection it is interesting to speculate on what happened after women were granted the right to vote. Did they vote independently of the males, fathers and husbands? Until very recently, sociological studies indicated that women followed their husbands' choices at the polls. This pattern tended to change after World War II, but, then, important changes had already occurred in occupational opportunities also. Recent female demands for inclusion are being codified in "women's liberation" movements.

22. Freud, "Autobiographical Study," XX, 36; (note added, 1935).

23. Freud, "Family Romances," IX, 238; also, "Some Reflections on Schoolboy Psychology," XIII, 249.

24. Schafer, "Loving and Beloved Superego," *Ps. St. Chi.,* XV (1960), 163-88.

25. Freud, "Some Psychological Consequences of the Anatomical Distinction Between the Sexes," XIX, 257.

26. Schafer, "Loving and Beloved Superego," 176-77. Actually, women can build up a strict and even punitive superego, and in any individual case there can be "no foregone conclusion about superego development based on a person's biological sex." Also see Edith Jacobson, "The Self and the Object World," *Ps. St. Chi.,* IX (1954), 118.

27. Talcott Parsons and R. F. Bales, *Family, Socialization and Interaction Process* (Glencoe, Ill., 1955).

28. This does not mean that the system cannot produce pathological individuals. It can, of course, and probably the most prevalent pattern in our culture is the continued identification on the part of the boy with the mother during secondary and later phases of socialization. The "danger" in this type of arrangement for the boy in particular is to seek in the contemporary situation the gratifications of primary dependency, a condition inconsistent with our activistic cultural standards. Talcott Parsons, "Definitions of Health and Illness in the Light of American Values and Social Structure," in *Social Structure and Personality* (New York, 1964).

Nor does this mean that there cannot be a loving father

or that the children do not love him. Rather, it means that by and large it is the mother's responsibility to inculcate in the children the primary motivation for the patterns of action that the family and society require. She accomplishes this on the basis of her unique relationship to the children. The father's relationship is more external and focuses rather on supplying normative content to the basic patterns established by the mother. The father's participation is increased in the oedipal phase when he makes himself responsible for the boy's inclusion in "the life of male responsibility, social contribution, and work," for the boy's identity as male, and so on. See Tess Forrest, "The Paternal Roots of Male Character Development," *The Psychoanalytic Review*, LIV (1967), 57-58, 63-66. It was Forrest's intention to locate the father's role as far back as infancy, presumably in contradiction to the point of view stressed here. But she does not draw a distinction between patterns of action and normative contents, and it seems quite clear in the context of what she writes that the father is in effect acting in an external way.

It is also interesting that Forrest speculates on the oedipal problem in the following way: "what Freud interpreted as the boy's desire to have mother for himself, and his competition with the father, are nothing more mysterious than the child's efforts to learn from father how much of mother one can keep as a boy, how boys act with mothers, what the similarities and differences are between boys and men, how much of a man a boy must be to venture safely into the world outside, and how much of a child a boy can remain at home." This weakened view of oedipal conflict is a reflection of the changing nature of the family structure, in which the father appears less as a coercive figure and more as a family guide; i.e., Freud's perception was probably accurate for his time and society. On the influence that social change has on psychoanalytic thinking see also, for example, L. B. Boyer and P. L. Giovacchini, *Psychoanalytic Treatment of Schizophrenic and Characterological Disorders* (New York, 1967), 310-11. "Insofar as we seldom saw a patient who could be formulated in terms similar to those outlined by Freud, the question as to whether the 'classical' psychoneurotic patient existed or just how frequently one encountered such a patient had to be asked. Frequently, the course of therapy reveals that what seems to be a psychoneurosis primarily based upon an oedipal conflict masks underlying primitive pregenital problems and ego defects. One cannot come to any definite conclusions but this book raises the question as to whether psychopathology has been modified, perhaps because of cultural changes, or whether our further understanding of transference phenomena, because of insight gained from the structural theory and ego psychology, has enabled us to see aspects of psychopathology that were not previously apparent." We would say that the two are intimately connected; increased insight is a function of social change, as different problems become available. Anna Freud ("The Mutual Influences in the Development of Ego and Id," *Ps. St. Chi.*, VII, 1952, 50), has also noted that because of the changed patterns in the family it takes longer for firm, well-developed ego structures to appear. "This may account for the fact that the less well-defined and fluctuating developmental disorders are on the increase at the expense of the real infantile neurosis which was more frequently recorded and treated by the analytic workers of the past."

29. From a historical and sociological point of view it is necessary to put some tentative temporal boundaries on these social arrangements; see page 182 above.

30. It is against this qualification that Freud's typical judgments must be measured. For example, Freud wrote that "women represent the interests of the family and of sexual life. The work of civilization has become increasingly the business of men, it confronts them with ever more difficult tasks and compels them to carry out instinctual sublimations of which women are little capable." Freud, "Civilization and Its Discontents," XXI, 103. For social as well as psychological reasons, of course, the role of women with regard to the functions of autonomy and inclusion are changing and will continue to do so in the future.

Parsons has described these aspects of socialization quite effectively, although he has not stressed the distinction between males and females. On the problem of object cathexis and separation, Parsons writes: "The discontinuity (sequential cathexis of object in early socialization) derives from the fact that each phase requires . . . a specific and extensive *reorganization* of the structure of the personality as a system. The main framework of this structure . . . consists of internalized social objects systematically related to each other. The process of differentiation of these objects . . . makes it necessary to establish new system boundaries and new relations as of relative strength and of integration." Parsons and Bales, *Family, Socialization and Interaction Process*, 40-41. We have pointed out that the discontinuities of early socialization in the modern family are more complex, more disparate for the boy than for the girl. It is for this reason that the boy terminates the oedipal phase with a more clearly differentiated personality than the girl.

31. The concept of separation anxiety resulted from Freud's revision of anxiety theory (1926). Quite early Freud had pointed out that the act of birth was the first experience of anxiety, the source for and the prototype of the affect of anxiety. Subsequently, motivated by Rank's *The Trauma of Birth,* as well as new inferences that had been drawn from the structural theory, Freud observed that birth itself was not decisive in the problem of anxiety, that ultimately the sense of danger is displaced from the economic situation (an unmanageable influx of stimuli) to the conditions that determine danger situations, i.e., the loss of object (and, later, the loss of the object's love). Anxiety, therefore, is related to the nonsatisfaction of a growing tension brought on by need, against which the child is helpless. This is analogous to the birth situation and repeats that situation of danger. But what the child carries with it from birth is the *way* of experiencing danger. When the infant learns from experience that an external perceptible object can put an end to the dangerous situation, the transition is made—the absence of the mother becomes the danger (i.e., separation). This process represents a transition from the automatic, involuntary appearance of anxiety to the intentional reproduction of anxiety as a signal of danger. On the basis of this transition Freud elaborated a scheme of phase-appropriate anxiety—in which each period of the individual's life has its own determinant of anxiety. "Thus the danger of psychical helplessness is appropriate to the period of life when the ego is immature; the danger of the loss of object, to early childhood when he is dependent on others; the danger of castration to the phallic phase; and the fear of his superego to the latency period." Freud, "Inhibitions, Symp-

toms and Anxiety," XX, 142; also see editor's note, 82. In addition see John Bowlby, "Separation Anxiety: A Critical Review of the Literature," *Journal of Child Psychology and Psychiatry*, I (1961), 251-69; "Grief and Mourning in Infancy and Early Childhood," *Ps. St. Chi.*, XV (1960), 9-52. On the problem of separation in the views of others (Klein, Winnicott, Balint) and for further comments on Bowlby, see W. G. Joffe and Joseph Sandler, "Notes on Pain, Depression and Individuation," *Ps. St. Chi.*, XX (1965), 400-414.

32. On Freud's appreciation of the mother see the following: "Three Essays . . ." VII, 222; "Narcissism," XIV, 87-88; "New Introductory Lectures," XXII, 122; " 'Civilized' Sexual Morality," IX; "Female Sexuality," XXI, 234; "Introductory Lectures," part 1, XV, 314; "Future of an Illusion," XXI, 24; "The Interpretation of Dreams" (The Dream of the Three Fates), IV, 204-8. Note Freud's use of Ferenczi's idea that the high degree of narcissistic value placed on the penis stems from the fact that this organ is the guarantee that the owner can be reunited to his mother. "Inhibitions . . ." XX, 139. "New Introductory Lectures," XXII, 87. Also see the very late "Outline of Psychoanalysis," XXIII, 188. "By her care of the child's body she becomes its first seducer. In these two relations lie the roots of a mother's importance, unique, without parallel, established unalterably for a whole lifetime. . . ."

The pre-oedipal mother came permanently into the literature in 1931 (Freud was then seventy-five), and, at that, Freud's new insight came as a surprise, "like the discovery, in another field, of the Minoan-Mycenean civilization behind the civilization of Greece." "Female Sexuality," XXI, especially 226-27. Freud understood that the lack of some relatively sophisticated formulation for the pre-oedipal period presented problems for the theory. But, as he explained, everything relating to this first attachment to the mother was so difficult to grasp in analysis that it was as if it had succumbed to an inexorable repression; this period, again, was too difficult for him to investigate. Freud, "Female Sexuality," XXI, 226.

33. Passages referred to in Freud, "Civilization . . ." XXI, chap I. On this interpretation of resistance see, for example, Loewald, "Ego and Reality," *The International Journal of Psycho-Analysis*, XXXII (1951), 13.

34. See, for example, John Bowlby, "Grief and Mourning in Infancy and Early Childhood," 14, 43: "There was little understanding of the long phase during which the child is intensely attached to his mother." Also Anna Freud, "Psychoanalysis and Education," *Ps. St. Chi.,* IX (1954), 56: "The idea that infants need a continuous and emotionally satisfying relationship to one person has been explicit in the literature for only a short time." Of course, Melanie Klein had an idea of the central position of the mother quite early, and rather earlier than was true generally for psychoanalytic writers at large. However, in terms of the frame of reference established here, we would conclude that Klein's insight was idiosyncratic and could not have entered into the mainstream of psychoanalytic thinking at that point. Indeed, David Rapaport has written that "The 'theory' of object relations evolved by Melanie Klein and her followers is not an ego psychology but an id mythology." (In Rapaport's introduction to Erikson's "Identity and the Life Cycle," *Psychological Issues,* vol. 1, no. 1, monograph 1, 11, note 4.) More recently, however, many of Klein's insights and suggestions have been integrated into psychoanalytic theory. This is in line with the recognition of other writers who had been excluded from consideration for a time, e.g., Jung and Adler. There is a very interesting note on Jung in Erikson's "Identity and the Life Cycle," 31, note 7.

35. Note the bibliography in John Bowlby's *Maternal Care and Mental Health* (Geneva, 1951). Of 158 multilingual items listed, five are dated from the period 1924-29, 22 from 1930-39, and 131 from 1940. Also see Sylvia Brody, *Patterns of Mothering* (New York, 1956), chap. III; and Michael Balint, "Changing Therapeutic Aims and Techniques in Psychoanalysis," *The Psychoanalytic Yearbook* (New York, 1951), VII, 179-80.

36. ". . . the early mothering experience is the most important single relationship in the child's life." Peter L. Giovacchini, "The Submerged Ego," *Journal of the American Academy of Child Psychiatry,* III (1964), 439.

37. Roy Schafer's introduction to W. Lederer's "Dragons, Delinquents, and Destiny," *Psychological Issues* (New York, 1964), vol. IV, no. 3, monograph 15, 1.

38. Perhaps this one interesting conclusion from the recent literature will reinforce the point: "In view of the immature ego

organization in the pre-oedipal phase and . . . [the possibility] of violent narcissistic injury . . . it seems to me that the influence of the pre-oedipal development on the ego structure (which, in the oedipal phase can be affected again by the injury associated with the castration fear) is of very great importance (possibly decisive) for the ultimate development of ego and personality." P. J. van der Leeuw, "The Pre-oedipal Phase of the Male," *Ps. St. Chi.,* XIII (1958), 371. Also, Jeanne Lampl -de Groot, "Preoedipal Phase in the Development of the Male Child," *Ps. St. Chi.,* II (1946), 75-83. Freud originally pointed out (in "Female Sexuality," XXI) that the pre-oedipal phase had far greater importance for women than it could possibly have for men. However, see, for example, the literature on the relationship of the pre-oedipal mother to learning and learning difficulties: R. R. Greenson, "The Mother Tongue and the Mother," *The International Journal of Psycho-Analysis,* XXXI (1950), parts 1 and 2, 18-23; Vivian Jarvis, "Clinical Observations on the Visual Problem in Reading Disability," *Ps. St. Chi.,* XIII (1958), 451-70; Emma and Robert Plank, "Emotional Components in Arithmetical Learning as seen through Autobiographies," *Ps. St. Chi.,* IX (1954), 274-93; John C. Coolidge, *et al.,* "Patterns of Aggression in School Phobia," *Ps. St. Chi.,* XVII (1962), 319-33. Also note the following: "The tendency of psychoanalytic investigators of Judaism and Christianity has been to stress the phallic and paternal elements even when their clinical and therapeutic work emphasized the importance of earlier stages." Richard L. Rubenstein, "The Significance of Castration Anxiety in Rabbinic Mythology," *The Psychoanalytic Review,* L (1963), 288-312. Loewald has written the following: "In psychoanalytic theoretical constructions concerning ego development and structure, the positive libidinal relationship to the mother and the hostile submissive relationship to the father had overshadowed, if not led to a neglect of, the role of the dread of the womb and of the primary positive identification with the father, in the constitution of the ego. The concept of reality had been dominated by the emphasis on the paternal castration threat, notwithstanding the introduction of the concept of primary narcissism and the investigation of early ego development." Loewald, "Ego and Reality," 17. Also see, e.g., René A. Spitz, "Autoerotism Re-examined," *Ps. St. Chi.,* XVII (1962), 313.

39. Balint, "Changing Therapeutic Aims . . . ," 179-80. See David Rapaport's introduction to Erikson's "Identity and the Life Cycle," *Psychological Issues* (New York, 1959), vol. I, no. 1, monograph 1, 11. "Psychoanalysis established the first conception of reality relations in terms of secondary process and in relation to danger situations, but did not generalize it into a concept of adaptation until 1937. Thus the theory of object relations remained outside the scope of psychoanalytic ego psychology and the psychosocial implications of reality and object relations remained unexplained theoretically." See also Erikson's comments in "Identity and the Life Cycle," 39. "Psychoanalysis came to emphasize the individual and regressive rather than the collective-supportive aspects" of adaptation and adjustment. It was therefore concerned "with only half the story." "For if a residue of infantile narcissism is to survive, the maternal environment must create and sustain it with a love which assures the child that it is good to be alive in the particular social coordinates in which he happens to find himself. . . . Widespread severe impoverishment of infantile narcissism (and thus of the basis of a strong ego) is lastly to be considered a breakdown of that collective synthesis which gives every newborn baby and his motherly surroundings a superindividual status as a trust of the community." John Bowlby has suggested in addition that Freud paid inadequate attention to the child's attachment to the mother because so many of his patients had been brought up by nannies. The only thing we can infer from this is that the absence of the mother did not lead to a sense of deprivation; if it had, this would have resulted in the expression of hostility. See Bowlby's review article, "Separation Anxiety. . . ." It should also be noted that Freud's overall paternal view of the world has been defended on theoretical grounds, particularly in terms of the nature of superego formation, i.e., Freud's view was not "a simple consequence of incomplete theoretical exposition, neglect of the psyche of women, or paternalistic bias." Schafer, "Loving and Beloved Superego," 176-78.

40. See Freud, "Little Hans," X, 140; "Civilization and Its Discontents," XXI, 120. "I remember my own defensive attitude when the idea of an instinct of destruction first emerged in psychoanalytic literature, and how long it took before I became

receptive to it." This statement alludes to the appearance of this hypothesis in Adler's work. See editor's introduction to "Civilization . . . ," XXI, 61-62; and "New Introductory Lectures," XXII, 103-4; Hartmann, Kris, and Loewenstein, "Notes on the Theory of Aggression," *Ps. St. Chi.,* III-IV (1949), 9.

41. Ernest Jones, *The Life and Work of Sigmund Freud* (New York, 1953, 3 vols.), I, 323. Freud confessed his error to Fliess *(The Origins of Psychoanalysis,* letter of September 21, 1897); he indicated it publicly in his paper, "Sexuality and the Neuroses," VII, 274-75. Also note that in the first two editions of "The Interpretation of Dreams" (1900, 1909), there was a passage in which it was assumed that children have no sexual desires. Jung called Freud's attention to it and Freud removed it from the third edition. Freud, "The Interpretation of Dreams," IV, 130; Jones, *The Life and Work of Sigmund Freud,* II, 285.

42. Freud, *The Origins of Psychoanalysis,* 227, letter of October 31, 1897.

43. On the personal level the reason for this insistence is reflected in Freud's prejudice that of all the possible human relationships the one between mother and son is the most stable, the one in which nothing can go wrong. "A mother is brought unlimited satisfaction by her relation to a son; this is altogether the most perfect, the most free from ambivalence of all human relationships," Freud, "New Introductory Lectures," XXII, 133; also see more or less the same in "Group Psychology and the Analysis of the Ego," XVIII, 101n; "Introductory Lectures," XV, 206; "Civilization and Its Discontents," XXI, 113.

44. Note, for example, the conclusions of a recent study on Rabbinic mythology: this work indicates that incorporation, rather than castration, occurs as the most feared punishment inflicted by God. "The traditions reflect fear of the preoedipal mother, rather than the father. This in turn calls into question the so-called dichotomy between matriarchal and patriarchal religions as well as the assertion, repeated to the point of tedium, that Rabbinic Judaism reflects fear of a tyrannical, castrating father. . . . Submission to the Father-God may well reflect a defense against a barely hidden greater fear of the Mother Goddesses." Rubenstein, "Castration Anxiety," 304-5. Compare Freud's opinion in XVII, 87: "In man's prehistory it

was unquestionably the father who practised castration as a punishment and who later softened it down to circumcision." See also Jung, "Symbols of Transformation," in "The Collected Works (New York, 1956, 7 vols.), V, 182, 213, 223-24, 236 (especially here), 251, 261, 263, 271, 297, 306, 312, 321, 329. Also see in Freud, "The Taboo of Virginity," X, 199; "A Seventeenth Century Demonological Neurosis," XIX, 104; "The Theme of the Three Caskets," XII, 301; and the "Dream of the Three Fates," in "The Interpretation of Dreams," IV, 204-8.

Another recent contribution takes the position that the great cultural battle occurs between the primordial forces of nature represented by the mother on the one hand, and the civilizing powers represented by the son, *in the service of the father,* in the father's business, on the other hand. According to this view Freud failed to recognize that the hero is one who slew his mother and not one who overcame his father. Sidney Halpern, "The Mother Killer," *Psychoanalytic Review,* LII, (1965), 215-18. Compare again with Freud's view in "Moses and Monotheism," XXIII, 12. Moreover, similar points of view have been elaborated for art, scientific work, and so on. It has been argued that the need and the ability to create come from factors of development occurring long before the oedipal stage. "Creativity is based on pre-oedipal levels and deals with the original destruction of objects and their recreation." Martin Grotjahn, *Beyond Laughter* (New York, 1966), 129; Edith Jacobson, "The Development of the Wish for a Child in Boys," *Ps. St. Chi.,* V (1950), 139-52; and van der Leeuw, "The Preoedipal Phase of the Male," *Ps. St. Chi.,* XIII (1958), 352-53.

45. There are a number of critiques of Freud taken from an anthropological or sociological point of view that tend to deny the central nature of oedipal conflict. However, there is one critique in particular that needs to be cited here: Anne Parsons, "Is the Oedipus Complex Universal? The Jones-Malinowski Debate Revisited and a South Italian 'Nuclear Complex'," *The Psychoanalytic Study of Society,* III (1964), 278-328. In this essay Parsons has dealt with the personal factors in Freud's discoveries (320), Freud's patriarchal bias (321), the relationship of psychoanalytic theory to American society and the changing nature of the family (322), although not always quite in the

terms employed here. But in particular she has indicated that although the oedipal conflict exists and is universal, it is not necessarily central to any particular culture at any given time, but rather the features of the complex vary with the features of the family and society it is found in. Thus, in general it should be said that there are "nuclear complexes" that vary with time, place, and social circumstances (310-12). This is the point of view employed here.

46. If we focus on the modern family, we can note four phases and four objects of significance in the child's development. The phases are (in temporal order) oral-dependency, love-dependency, oedipal, and latency. The object relationships involved in the first three phases (we need not consider latency here) are as follows: in the oral-dependency phase, the child and mother as unit (the early narcissistic phase at which point the child is incapable of making a subject-object dichotomy); in the love-dependency phase, the child and mother as separate but still affectually bound and bound also by particular expectations (i.e., the child can now make subject-object distinctions but is tied to the maternal figure or the two are tied to each other by various psychological and social mechanisms); and, in the oedipal phase, child-mother, child-father, and child-parents. The crucial difference between this modern family pattern and the pre-modern one is in the (second) love-dependency phase—i.e., the pre-modern father and the parents (as unit) entered the child's object world at this point, much earlier in the child's development than was to be the case in the modern family. And from the point of view of the pre-modern child, it was the parents and the father, as well as the mother, who could and would satisfy needs during this phase. This structure is in part based on the relations described by Parsons and Bales in *Family, Socialization and Interaction Process.* In pre-modern families, then, there was in this sense a "maternal" father, internalized at the most primary levels.

Perhaps Kafka's story "The Verdict" should be examined from this point of view. Georg's solution to the conflict can be interpreted in more oedipal terms, i.e., in terms of a negative, passive, masochistic, dependent, homosexual solution, with a good deal of unconscious guilt. The question is, though, can one derive such compliance, compliance to the point of self-destruction, from such a solution? It is interesting that the whole sense of being empty, no good, completely without confidence in one's ability to deal with the environment, as manifested by Georg, is indicative of identification with the father at more primary levels.

47. Smelser, *Social Change*.

48. It should be pointed out that socialization was so intensive in the family also because the father was not connected to extrafamilial sources of economic and political authority. In the pre-modern family, therefore, autonomous activity would have violated simultaneously status, affectual, integrative, and evaluative relations. The realignment of authority has come to mean that the son can both withdraw from the family and surpass the father; indeed, the son is *expected* to surpass the father. There are many examples of this change, but one in particular is interesting. In 1943, Margaret Ribble published a book entitled *The Rights of Infants;* the book went through eight printings between 1943 and 1947. The first thing that must be pointed to is the title itself—in what kind of society can infants be conceived as having *rights* irrespective of the status, occupation, or family background of the parents? Further, in a work of some 120 pages the author devoted two pages to the father. Ribble did write: "In a woman's greatest creative venture, the bringing into the world of new human beings and guiding them psychologically through infancy, *her husband is the power behind the throne,* and the success of her undertaking depends upon the constancy of that power." (Ribble, 102, emphasis added.) However, this should be taken to mean that the father has power *external* to the family, in his connections to the economic order. Psychologically the mother has the power and the father is no longer so integrated into the child's affective life.

49. Freud, "A Disturbance of Memory on the Acropolis," XXII, 247.

50. The retreat to passive dependency has been recognized as one of the most important forms of reaction to the demands for autonomy and activistic behavior (see, for example, the comments in note 28 above). However, there has been typically less emphasis in the sociological literature on the so-called compulsive masculine response to these demands. This has been the case for two reasons: much of the compulsive's masculine

response has gone relatively unnoticed in the activistic context of our culture; when this response has been observed it has been explained solely in terms of reactions to maternal dependency and fears of latent homosexuality. The contribution to stress of demands for autonomy and activism rarely enters the picture. See for example, Talcott Parsons, "Age and Sex in the Social Structure of the United States," *American Sociological Review,* V (1942), 604-16; John I. Kitsuse and David C. Dietrick, "Delinquent Boys: A Critique," *American Sociological Review,* XXIV (1959), 208-15.

51. In the traditional family and society the child may have entered into adult role obligations chronologically earlier than the child in modern society. For example, the boy in his early teens may have been expected to work in the factory or on the farm, or he may have married while still relatively young. These possibilities raise two sociological problems for the ideas presented here. One concerns fulfillment of age-graded role obligations, whereas the other concerns the psychological and sociological authority structure related to kinship and family in traditional society. With regard to the first problem, it would appear, from a behavioral standpoint, that children in traditional families and societies entered what is presently considered to be the adult world at an earlier stage in life than children in the contemporary world do. However, with regard to the second and more important issue, that of authority structure, children in traditional societies remained children until they established independent places of work and residence, and even then their status was perhaps not fixed until the death of the parents. It should also be pointed out that the process of differentiation continues in the family and is leading to other forms of functional and dysfunctional behavior. For this reason, again, it is not possible to stress oedipal conflict to the extent that Freud insisted upon. In fact, in the United States, the most pluralized of industrial societies, the principle that legitimates the distribution of influence in the family seems to be taken on a rather collegial form, among the males but to an increasing degree among the females too. This has implications for the ability of the female to win support for her desires to participate in the family and in political and occupational orders outside the family.

52. Loewald, "Ego and Reality," *The International Journal of Psycho-Analysis*, XXXII (1951), *passim*.

53. It is obvious that there cannot be absolutely equal inclusion in the family decision-making process for all members regardless of age (which is achieved in politics in the sense of one man, one vote). For various reasons the parents must have the final say. Nevertheless, it is true that the children have been included in decision-making and they influence decisions to a remarkable degree—far more so than at any other time in the history of the world. It is on this basis, keeping in mind the distinction between power and influence, that the analogy between family and political structure has been drawn.

The sociological processes of differentiation, inclusion, value generalization, and up-grading (described by Parsons in his *Societies*) were involved in these family changes. We have described the processes of differentiation, inclusion, and value generalization but we have not stressed the process of up-grading, involved, for example, in the inclusion of the children but also in an interesting way in the inclusion of mothers/wives in familial decision-making. There is an excellent discussion of the latter in the Banks's work *(Feminism and Family Planning in Victorian England)*. In their attempt to explain family planning and the decline in family size in the late Victorian era, the Banks's emphasized by way of explanation the inclusion of the wife in the family authority structure, rather than the influence of the contemporary feminist ideologies: "family planning now became possible because men found it easier to talk about such matters with their wives, having already become accustomed to a greater measure of joint discussion on other issues." But the Banks's are at a loss as to what the more general factors involved in these changes were. However, they write that "the growing participation of the middle-class wife in decisions of this kind, could only have come about in consequence of a change in attitude on the part of her husband . . . [and this] could have been *produced by events far removed from the activities of the feminists.*" (127-28, emphasis added).

We have already indicated what kind of external events would account for such changes in the structure of the family. But we also suggest that structural changes took place internal to the family and were particularly important in the up-grading of the authority of mother/wife and her involvement in the decision-making processes. The specialization of functions, that is, the father's involvement primarily outside the house, left the mother as the only "older" family member in the house. This led to the up-grading of her everyday "managerial" functions—e.g., the rearing of the children, marketing, household budgeting, the direction of maids and servants where applicable, and so on. This enhanced her authority and control over the household and it is not unlikely that the husband had to compromise with his wife for these reasons. The result was a joint decision-making process as an institutionalized feature of middle-class homes. This accommodation within the family to the authority of females should have had an effect on family planning and on the decline of family size. Some of this general process is implied by Smelser in his *Social Change,* and in his more recent *Essays in Sociological Explanation* (Englewood Cliffs, N.J., 1968), 76-91.

54. The same is generally true for behavior in the economic marketplace. Because the technical–industrial system aims to achieve more rational control over means and ends, every father's occupational role is ideally or logically threatened by every son. However, the possibility for conflict and guilt is reduced by the abstract criteria for selection, recruitment, and retirement, as well as by social, ethical, and moral values that at least contemporarily prohibit the total rationalization of the economic processes.

55. In addition, though affectual ties remained the primary binding force for members of the family, two changes occurred that allow for a further distinction between traditional and modern families. First, there developed a quantitative (if not a qualitative) difference in the expression of affect between the family unit (father, mother, children), and those outside the unit (grandparents, different relatives, and so on). Second, the democratization legitimated a broader exchange of affect among different members of the family, and this supplanted a more exclusive parental domination over emotional expression. It was as a result of these changes also that each member gained a degree of influence and authority in the family regardless of age.

56. It is interesting that this permissiveness has typically

been justified by reference to psychoanalytic theory and therapy
—as if Freud ever counseled the abandonment of standards or
of the prerogatives of paternal authority. Permissive behavior
is legitimated on the grounds that the repression or inhibition
of impulses will damage the natural ability of the individual
to perform. It is difficult to understand the origin and continued reference to this rationalization unless it is assumed to
serve the purpose we have indicated. Of course, the question
of varying resolutions to conflict in different institutional dimensions, as well as the question of permissiveness in the family, have further vital empirical and theoretical significance, but
this cannot be pursued here. See Wolfgang Lederer, "Dragons,
Delinquents, and Destiny," *Psychological Issues*, vol. IV, no. 3,
monograph 15. Also see Christine Olden, "Notes on Child
Rearing in America," *Ps. St. Chi.*, VII (1952); and Herbert Marcuse, *Eros and Civilization* (New York, 1955), 88-89.

7: UNIVERSAL REACTIONS TO MODERNIZATION

1. This is not the only light in which these events can be
viewed. Herbert Marcuse, for example, has interpreted these
revolutionary actions as the revolts of sons against fathers, with
a consequent restructuring of patriarchial domination. This
view, however, is based on the perception of some ultimate
freedom, on the possibility of a society "without the father—
that is, without suppression and domination." The argument
rests on inferences that can be drawn from Freud (though it is
unlikely he would have drawn them), and on intuition, i.e., the
immortal wish that man may escape conflict, aggression, and
anxiety. This view is ahistorical and asociological; as will be
observed below, there is at present no objective basis for such
a conclusion. The level of control that is implied in such a
resolution of the human condition is beyond anything that one
can imagine being derived from social processes as they now
exist. To some extent the problem lies in Marcuse's view that
society is unnecessarily and dangerously repressive and punitive, and that a qualitatively different society can be organized.
All that can be said on this score is that if society is measured
against these particular ideal goals, then all present actions are
failed actions. But if contemporary society is viewed with

reference to the past, then it is possible to say that man has achieved a measure of control over internal and external processes, and perhaps that is all he can achieve. See Marcuse's *Eros and Civilization* (New York, 1962), 60-65, especially, for our purposes, the materials quoted from Rank's *The Trauma of Birth*. Norman O. Brown has also addressed himself to this issue, in his own terms, in *Life Against Death*, and *Love's Body* (New York, 1966). Also see Erich Fromm, *Escape From Freedom* (New York, 1964), 101.

2. Max Weber, *The Protestant Ethic and the Spirit of Capitalism*, trans., Talcott Parsons (New York, 1958). (Hereafter, *The Protestant Ethic.*) For Weber, what had to change (in order to account for the economic style, or "ethic," that he described) was not "religion" as such, but the values (the morality) undergirding the religious and economic life. That the change in religion as such is not determinative for behavior on other institutional levels is identified by the many areas that were affected by the Protestant Reformation where such capitalist relations as Weber described did not develop. The distinction that must be made is this: the economic changes did not occur where Protestantism remained limited to the religious sphere, i.e., where its dictates remained directed only to religious practices (e.g., freedom personally to read the Bible in a native tongue and interpret it for oneself). Where the values became secularized and generalized and thereby became normative directions for everyday activity (e.g., man is free to make his own decisions and has the right to do so without reference to any superior external authority, priest or king), economic and other kinds of institutional changes could take place. The transition from the religious sphere to other areas, and from the cultural to the social, need not have occurred at all, nor did it have to occur at any given pace, or in all areas. However, it must be emphasized that the transition from the religious to the secular depended on the conscious and unconscious relationships to authority as described here, and not on the ideas. Neither the religious changes themselves nor the ideas associated with them are determinative for change in the economic sphere, or any other one.

3. Weber, *The Protestant Ethic.* The quotation is from 119. The various aspects of behavior can be found in Chapter

IV. On the effects of these mandates after the religious commitment waned, see 72, 176, 180.

4. Weber, *The Protestant Ethic,* 171.

5. Weber also distinguished pre-modern from modern social structures. This is relevant because the kind of structural differentiation he described was articulated with personality orientations and constituted the institutional framework within which personal autonomy and rational calculation could be pursued.

6. Weber, *The Protestant Ethic,* 51-52, 55.

7. Weber, *The Protestant Ethic,* 54. One's duty in a calling "is what is most characteristic of the social ethic of capitalist culture, and is in a sense the fundamental basis of it."

8. Weber, *The Protestant Ethic.* The quotations are from 167 and 156. See Chapter V.

9. See Benjamin Franklin, *The Autobiography and Other Writings,* ed. L. J. Lemisch (New York, 1961), especially 185-97. The quotations are from 195-96.

10. See C. B. Macpherson, *The Political Theory of Possessive Individualism* (London, 1962), especially 38-61.

11. Michael Walzer, in *The Revolution of the Saints* (Cambridge, Mass., 1965), has addressed himself to the problem of reactions to the withdrawal from traditional societies and structures and the relationship of ascetic mandates to radical revolutionary activity. On the basis of his analysis of Puritan endeavor and aspiration Walzer has elaborated a model of radical political behavior in terms of the punitive, unconscious superego reactions to withdrawals from traditional values. Walzer assumes that the kind of social unrest that produces the behavioral mandates in this punitive form finds stabilization in political activity, which is the vehicle both for the institution of a new order and for the maintenance of control over the hostile environment in the interim period. He seems to suggest that such value change cannot be accomplished on the basis of controlled moderate activity, that it can follow only upon radical disruptions of the past. This is not the case, however, and the problem is more complex than is indicated in Walzer's work. Walzer also discussed the Weber thesis, and although he disagreed with Weber he did not himself suggest the source for the characteristic normative stan-

dards that appeared also in the economic sphere of activity. (On this see, e.g., R. Bendix, *Work and Authority in Industry,* [New York, 1963], especially 99-116 on the formulation of an entrepreneurial ideology, and the references to Samuel Smiles on 109 and 111.) Walzer made no references in this connection to subsequent developments in the family either. See his concluding discussion, 300-20.

12. *From Max Weber: Essays in Sociology,* eds. and trans. H. H. Gerth and C. Wright Mills (New York, 1958), 343-50.

13. Talcott Parsons and R. F. Bales, *Family, Socialization and Interaction Process,* 154.

14. See Peter T. Cominos, "Late-Victorian Sexual Respectability and the Social System," *International Review of Social History,* VIII (1963), *passim.*

15. Ivan Goncharov, *Oblomov,* trans. N. Duddington (New York, 1960).

16. N. A. Dobroliubov, "What is Oblomovshchina?" in *Selected Philosophical Essays* (Moscow, 1956), 182. (Hereafter, *Oblomovshchina.*)

17. Dobroliubov, *Oblomovshchina,* 187-88, 185. Dobroliubov's emphasis.

18. Dobroliubov, *Oblomovshchina,* 189, 194, 197, 201. The quotation may be found in Goncharov, *Oblomov,* 118. Goncharov's view of this society is a quite maternal one, beginning with the preoccupation with food (see 107). Also, Goncharov described Oblomov's conception of his professional role in these terms—i.e., Oblomov's view was emotional and familial rather than abstract and bureaucratic. Oblomov "imagined that the officials in the same department were one friendly, closely knit family, unceasingly striving for one another's peace and pleasure . . ." (53).

19. Dobroliubov, *Oblomovshchina,* 182-84.

20. See N. Leites, *A Study of Bolshevism* (Glencoe, Ill., 1953), 223. In general, Leites also contrasts passive-dependent attitudes with competitive-autonomous attitudes and with the paranoid symptoms that follow from unresolved guilt accruing from the latter position. Leites's work provides a useful base for a quick survey of the points made here, since it is psychoanalytically oriented. Also note, incidentally, this reported comment of Lenin's: "I'd like to take not just anyone, but even

many of our party comrades, lock them in a room and force them to read *Oblomov*. Then: Have you read it? Good, well do it again. And when they beseech, we can't go on any more, the interrogation would start. Have you understood the essence of *oblomovism*? Have you realized that it's present in you, too? Have you sternly resolved to rid yourself of this disease?" In Peter Reddaway, "Literature, the Arts and the Personality of Lenin," *Lenin: the Man, the Theorist, the Leader,* eds. Leonard Schapiro and Peter Reddaway (New York, 1967), 47, 52. On page 62 of this text, Gorky is quoted as having described Lenin to H. G. Wells as a "puritan." Again, see Leites, *A Study of Bolshevism,* 270. Lenin said it would finally be necessary to make a man of Oblomov.

21. Goncharov, *Oblomov,* 162-65.

22. N. G. Chernyshevskii, *What Is to Be Done?* trans. Benjamin Tucker (New York, 1961). The novel is subtitled "Tales of New People," and the "new man" whom Chernyshevskii had created and who he hoped would come to dominate Russian life was characterized by "tact, coolness, activity, all well balanced, the realization of common sense in action." This man would act only "for mankind in general"; i.e., what he did would be on the basis of principle rather than passion, "from conviction and not from personal desire." The ethic is here intact, but the emphasis is on work, especially. "Now, the principle element of life is labor," Chernyshevskii wrote, "and consequently the principal element of reality is labor, and the characteristic by which it can be most surely recognized is activity." See pages 174, 229, 145.

One of the principal themes of Chernyshevskii's novel, in fact, is the usefulness and practicality of rational, systematic economic endeavor. Vladimir Nabokov has already pointed out how incomparably bourgeois these radicals were, given their interpretation of social democracy—bourgeois, that is, in the sense that all the imperatives that typically identify middle-class, capitalist endeavor are repeated here to the letter. The desire to rationalize time, the disposition to see harmfulness in idleness and luxury, or in allowing emotion and sentiment to interfere with the objective analysis of events, the scorn for any sign of weakness, the rigid commitment to duty and self-discipline—all are vital elements comprising the "new man."

For example, one of Chernyshevskii's characters founded a cooperative workshop. "The founders were directly interested in the success of the business, and naturally it went on very well. The shop never lost customers. . . . They soon had more orders than the working girls originally employed could execute, and the force went on steadily growing. . . . One of the first measures of the collective administration was a decision that Vera Pavlovna [the organizer of the shop] no more than the others should work without reward. . . . The business was already so large that Vera Pavlovna could not do all the cutting; they gave her another cutter to aid her. Both received the same wages, and Vera Pavlovna succeeded at last in inducing the society to receive into its treasury the sum of the profits it had obliged her to accept, first deducting that to which she was entitled as a cutter. They used this money to open a bank." (156-57.)

Another of Chernyshevskii's characters, a thoroughly punitive individual fiercely determined to keep control—although obviously admired by those interested—was Rakhmetov, "the rigorist." Rakhmetov would say, "I have no right to spend money on a whim which I need not gratify," and he admonished himself and others for the useless expenditure of time. His only vice was the enjoyment of good cigars which he called an "abominable weakness." Rakhmetov slept on a bed of nails to test his endurance: "A trial. It was necessary to make it. Improbable, certainly . . . but it was necessary to make it. I know now what I can do." Rakhmetov scolded Vera Pavlovna, when she wanted to leave her work in the shop, on the grounds of duty and the need to invest in impersonal social objectives. "You risked an institution, which more or less aptly served as an important affirmation of their practicability. . . . You submitted this institution to the risk of changing from a proof of its practicability into evidence of the impracticability and absurdity of your convictions, into a refutation of your ideas which were so beneficial to mankind." And Vera Pavlovna responded by confessing that her actions had been based on sentiment, not reason: "Yes, I should not have had this feeling. But I did not invite it; on the contrary, I tried to suppress it." (40, 229, 230, 237, 250.) Also note the great effect Chernyshevskii's novel had on those who followed in the radical movement. See Franco Venturi, *Roots of Revolution* (London, 1960), 351; and Leopold H. Haimson, *The Russian Marxists and the Origins of Bolshevism* (Cambridge, 1955), 97-102, on Chernyshevskii's influence on Lenin's attitudes.

23. See, for example, V. C. Nahirny, "Some Observations on Ideological Groups," *American Journal of Sociology*, LXVII (1962), 397-405. Vera Figner noted that members of the *Zemyla i Volya* (Land and Freedom) group were expected to forget "all ties of kinship and all personal sympathies, love and friendship. . . ." She also noted that the least disciplined and least integrated of the group tended to give way to spontaneous behavior. Also note Nechaev's statement that the nature of a true revolutionary "excludes all romanticism, all sensibility, all enthusiasm, and all spontaneity; it excludes even personal vengeance. . . . Revolutionary passion becomes for him [the revolutionary] an unceasing habit and allies itself with cold calculation." See Leites, *A Study of Bolshevism*, 187.

24. Such a brief summary statement raises problems. The explicit reference to Lenin should not be taken to imply that more moderate elements, Marxist or otherwise, were not committed to essential aspects of the code of conduct. Lenin was not the only one to insist upon discipline, emotional constraint, systematic effort, and so on. His approach, however, does have the virtue of clarity. Further, it must be noted that Lenin was never able to bring the personality mandates under ego control, and they therefore remained harsh and punitive—i.e., regressive, in the sense described in chapter 1 and in the present chapter. Finally, it should be noted that in this context "spontaneity" was susceptible of several definitions: it could mean unplanned, isolated, individual acts based on an explicit emotional content; or, mass acts that had no broader view, organizationally or ideologically, than the immediate event; or, mass acts that, from a Marxist point of view, had a too-limited and shortsighted content. More moderate Marxists were willing to accept this last kind of "spontaneous" activity on the assumption that consciousness would develop out of continued, protracted struggle. Lenin, however, rejected all three possibilities.

25. Haimson, *The Russian Marxists and the Origins of Bolshevism*, 76-77, 83, 119, 133-35, 138, 192. Leites, *A Study of Bolshevism*, 186-268. Walzer, in *The Revolution of the Saints*,

also quotes from Lenin in this regard, 313-14. Lenin's insight into the problem of passivity is further reflected in this appraisal of terror: "individual acts of terrorism . . . create only a short-lived sensation, and lead in the long run to an apathy, and the passive awaiting of yet another 'sensation.'" Quoted in Adam Ulam, *The Bolsheviks* (New York, 1965), 13.

26. See chap. 1, above.

27. See, for example, Alasdair MacIntyre, *Secularization and Moral Change* (London, 1967), 45, 49, 51. "It is for fewer and fewer people in England the case that there is any unambiguous and single moral form within which they could work out their lives." The same is true for the United States.

The strict superego control reinforced by the actions of punitive external agents in the initial stages of value change has already been noted. The two-level system of self-observation and the watchfulness of the community is noted by Walzer (in *The Revolution of the Saints,* 221),who writes: "[The saints] . . . examined and admonished one another. The saints were thus bound together in a close system of collective watchfulness, which might occasionally turn into a kind of spiritual terrorism. In his Kidderminster parish, Baxter reported, the enforcement of the moral discipline was made possible 'by the zeal and diligence of the godly people of the place, who thirsted after the salvation of their neighbors, and were in private my assistants.'"

Nahirny, "Some Observations on Ideological Groups," 400, quotes a member of the *Narodnaya Volya* (People's Will) group to this effect: "I enjoin you brothers, to keep guard over each other in every practical activity, in all the small concerns of everyday life. It is necessary that this guarding should enter into the conscience and thus turn itself into a principle, that it should cease to seem offensive, that personal considerations should be silenced before the demands of reason. It is necessary for all the closest friends to know how a man lives, what he wears, how he takes notes and what kind of notes he takes, how careful, observant, and resourceful he is—in this is our power, in this is the perfection of our organization."

28. Talcott Parsons and Victor Lidz, "Death in American Society," in *Essays in Self-Destruction,* ed. Edwin Shneidman (New York, 1967). It seems to us that this mandate to action is

the sociological background for the psychoanalytic emphasis on the organization and elaboration of an ego psychology, and the reason for the changing nature of therapeutic styles as well. Modern "character disorder" is typically viewed in terms of ego weakness, in terms of the inability to determine one's own existence, to be rational, calculated, conscious, to withhold affect from inappropriate objects, and so on. The analytic "cure" consists in rationalizing psychic process and in forcing the ego to act on its own behalf in terms of the numerous legitimate ends and means.

29. Marx's feelings about the destructive nature of bourgeois civilization pervade everything he wrote. The particular quotation is from "The Economic and Philosophical Manuscripts," in *Karl Marx, Early Writings,* trans. and ed. T. B. Bottomore (New York, 1964), 121. The absence of aggression refers to the social level of activity, not the personal; that is, there will be no aggression stemming from the reorganized social structure.

30. Weber, *The Protestant Ethic,* 180-82.

31. The possibility for ego control over object choices and relations, particularly with regard to "external" activities, i.e., political and economic activities, has been suggested by Hartmann, Rapaport, and others. Their position is that actions which originate in response to intrapsychic conflict, or become bound to such conflict, can undergo a change and become (relatively) autonomous actions. As ego interests become more independent of instinctual origins, the feelings of pleasure that derive from mastery and control are no longer so closely connected to libidinal and aggressive sources. Such activity may then become a part of the "conflict-free" ego sphere that pursues activity for its own sake and not in relation to id or superego mandates. Of course, the regressive alternatives always exist, and these are not to be forgotten or underestimated. Heinz Hartmann, *Ego Psychology and the Problem of Adaptation* (New York, 1958); also, Hartmann, "Comments on the Psychoanalytic Theory of the Ego," *Ps. St. Chi.,* V (1950), 74-96. Robert W. White has recently argued for the existence of autonomous functions at birth, functions that are not subsequent, secondary developments originally related to libidinal or aggressive sources and are not originally instinctual, although in-

dependent of libidinal and aggressive sources (in the sense in which Ives Hendricks has stated this problem). However, because of the consistent failure of various radical actors to maintain ego control under pressure, and because of the sexualization and aggressivization of mastery and control, we prefer the hypothesis of an instinctual basis of activity. Robert W. White, "Ego and Reality in Psychoanalytic Theory," *Psychological Issues* (New York, 1963), vol. III, no. 3, monograph 11, *passim*. In any case, ego support, various forms of control, and different patterns of behavior are provided by or within the context of the family.

32. Erik Erikson, "Identity and the Life Cycle," *Psychological Issues* (New York, 1959), vol. I, no. 1, monograph 1, *passim*.

33. Freud, of course, did not think that control over external agencies would significantly abate the functions of guilt and aggression. Freud, "Civilization and Its Discontents," XXI.

Index